# CONTEMPORARY TRANSPORT TRENDS

# Contemporary Transport Trends

*Edited by*

MICHAEL ASTERIS

*Principal Lecturer in Economics*
*University of Portsmouth*

PETER GREEN

*Director*
*Institute of Transport Administration*

# Avebury

Aldershot · Brookfield USA · Hong Kong · Singapore · Sydney

Published by
Avebury
Ashgate Publishing Limited
Gower House
Croft Road
Aldershot
Hants
GU11 3HR
England

Ashgate Publishing Company
Old Post Road
Brookfield
Vermont 05036
USA

A CIP catalogue record for this book is available from the British Library and the US Library of Congress.

ISBN 1 85628 284 8

Printed and Bound in Great Britain by
Athenaeum Press Ltd., Newcastle upon Tyne.

# Contents

# The Institute of Transport Administration

The Institute of Transport Administration (IoTA) is an organization of professional managers and administrators from all segments of the transport industry. It was founded in 1944 as the Institute of Traffic Administration: the name was changed in 1981 to reflect more accurately the composition of the membership.

The principal aim of the organization is to improve the knowledge and skills of its members in the efficient management of transport, regardless of specialization within the industry.

Membership is open to anyone involved with the business of transport - the Institute has never insisted upon a minimum educational standard on the part of applicants. IoTA is, however, proud of its educational provision. In conjunction with Henley Management College, a programme of distance-learning and residential tuition is offered to both existing members and non-members, who appreciate the advantages of obtaining a Management Diploma from Henley which guarantees corporate membership of the Institute.

There are more than four thousand members in the United Kingdom, all of whom are allocated to one of the 30 semi-autonomous Centres located throughout the country. There are also a number of thriving centres overseas. Each centre arranges a programme of presentations, seminars, visits and social events. All Centres are represented on the National Council; this is the governing body which formulates rules and policy. Council is advised by six functional committees.

In October each year, IoTA holds a National Conference. The programme generally consists of a mixture of presentations on a specific theme by eminent speakers, together with an active social programme for delegates and their guests.

The membership of the Institute forms a significant body of informed opinion and this fact is recognized by the inclusion of IoTA representatives on committees and discussion groups concerned with transport policy. The organization also promotes independent analysis and public discussion of contemporary issues. For example, it has recently commissioned a firm of consultants to produce a comprehensive study aimed at assisting British manufacturers and distributors to take advantage of the Single European Market in terms of the physical distribution of their products.

The Institute's bi-monthly journal **Transport Management,** which is the source of the reprints contained in this volume, constitutes an authoritative publication containing articles and features on issues confronting the industry.

The Headquarters of IoTA is located in Southampton. the Director and his staff are always pleased to answer questions and give advice to potential members. Enquiries should be addressed to The Director, The Institute of Transport Administration, 32 Palmerston Road, Southampton, Hants, SO1 1LL, England.

# Acknowledgements and notes

The editors are indebted to the authors of the papers that are reprinted in this volume and also to The Institute of Transport Administration for permission to republish them. The manuscript of the book was typed with speed and efficiency by Julie Crook, Margaret Jarman and Jane Coomber, at the University of Portsmouth Students' Union; and we thank them also for a number of useful suggestions.

## NOTES

Note 1.  The authors' affiliation, where indicated, was that at the time of the original publication.


Note 2.  UK Currency.

Pre-Decimal:12 pence (d) = 1 shilling (s); 20 shillings = 1 pound (£) sterling.
Decimal (1971): 100 'new' pence (p) = £1 sterling.

# Biographical notes

Michael Asteris, Visiting Fellow at the Mountbatten Centre for International Studies University of Southampton, Honorary Fellow of the Institute of Transport Administration, is currently Principal Lecturer in Economics at the University of Portsmouth. Dr Asteris has taken a special interest in transport and defence, and has written extensively on these subjects.

Peter Green is Director of the Institute of Transport Administration, Southampton and was Editor of Transport Management between 1985 and 1989. Wing Commander Green served in the Royal Airforce for 36 years and held various appointments in the United Kingdom and overseas, including command of a NATO strike base in West Germany.

# Preface

For a number of years after its foundation, the Institute had a section within the trade magazine **Transport Management**, published by one of its founder members, the late Mrs Christine Taylor. Ultimately, it was considered expedient that the rapidly growing Institute should have its own Journal which was launched in October 1958. For some years this was known as The Journal of the Institute of Traffic Administration. Later this was shortened to Traffic Administrator but in 1974 the present title, **Transport Management**, was adopted by kind permission of Mrs Taylor.

After more than 30 year continuous publication of the Institute's Journal, we considered it appropriate to make readily accessible in one volume a selection of those articles which have appeared during this period. As indicated by its logo, the principal aim of the Institute is the improved management of transport by road, rail, sea and air. It thus seemed natural for the present collection to mirror these major subdivisions of transport. Consequently, the compilation consists of eight representative works drawn from each of the four modes. It must be admitted, however, that several of the reprints contain material that could fall comfortably under two or more headings. Deciding which essays to include was no easy task: inevitably, limitations of space and the need to maintain a balance between each topic area implied the omission of many excellent articles.

Many of the papers which are included in this volume were originally presented at Institute conferences or UK regional centres; most of the others were written specifically for the Journal. All have been reproduced unaltered, save for some relatively minor amendments and the omission of photographs. They therefore reflect the views of their authors at the time that they were written. Each essay is, of course, independent of the remainder but an introduction focusing on the main trends in transport since the late 1950s is included so as to place the various contributions in context.

Michael Asteris
Peter Green

# Transport trends:
# An overview

*Michael Asteris*

The Institute of Transport Administration first published its own periodical in October 1958 because, in the words of the founding editor, 'we had progressed to a stage where it would be prudent and desirable to have our own Journal'[1]. Fortuitously, late 1958 was a significant time in the history of domestic and international transport: it witnessed both the opening of Britain's first length of motorway and the initial trans-Atlantic jet airliner service. The articles reproduced in this volume can thus be regarded as encompassing the 'motorway age' and the 'jet airliner age'.

In order to set the scene for the various contributions which follow, this introduction seeks to provide an overview of trends in both domestic transport and in international transport to and from the United Kingdom, with particular reference to the period since the late 1950s.

## DOMESTIC TRANSPORT

Transport is a vital element of civilized life: it enables individuals to take advantage of a wide range of social and employment opportunities and permits production to take place on the basis of geographical specialization. The importance of transport to the United Kingdom can be illustrated in a number of ways. To begin with, on a value added basis, it comprises about 4.5 per cent of the Gross Domestic Product. With a labour force not far short of

1

one million, the sector also constitutes a significant source of employment.[2] Moreover, about 30 per cent of all energy use by final consumers can be attributed to it.[3]

## Government policy

The importance of the transport sector is reflected in the complexity of its problems. In attempting to deal with them, government policy over the long term has tended to oscillate between two approaches: nationalization and regulation on the one hand, and privatization combined with free markets on the other. Both approaches have efficiency as a dominant objective but interpret it differently.

Those who espouse the regulatory path argue that profitability based on the market mechanism is a poor indication of efficiency for two principal reasons. First, because large sectors of transport display monopoly characteristics. Secondly, because transport systems create highly undesirable 'externalities', such as noise and pollution, which the market system does not take fully into account.[4] Detailed planning is thus viewed as the only reliable means of promoting efficiency, by directing each facility to those transport functions where its advantages are greatest.

In marked contrast, many politicians and economists regard the efficiency objective as achievable only when the price mechanism is the prime instrument of resource allocation. This does not imply an unfettered or disorderly situation where everything is acceptable. Rather, one may view the free market as in some ways analogous to the game of cricket. This field sport is played according to a set of laws; if these are transgressed then penalties are incurred. The nature of the laws are laid down, and occasionally changed, by the cricket authorities. Similarly, the free market requires a framework of policies and regulations which can be amended as circumstances warrant.

Both safety and need can be incorporated in the competitive ground rules. With respect to the latter for example, there are services which are widely considered to be desirable, even though they cannot be justified on a commercial basis. In such cases, a direct subsidy, rather than some form of cross-subsidization, should be the rule because then the cost is transparent.[5] Society is thus placed in a position where it can judge whether scarce resources are being put to best use.

In the immediate post-war years, state ownership and central direction were the dominant transport themes. These were epitomized by the British Transport Commission, established under the Transport Act of 1947 to oversee a vast nationalized undertaking comprising the railways, London

2

Transport, large sections of the bus industry, long distance road haulage, ports and inland waterways. Transport was treated as a 'public service', in the context of which the profit motive was a decidedly secondary consideration. The Commission was charged with providing a 'properly integrated system' of transport. However, this objective was difficult to realize in the face of the continued existence of a substantial private sector.

Though the path has certainly not been direct, from the first half of the 1950s onwards, the general thrust of transport policy has been towards market-oriented solutions. The process began with the Transport Act of 1953 (which led to the return of many road haulage vehicles to private ownership by 1956) and may be traced through subsequent transport related legislation, including the Acts of 1962, 1968, 1980 and 1985.

Following British accession to the European Economic Community (EEC) in 1973, there has also been a growing international dimension to policy making. Attempts to implement a 'Common Transport Policy' have been hampered by the diversity of the Member States. Nevertheless, considerable progress has been made in creating a broader competitive market within the Community. Indeed, the liberalization of transport services is a key element in the attempt to complete the Single European Market by 1993.

**Traffic trends**

This is not the place for a detailed discussion of the numerous changes in the transport scene between 1958 and the present. It is possible, though, to identify two outstanding developments in the distribution of traffic in the UK during this period. The first, has been the increasing domination of the road vehicle in both passenger and freight movements and the consequent decline in the importance of the railways. Table 1 reveals that rails' share of the UK passenger market has more than halved since 1958, while its share of the freight market amounts to less than a third of its level some 30 years ago.

## TABLE 1
## DISTRIBUTION OF UK PASSENGER AND FREIGHT TRAFFIC,
## SELECTED YEARS
## 1958-89

|  | 1958 | 1968 | 1978 | 1988 | 1989 |
|---|---|---|---|---|---|
| **Passenger Traffic (billion passenger kilometres)** | | | | | |
| Cars and Cycles (1) | 131 | 292 | 351 | 528 | 568 |
| Buses and Coaches | 70 | 59 | 40 | 41 | 41 |
| Rail | 41 | 34 | 25 | 41 | 40 |
| Air | 0.5 | 1.9 | 2.7 | 4.6 | 4.9 |
| All Modes | 242.5 | 386.9 | 438.7 | 614.6 | 653.9 |
| **Freight Traffic (Goods moved: billion tonne kilometres)** | | | | | |
| Road | 41 | 79 | 99.3 | 130.2 | 137.4 |
| Rail | 30 | 23 | 20.0 | 18 | 17.3 |
| Water (2) | 21 | 25 | 47.6 | 60.9 | 57.3 |
| Pipeline | 0.2 | 2.4 | 9.8 | 10.8 | 9.4 |
| All Modes (3) | 92.2 | 129.4 | 176.7 | 219.9 | 221.8 |

Notes:  1    Including taxis, motorcycles and pedal cycles.
2    The data for 1978 and onwards is not strictly comparable with that for earlier years because of adjustments in the method of calculation necessitated by substantial changes in the character of the coastal shipping industry.
3    Air freight in the UK, while sometimes important in terms of speed of delivery, is insignificant in volume.

Sources: Derived from Department of Transport, Transport Statistics Great Britain, various editions.

The growing importance of road transport is, of course, the continuation of a trend which, apart from a brief interlude during and immediately after the Second World War, has been a feature of the twentieth century.

Table 1 also highlights the other major change in traffic distribution viz. the growth of private passenger transport and the decline in the importance of public passenger transport. This shift is attributable to rapidly growing car

4

ownership and has led to the closure of many rail and bus services since the late 1950s.

The rail network first began to feel the impact of increased competition from road transport in the mid-fifties. By then it had become clear that the poor physical state of the system placed it in a very weak market position, so a modernization programme was embarked upon. In the event, changes in the pattern of demand for both passenger and goods transport prevented the industry achieving a secure financial footing. Network rationalization therefore became a distinctive feature of the railways following the publication of the 'Beeching Report' in 1963.

While the railways modernized and rationalized in the struggle to remain competitive, two particularly important developments were taking place in road transport. First, the infrastructure was being extended and improved by the building of new roads. Thus, by the late seventies, the core of the motorway system was virtually complete. Secondly, between the early sixties and the mid-eighties, regulations relating to lorry weights and proportions were relaxed. Between them, improved infrastructure and legal changes substantially raised productivity in road freight transport.

Faced with intense competition from the road sector, British Rail has sought to exploit those segments of the transport market to which it is best suited. This approach has enjoyed a considerable measure of commercial success. Moreover, the privately funded £7.6 billion Channel Tunnel promises to revolutionize British Rail's long distance passenger and freight prospects, by adding a major international dimension to services from mid-1993 onwards.

## INTERNATIONAL TRANSPORT

To a degree, the growing importance of road relative to rail in domestic transport during the past 30 years is mirrored in the expansion of air relative to sea in an international transport context.

### Sea transport

The most decisive change in the relative position of the latter modes of transport has taken place in long-distance international travel. In 1958 a dense network of scheduled passenger routes still linked Great Britain with maritime states around the World. During the 1960s and 1970s these services were gradually relegated to history in the face of overwhelming competition from civil aviation. On the other hand, largely as a consequence of the growth of tourism, short-sea travel between the UK and near Continental countries has risen very rapidly since the late 1950s. Thus Dover, the leading cross-Channel port, dealt with over fifteen million passengers in 1989, compared with less than two million in 1957. Other ferry ports in South East England, including Harwich and Portsmouth, have also experienced a dramatic rise in passenger traffic in recent decades.

As a result of shifts in the pattern of UK trade and technological change, terminals on the eastern side of Britain also dominate seaborne freight traffic.

In the late 1950s trade links with former Empire countries were still very strong; only a quarter of UK trade was with the present members of the European Community. By contrast, today the proportion exceeds one half. There has thus been a shift in the pattern of trade from deep-sea to near-sea destinations. In terms of individual ports, the main losers have been the west coast terminals, together with London: the beneficiaries have been ports - such as Dover and Felixstowe -situated close to the prime markets of Europe.

Containerization - one of the most significant innovations in the history of international freight transport - reinforced the shift from west to east. The high cost of the new container terminals and vessels, together with the desire of shipowners to maximize sea time resulted in a reduction in ports of call. Where possible, the UK and the Continent are served by a single vessel so as to ensure a high load factor on regular services. Convenience often requires that the UK port of call be close to the main European trade routes, thus providing custom for terminals in the south-east.

Changes in the patterns of sea travel, trade and technology go some way towards explaining the decline in the merchant fleet registered on the UK mainland from almost 50 million deadweight tons in 1975 to less than 4 million tons in the early 1990s. However, the fundamental causes of the contraction are to be found in the long shipping recession, which began in the early 1970s, and the relatively high cost of sailing under the Red Ensign. During the 1980s, this latter factor led British owners to seek lower costs and less restrictions by registering many of their vessels 'offshore', in places such as the Isle of Man, Bermuda and Hong Kong. The gradual deregulation of domestic transport thus has its counterpart in the liberalization of shipping.

**Air transport**

During the post-war era, civil aviation has displayed two distinctive characteristics: rapid technical progress and falling real costs. These features, together with economic growth, have led to a dramatic expansion in both air

6

travel and air freight. Thus annual UK air passengers increased from about half a million in 1946 to over 86 million in 1988. During the 1980s alone, demand for air travel approximately doubled.

On the freight side, UK international air traffic has assumed great importance since the end of the fifties. At that time it accounted for about one-twentieth of Britain's exports and imports, by value; today, despite a massive rise in foreign trade during the intervening period, the proportion is in the region of one-quarter.

The state has been very influential in airline operations. Indeed, for much of the post-war period, the UK industry was dominated by two publicly owned concerns: British European Airways (BEA) and the British Overseas Airways Corporation (BOAC). These were merged to form British Airways in 1972.

As in other sectors of transport, the policy in recent years has been to encourage greater efficiency and liberalization in airline operations. In pursuit of these objectives British Airways was privatized in 1987 as was the British Airports Authority, which managed and operated London's Heathrow and other state-owned airports. Meanwhile, new airlines, for example, Air UK, have come into existence, while major tour operators have established their own airlines.

## THE WAY FORWARD

This brief survey of UK transport has highlighted the ways in which the sector has developed in recent decades. Looked at as a whole, the present network is far more extensive and sophisticated than that of the late fifties. But despite all the progress of the intervening period, transport in the early nineties constitutes a major problem area. The reason for this is that rapid economic expansion has generated a growth in demand for transport well in excess of the growth in the capacity of the system. The excess demand manifests itself in congestion across a broad spectrum, including motorways such as the M1 and M25, British Rail's InterCity Network, the London Underground, and Heathrow airport. An improved transport infrastructure is therefore highly desirable, not least to derive maximum benefit from the opening of the Channel Tunnel and the completion of the Single European Market.

In attempting to deal with present problems in an acceptable time scale, the Government, in addition to increasing public spending on transport infrastructure is contemplating extending privatization to roads and railways. If toll-financed major highways and a denationalized rail network do become

7

features of the opening years of the twenty-first century, then policy towards the transport sector will have travelled a very long way from the early post-war philosophy of state ownership and central direction.

## THE ARTICLES

The selection of reprints from **Transport Management** has been arranged on a modal rather than a thematic basis. Even so, the concepts which have provided the framework of this overview reflect those contained in the essays which follow. Hence, recurring themes in the remainder of the volume include the role of the state, efficiency, pricing and investment strategy, and the impact of change.

## NOTES AND REFERENCES

1. See J. Parker, Transport Management, December 1975 p.4.

2. Rising productivity has, however, resulted in a steady fall in numbers employed. See Department of Transport, Transport Statistics Great Britain, 1979-1989, HMSO, London, 1990, p.44.

3. Ibid., p.8. Of the transport energy used, 80 per cent is attributable to road transport. Petroleum provides 99 per cent of transport energy requirements.

4. Sitting in a suburban garden close to the end of the flight path leading to London's Heathrow airport and lead deposits on the verges of the M25 motorway, provide two excellent illustrations of unwanted externalities.

5. Cross-subsidization occurs when revenue from a profitable activity is used to finance the loss on one which does not cover its costs.

# Section One
# Road Transport

The first two selections are devoted to the bus industry. Hindle's chapter provides a picture of the sector following the major restructuring initiated by the 1968 Transport Act. At that time, public ownership was considered the most effective way of dealing with the industry's problems. By the mid-1980s, however, the climate of opinion had moved in favour of deregulation and privatization. Consequently, the second chapter, by Knowles, examines how the new framework created by the 1985 Transport Act has affected operators.

The next two works provide different perspectives on the road haulage industry. Buck in Chapter 3 focuses on contract hire, a specialized service which has grown rapidly in the last 20 years, while the chapter by Mrs Chattle examines the likely impact of 1992 on road haulage and concludes that in many respects the European Commission's proposals are similar to conditions already prevailing in the United Kingdom.

The road vehicle has brought numerous benefits to society, but it has also involved environmental costs. Sharp looks at these costs in the context of the goods vehicle, while Rhys selects one particular problem, smoke emission, and cautions against expending a disproportionate amount of resources on it. Motorways were welcomed as a solution to many of the problems arising from extensive use of vehicles. However, as Diment makes clear in Chapter 7, motorways though safer than other roads, suffer severe congestion which results in increased accidents.

The final chapter in Section 1 was written a quarter of a century ago, yet Jones' discussion of the role computers can play in road transport remains surprisingly fresh and relevant.

# 1 Bus operation

*Paper presented to the Southampton Centre by*
*S. Hindle*
*Borough of Bournemouth Transport*
*December 1971 issue*

One hundred and forty-two years ago a Mr. Shillibeer announced that he was building two new vehicles and that when these were completed he intended to operate them along the Paddington Road in London.

Surely enough, on the 4th July 1829, George Shillibeer introduced, between Paddington Grove and the Bank, his two new coaches, each drawn by three horses and each coach capable of carrying eighteen people, the coaches picking up and setting down passengers on the public highway.

This was the birth of the bus industry in this country - an industry which last year carried 10,000 million passengers, and which has grown over those 142 years from the operation of two horsedrawn coaches to a massive industry which operates 70,000 vehicles, employs a quarter of a million people and covers over 2,000 million miles every year.

This is the bus industry today, and I propose to look at the general structure of the industry and the organization of a typical bus operator.

Then, I would like to indicate some of the problems which face the industry - not only the problems but also what we are doing about them.

Finally, I should like to look into the crystal ball at the shape of the industry in years to come.

Many of the statistics that I shall quote will refer to the Bournemouth undertaking, but these apply generally to bus operators throughout the country.

# GENERAL ORGANIZATION

One of the peculiarities of the bus industry over the years has been the fragmentation of the industry. Many operators have been restricted by artificial boundaries, whilst in other areas operations overlapped causing wasteful competition and inefficient operation.

During the last two years a major reshaping of the bus industry has taken place following the passing of the 1968 Transport Act and operators now fall into three well-defined groups.

## 1. State controlled

The National Bus Company and Scottish Transport Group were formed by taking over most of the major bus companies, e.g., Hants and Dorset, Southdown, Ribble, Midland Red, etc. The NBC operates over 27,000 vehicles and controls the activities of seventy subsidiary companies which range in size from 26 to 1,740 buses.

The NBC operates as a commercial body, each subsidiary company being responsible for its own management but responsible to the NBC Board, which is comprised of high ranking professional transport men.

## 2. Municipal control

### (a) Local authorities
Under this heading we have seventy municipal undertakings operating 10,850 buses, the undertakings ranging in size from Bedwas and Machen with 5 buses to Glasgow Corporation with 1,220 buses.

Each undertaking is controlled by professional management, responsible to a transport committee comprised of elected representatives.

### (b) London transport
This is the largest single bus undertaking in the world, operating 6,590 buses. It is controlled by a Board of professional transport men, responsible financially to the Greater London Council.

### (c) Passenger transport authorities
These were set up under the 1968 Act in certain densely populated areas of the country, the authorities taking over control of all the municipal operators in the area.

The actual planning and operations are performed by a Passenger Transport Executive comprised of professional transport men, responsible for policy to the Passenger Transport Authority, which is comprised of representatives of Boroughs and County Councils within the area.

It is interesting to note that the PTA's are responsible for the overall planning of all passenger transport services within the area, including railways and ferries.

## 3. Independent operators

In this final group are hundreds of small operators, many of whom operate mainly contract and private hire work; and whilst the number of vehicles operated is 14,500 they are not really of great importance in connection with this paper.

## ORGANIZATION OF AN UNDERTAKING

What does bus operation mean to the average person?

I suppose it is the operation of a bus from Point A to Point B picking up and setting down passengers and collecting fares.

Quite a simple operation on the face of it, but behind it there is a rather complex organization.

We could say that the engineer provides a serviceable vehicle, the traffic department operates the vehicle, and the commercial department pays the wages and counts the cash, but there is more to it than this.

### Engineering department

This department provides serviceable vehicles. This involves major over-hauls and repairs of mechanical parts and bodywork, and re-paints, together with routine preventative maintenance. The highest standard is required to pass MOT tests and obtain certificates of fitness.

The engineering section also investigates vehicle design with a view to obtaining the most suitable type of vehicle for a particular purpose, e.g. low step entrances for Bournemouth's elderly passengers, open top buses for pleasure summer services, and special equipment for one-man operation.

The engineer avails himself of modern materials and takes advantage of the latest techniques in work study and incentive bonus schemes.

The object is the highest standard of reliability and safety coupled with maximum availability.

## Commercial section

Responsibility is accepted in this section for all financial aspects including wages, salaries, stores control, accounts, cash counting, ticket analysis and the preparation of statistics. Here again the latest equipment is in use, i.e. electronic cash counting, computers for wages and stores control, whilst the operation of budgetary control ensures that financial targets are reached.

## Traffic department

The traffic department is responsible for the operation of the buses together with control of platform and inspectorate staff, the control of fares, and liaison with the traffic commissioners, police, borough engineer and other council officials.

The main task is deciding the level of services needed by the public and the most efficient and economical way of providing them.

This involves operational research to establish the demand for services, the preparation of time-tables to meet that demand, the preparation of bus schedules to cover all journeys in the most efficient manner with a minimum of standing time.

## Buses must be kept running

The Traffic Manager will decide how best to operate his schedules - by a traditional two-man bus or by one-man operation. This will depend on the economics of the route in question, the type of route and the availability of suitable vehicles.

The next process is the production of crew duties to ensure that every bus is manned. Duties must comply with the law regarding drivers' hours, union agreements and must involve a minimum of non-working time. For eight hours pay we require eight hours work if possible.

All this work is useless without an extensive follow-up by way of inspectors' reports, traffic census, letters from the public and discussions with ratepayers' associations in order to ascertain that services are working satisfactorily. If they are, all well and good, but if not, then we go back to square one.

This meticulous attention to detail is in my view the hall-mark of the efficient bus operator. Bus operation is so completely different from those services which can be charged for as they are used or sold, in that cost is incurred whether any seats are sold or not.

Therefore the continuous detailed attention to time-tables, schedules and duties can make the difference between a surplus and a loss at the end of the year.

## SERVICE PLANNING

How can we, the bus operators, decide what our customers, the public, need or may need in the future in the way of services, routes and frequencies? There are many methods of investigation including:-

Questionnaires;

Use of personnel to ask questions and record journeys taken;

Use of personnel at bus stops to speak to passengers; discussions with ratepayers' associations.

In Bournemouth, during recent years, we have successfully used a travelling census technique to determine frequencies and heavily loaded portions of routes.

These methods are of little use, however, when assessing the demand for a new service. When investigating the possibility of introducing a new off-peak shopping service two years ago, we had to decide on the advisability of routing the service through an area which previously had never had a bus service. In order to assess the public demand, inspectors were sent out with instructions to walk along the proposed new section of the route and to stop all pedestrians and ask them set questions, i.e., How far were they walking? Would they ride if a bus service was provided? How many times a day did they make the journey? What time did they return? and many more questions.

From the information provided it was clear that a service would be patronized and this has operated for two years and is a financial success.

All these methods of investigation are extremely limited in their use as they fail to reveal the points of origin and destination, especially when a changeover of bus is required.

In 1965 and in 1970 extensive origin and destination surveys were conducted in the Bournemouth area, whereby questionnaire cards were issued to all passengers on every third bus on each service. The cards had the postage pre-paid and the detail received was processed by computer, valuable information being received on passenger flows, origin and destinations and the reasons for travel.

15

From this information in 1965 the whole of the services in the western half of the town were completely re-organized and co-ordinated, substantial savings made, and better services provided.

## PROBLEMS OF THE INDUSTRY

|  | 1950 | 1970 |
|---|---|---|
| Cost of double-deck bus | £4,500 | £9,000 |
| Cars in Bournemouth | 11,000 | 42,000 |
| Bournemouth Corporation Transport Passengers | 64m. | 26m. (less 60%) |
| Bournemouth Corporation Transport mileage | 5.3m. | 4m. (less 12%) |
| Wages - driver for 48 hours | £6.5.0d. | £34.15.0d. |
| Total Expenditure | £½m. | £1m. |

These are just a few facts which give rise to major problems in the industry at the present time, but before discussing these problems I should say that Bournemouth Corporation Transport is not a profit-making concern but neither is it a burden on the rates. The Bournemouth council has decreed that the undertaking should be self-supporting, i.e. the income from fares must cover all items of expenditure - and this applies to most municipal bus operators.

There is no doubt that of the figures given the most significant are the fall in Bournemouth Corporation Transport passengers from 64m. to 26m. over twenty years, and the increase in total expenditure from just under half a million pounds to just over one million pounds.

Why has the passenger traffic declined? Car ownership has increased by four times in twenty years. This is especially noticeable with the holidaymakers who form a substantial part of our trade.

Television has also had a great impact, and our revenue for evenings and Sundays has dwindled to almost nothing.

We also realize that increases in bus fares have played their part in driving away passengers.

These factors have all helped to reduce the number of passengers carried and therefore the revenue.

On the other side of the account, we find that constantly increasing wages and prices have pushed up our expenditure from under half a million pounds to over one million pounds in twenty years.

It must be obvious, therefore, that a constant review must be made of our financial position for, if expenditure is constantly rising and revenue is falling, the only possible result at the end of the year is a deficit.

## SOLUTIONS TO DEFICIT

When faced with an anticipated deficit what can be done to meet the situation? There would appear to be three possibilities.
1. Reduce expenditure;
2. Increase the revenue from fares;
3. A subsidy.
Let us take a closer look at these possibilities.

### 1. Reduce expenditure

As 70 per cent of our expenditure is in wages and salaries, it follows that substantial savings can only be made in this particular field. This means better operating methods or reduced services. Every undertaking has closely examined its timetables with a view to effecting service economies but it must be accepted that if services are constantly reduced we shall only lose more and more passengers. It is important to note that in the case of Bournemouth 21 per cent of our mileage is unremunerative, i.e. the revenue does not cover the cost of operation. Consequently the NBC and other operators are now saying: "If a service does not pay its way, it must be taken off unless we get a subsidy." Bournemouth Corporation Transport has not taken this line of action so far because we feel that some inconvenience would be caused to the public.

It must be stressed, however, that savings are constantly being made by improving schedules and duties, by conversion to one-man bus operation, and by streamlining the administration of the Department, e.g. the use of computers, electronic coin counting, improved management techniques and productivity deals. There is, therefore, not much hope of further substantial economies in this field.

## 2.  Increase the revenue from fares

No doubt everybody has the solution to this problem and I think it would be useful to look at the various suggestions which have been made to us in the past.

### (a)  Don't put up the fares - reduce them and get more revenue
This would be revolutionary but people say we ought to try something new. My answer is that if Bournemouth Corporation Transport put the fares back to the level of twenty years ago, and if we had the same number of passengers that we had then (64m.) our total revenue would be £500,000

Our total expenditure in the last financial year was one million pounds, which leaves a deficit of £500,000 to be found from some other source.

Our advisors never indicate the nature of this source.

### (b)  Reduce fares during off-peak periods to fill the buses
No-one would like to see full buses more than I but we must again look at the facts closely.

In Bournemouth our off-peak revenue is approximately £500,000 and if, say, a half fare concession was granted then half this amount - £250,000 - would immediately be lost. It could be argued that this would be compensated by additional passengers who would take advantage of this concession. It is calculated that to do this an additional ten million passengers per year would have to be carried and this is not thought feasible on our existing passenger figure of 26 million.

### (c)  Flat fare
Many people will argue that a flat fare would solve all our difficulties and quote various figures from 3 new pence (p) to 5p. This would certainly simplify our operations.

What sort of flat fare would meet our requirements? The average fare paid on our system is 5p per journey, therefore to make the same revenue every passenger would have to pay 5p. But we must consider the effect of this on the various sections of the travelling public.

The short distance rider would have to pay a tremendous increase and many passengers would be lost. On the other hand the long distance riders would enjoy a reduced fare with consequent loss of revenue.

If we charged a flat 3p this would no doubt please everyone but with a current average fare of 5p we would have to double our passengers to break even - and still have the  deficit to tackle! Is this possible?

Five years ago Sunderland Transport embarked on a flat fare policy. Sadly, however, the undertaking ended up in the red, the deficits presumably having to be made good by the rates, and the flat fare has since been discontinued.

Flat fares may succeed in certain areas, but the decision to use them cannot be taken lightly.

### (d) Free travel

This possible solution has been suggested in different quarters on many occasions - even in London Transport last year. The theory is that no fares should be charged, the costs of operation being met from the local rate fund.

The costs of operation would, of course, be considerably reduced as we should be able to dispense with all conductors, ticket machines, cash office clerks and ticket inspectors.

But there would be considerable expenditure to meet and my estimate is that to provide the existing level of service to the public would involve an increase of 8p on the rates to pay for it.

What would be the reaction of the ratepayer who did not use the buses but had to subsidise his neighbour who did?

On the other hand, what about the ratepayer who has to pay for libraries but who does not read books, pays for schools but has no children?

There is no doubt in my mind that the only way to increase revenue is to increase bus fares. Having said that, I make the following points -
(a)    If we fail to put up fares we cannot meet our increased expenditure.
(b)    If we put up fares we lose passengers, so that over a period of time there
       are fewer passengers paying much  higher fares.
This is the biggest problem facing bus operators at the present time - not only in this country but all over the world.

The future of our industry depends very largely on this acute problem. Do we increase or don't we?

### 3.  Subsidy

This is the third possible way of meeting a deficit. If ever there was a dirty word to a bus operator it is 'subsidy'; whereby fare increases are avoided by meeting losses from the rates or other sources.

Transport managers have always felt that they were quite capable of standing on their own two feet without any financial assistance. It has also been felt that the passengers making a bus journey should pay the full economic cost of providing it.

There has, however, developed a thought that constant increases in fares drive away too many passengers to the private car, and that in time these cars will completely overwhelm the centres of our towns and cities. Would it not therefore benefit the community if fares were kept down, so helping reduce the congestion which will inevitably be caused, also saving the cost of car parks, new roads and land acquisitions?

Subsidies have, of course, been in existence in transport in some form for many years, e.g.

1.  Passengers on good paying routes subsidize passengers on non-paying routes;
2.  Short distance passengers have subsidized longer distance passengers;
3.  Town services have subsidized country services;
4.  Children's fares have been subsidized although they occupy the same space as an adult;
5.  Where education authorities pay school children's fares, the transport operator is subsidizing the education department by providing cheap fares.

It may be argued that a bus service for a person who cannot afford to run a car is surely as essential as swimming baths, public parks, putting greens, museums and libraries, not to mention financial support for music, drama and the arts.

On the other hand, if a local council subsidized bus services would it be fair that people who reside outside the area and who make no contribution should also be subsidized? I am not trying to make a case for or aga nst subsidization in the future but merely giving you a few basic facts. I leave you to think about it.


## TRAFFIC CONGESTION

Have you ever stopped to think what traffic congestion is costing you as a transport operator, whether you operate a fleet of trailers, delivery vans or buses?

If Bournemouth Corporation Transport could increase their average operating speed by one mile per hour we could save £50,000 per annum and this only means an increase form ten miles per hour to eleven miles per hour.

This is just an indication of the effects of traffic congestion on the bus operator, and apart from the effect on operating costs there is a disastrous effect on our passengers.

20

Congestion to us is just a part of a vicious circle - it slows down buses, passengers get aggravated and transfer to a private car, which creates more congestion.

This is a problem which must be solved in the near future but what can we do about it?

The two main factors which influence congestion and speed are -
1.    Car parking on the main highway;
2.    The creation of detours for new road schemes.

A Ministry of Transport Experimental Traffic Management Scheme in Bournemouth some four years ago banned all parking on a major highway for approximately one mile, and the effect was to increase our average speed through the area from eight miles per hour to sixteen miles per hour.

I am not advocating the wholesale banning of car parking but merely pointing out what can be done - because if something is not done within ten years our town and city centres will be completely strangled.

Every major road scheme in Bournemouth has involved buses making detours via circuitous routes - more mileage, more time and more frustration for the passengers.

## Bus priorities

Many towns and cities are meeting such problems by the introduction of priorities for buses. These schemes have the approval and backing of the Government. In some cases buses are allowed to make turns which are prohibited to other vehicles. In Leicester, buses activate traffic lights which then turn green to allow the buses through. Other towns have reserved lanes for buses, both with or against the normal traffic flow. In Reading, six separate priority facilities are in use and it is important to note that passengers are increasing by 3 per cent whilst other services are falling. They have recently banned all traffic from the main shopping street except for buses and service vehicles, which means that pedestrians can move about more freely without impeding social transport services.

If this appears to be a selfish attitude, I assure you it is not.

The criterion for the future is - can we move a greater number of people in this way than under a free for all? I think we can, but we must have the co-operation of all parties in order to succeed - planners, operators and the public.

## VEHICLE UTILIZATION (PEAKS)

You all know that one of the important features of running any successful business is to make the maximum possible use of all assets - machinery, plant, vehicles, staff and capital.

Every bus we buy costs approximately £10,000 and lasts approximately twelve years. If purchased on loan, the annual costs is £1,500 per bus. Some buses operate for as little as two hours per day and it must be obvious to everyone that this is a very inefficient way of doing business.

It has, of course, always been said that we are a public service and therefore the public must have their transport just when they want it and this is the result. It is ironical to realize that the better the service provided at peak hours the more inefficient one becomes in terms of vehicle utilisation. If it was decided to reduce the peak and make every passenger wait an extra two or three minutes, this would provide a worse service but would increase efficiency.

What solutions are there to this problem and what have we done about it?

The perfect solution would be for all branches of industry, commerce, shops and schools to stagger their starting and finishing times to such an extent that the peak would almost disappear.

This, of course, is utopian but some success with staggering has been achieved in various parts of the country, but not sufficiently to make drastic improvements.

In Bournemouth an effort to stagger school starting and finishing times met with great resistance but has partially succeeded.

I doubt if we shall ever get voluntary agreement to stagger and compulsion is not our way of life.

Some operators are taking positive steps to cut their losses by applying for higher fares during the peak periods to offset the higher costs. Similarly, in some cases children are to be charged adult fares if they travel during the peak periods. This I agree with and for the future we must look at the cost of carrying children very carefully. But we must be very careful in case, by increasing children's fares, we lose them and their parents.

Just to complicate the vehicle problem even further, Bournemouth has, in addition to its a.m./p.m. peaks, a summer peak when the revenue doubles, and extra buses are required which we de-licence for the winter months.

# THE FUTURE

We have looked briefly into the history, then at the present organization of the industry and also at some current problems.

What of the future and how do I see the role of the bus operator during the next ten to twelve years? Some of the problems are formidable.
You may have heard the prophets refer to a dying industry. Are we a dying industry? Are we going to see large towns and cities swamped by the motor car? Looking at the trend, this does appear to be the future picture, but there is a problem.

If we plan large towns and cities on the basis that all future journeys will be made by private transport, we find that we have neither the physical space nor the financial resources needed to provide the roads, car parks and land to accommodate this increase in car traffic. This would demand an investment so great that the country could not possibly provide it. This is not my theory - I am quoting Government statements. This thinking also completely ignores the needs of the old, the young, the housewives and the poor, who cannot afford private transport.

At the other extreme, do we seriously think that we can discourage the private motorist from entering the town or city centre area either by direct physical control, e.g., parking restrictions, or by financial restraints, e.g. parking charges, local licensing fees or road pricing? Do we think that we can provide sufficient peripheral car parks for 'park and ride' schemes to keep a central area clear. As a bus operator I do not think that this is feasible, nor I am sure, do you.

What therefore is the picture for the future?

Obviously compromise at some point between the two extremes which I have outlined, where we must have a policy and a plan for transportation. In this connection we mean not the movement of cars nor the movement of buses, but the movement of people, without ruining the character of the towns and cities we live in.

This needs a new dynamic role for public transport, whereby we are constantly aware of the public demand for services and of the most efficient and economical way of meeting this demand. To achieve this we need the utmost co-operation of the authorities in providing priority schemes for our service.

We must find out more about public preference for various forms of transport and the importance which the public attach to speed, comfort, regularity, reliability or cost in determining their choice. We must make the most effective use of all the resources at our disposal - staff, equipment and capital. We must allow more and more scientific, economic and operational research to influence our thinking. In operating our businesses, management must be fully up-to-date with all the latest management techniques. We must experiment and encourage the development of new vehicles, and systems, electric buses, dial-a-bus, precinct services and rapid transit systems using reserved bus lanes.

The object would be to provide an attractive, reliable and efficient system of public transport which will dovetail with plans for private transport and produce an effective transportation system which will be satisfactory to everyone.

I would like to end by quoting two paragraphs from the publication "Public Transport and Traffic", because on the first page it contains what I consider to be pearls of wisdom and sums up the whole transportation problem.

'One of the most precious achievements of modern civilization is mobility. It enriches social life and widens experience. To build mobility into the urban and rural life of this crowded island without destroying the other elements of good living must be one of the major purposes of transport policy.

Nearly half of our people live in large towns and cities and about 80 per cent of them in urban areas. The quality of urban life depends to a large extent on the excellence of the transport services available both to those who live in the cities, and to those who come there for work, shopping or pleasure. The freedom to move easily about the city - to go places and see people - is something of great value. Yet this freedom can, if ill-used, do great damage to the quality of urban life'.

I hope that I have indicated to you how the bus industry is contributing to this mobility, and how we must continue to contribute not only to the preservation, but to the expansion of that mobility in the transportation plans of the future.

# 2 Trends in the bus industry

*Article by T.W. Knowles*
*Lancaster City Transport Limited*
*December 1990/January 1991 issue*

Last year in an article for **Transport Management**, I considered some of the trends that seemed to be emerging in the bus industry within the new framework created by the 1985 Transport Act. In this article, I attempt to show where some of those moves have been consolidated and, at the same time, I try to make some predictions for the future.

It would seem that many of the future changes in the structure of the bus industry are going to be determined by political decisions, and many of the current trends may well be reversed if there is a change of Government at Westminster; whilst, at the same time, bus operators must keep an eye on 1992 when harmonisation with Europe takes place.

## OWNERSHIP

There have been surprisingly few changes in the actual ownership of bus companies during the last 12 months, although we have seen the growth of the Badgerline Group, whilst the Stagecoach Group has continued to expand; albeit in doing so, incurring the wrath of the Office of Fair Trading on the South Coast. In the North West, there has been some rationalization involving Stagecoach and Drawlane, whilst the municipal sector has, thankfully, seen no more of its number go out of business and, at first sight unexpectedly, the move towards privatization has almost ground to a halt.

It may seem to the observer that these two municipal features are somewhat contradictory, bearing in mind that at long last the Scottish Bus Group is beginning to be sold off. But let us perhaps consider the situation a little more closely. Firstly, the Scottish Bus Group has been forced to be sold off by the Government whereas, in spite of various pronouncements made by the former Minster of State for Transport, Michael Portillo, the municipal companies have only been encouraged to become wholly privately owned.

There was great enthusiasm amongst municipal managements to own their own companies, particularly at the time of the National Bus Company sell-off, but since then interest rates have soared and profit margins have to be considerable to repay the financial institutions for their backing in achieving a buyout. Furthermore, as these financial institutions expect a personal commitment from the management, considerable risks are incurred by the latter in terms of second mortgages and the like. This is one of the fundamentally unfair aspects of ESOP's (Employee Share Ownership Plans), in that those that have been achieved thus far seem typically to give the management, say, 51 per cent of the equity and the employees 49 per cent. However, the management have to put up some security against their loan, whilst the workforce do not. Put in this position, many managements find that their companies are making insufficient profits to repay the loan, added to which, present polls show the current Government to be somewhat unpopular and since it is past mid-term, there is a possibility of a change in Government in the fairly near future. The Labour Party have already said that they feel public transport should be regionalized and, therefore, it could be found that the company one has bought out and nurtured, suddenly becomes part of the public sector again. The owner is not guaranteed to get full compensation should such a situation arise.

Another factor mitigating against the municipal sales is that of civic pride; where in the same way that many local authorities fought deregulation because they would lose control of their bus undertakings, a similar argument is also put forward by local politicians in connection with their sale.

It could well be that very high interest rates have been a factor which has helped the larger groups to acquire companies which have previously been subjected to a management buyout. Clearly, one cannot comment on individual cases, but it does seem reasonable to assume that in a number of instances, the higher interest rates have squeezed the new owners to a point where it has been better for them to sell to one of the groups, who may be able to make economies of scale.

However, where this has happened on the South Coast, Stagecoach have got into trouble with the Office of Fair Trading and the Monopolies and Mergers Commission, who declared it anti-competitive for them to own both the former Southdown operation and the Portsmouth Citybus operation in Pompey. This is a most interesting decision and one suspects that in making probably his next to last (!) public announcement, the former Secretary of State for Trade and Industry, Nicholas Ridley, could not have been totall· au fait with the implications of the decision he made in relation to the integration that had already taken place in Portsmouth.

In telling Stagecoach to divest themselves of the Portsmouth Citybus operations, the following questions come to mind:

(a)  How do you unscramble the network that has been put together to serve most efficiently the residents of Portsmouth?

(b)  Following closure of the Southdown depots in Portsmouth, will any new purchaser of Portsmouth Citybus have suitable premises from which to operate?

(c)  Who in their right minds is going to purchase a company whose prime initial objective is going to be to set up in head-to-head competition with Stagecoach and all their resources?

(d)  Since it is going to be very difficult to sort out which staff transfer, assuming rationalization of conditions has taken place, there are potential redundancy payments which could have to be paid, and who pays these?

Mr Brian Souter of Stagecoach has been waiting a long time for this decision which, quite frankly, has shattered the bus industry since it flies in the face of the trends for ownership of big bus companies in this country.

Furthermore, a similar situation now exists in Sheffield, where South Yorkshire Transport now have to divest themselves of various small operators they had acquired. No doubt there will be more examples in the future, unless the OFT develops a better understanding of the bus industry.

## VEHICLES

Twelve months ago the manufacturing industry was experiencing something of a boom and although the speed of build and development of minibuses had slowed down, midibuses and full sized vehicles seemed to be attracting orders.

It has been a surprise to many that this upturn in deliveries has not been continued and no doubt, once again, interest rates make a significant contribution towards this downturn.

Even on straight line depreciations, a lot of profit has to be made just to cover charges for a new coach. The coach operator really has to have high quality regular work to justify purchasing new vehicles at frequent intervals and, of course, many small, and not so small, coach operators have fallen by the wayside by overstretching themselves in terms of their capital expenditure. Perhaps some of the remaining coach operators have taken heed of the difficulties of their former colleagues, and this is another reason for the slowing down of new vehicle deliveries. However, secondhand vehicles are going to become scarcer as time goes on and this eventually will inflate their price above their true value, and maybe in due time this will cause an increase for new vehicle purchasers.

The European manufacturers have made a large impact on the coaching industry, and now are commanding a substantial share of the chassis production for buses purchased new in the UK. With Optare now becoming part of a large European Group -United Bus - it is becoming apparent that Britain is perhaps in the foreseeable future, not going to be a substantial enough market to support indigenous important suppliers, and we may well have to cast our net for virtually all our vehicle acquisitions overseas or, at least, rely on home-based subsidiaries of multi-national organizations.

One of the problems, as I see it, is that the British market suffers from the fact that, compared with most of the rest of the world, we drive on the 'wrong' side of the road and, therefore, to construct vehicles to penetrate say the European market, means a considerable number of development modifications and design variations which complicate the issue when one's own market is the odd-man-out. For the continental manufacturers, who will perhaps already be exporting to countries who drive on the same side of the road as them, the development costs involved to expand their export market into the UK is not as great in relation to their total turnover. Once we are Europeanized in 1992, it will come as no surprise to me if, in due course, pressure is put on Britain to change to driving on the right-hand side of the road. I also believe that harmonization will, in due course, bring regulations such as speed restrictions, under a common standard, which will make life for operators much easier. One just hopes that the new standards are not the most restrictive of all the options, since otherwise coach travel could then become unattractive.

# EUROPE

One of the big worries about harmonization with Europe, is the effect that our present licensing system will have in terms of ease of entry for new operators compared with the difficulties that British operators might have in trying to penetrate the European market. At present, so long as somebody can obtain an Operator's Licence through establishing themselves as being professionally competent and of good repute, all one then need do is register a service in the hope that the operation proposed is a viable activity. With the services for normal bus operation in most parts of the continent being heavily subsidized, a commercial British operation may find itself unable to compete on equal terms.

This could well make bus operation, particularly in the areas where access from the continent is easy, subject to even greater competition than exists at present.

# NEW MODES

A lot is currently being said about light rapid transit and it seems fashionable at the moment for most medium and large sized British cities to be developing plans for this type of facility. I would guess that at the end of the day, much of the effort expended in discussing these schemes will prove to be wasted . Only the largest cities will successfully operate such systems on account of the cost of the infrastructure being totally disproportionate to the frequency of service that can be operated and, therefore, the cost per capita for each person carried. In those areas where LRT does become a reality, the interesting question is then raised as to whether they should compete with or coordinate with, normal bus services. Where the bus operator obtains the franchize to operate a system, then clearly co-ordination is much simpler. But if, as may happen, another party obtains the rights to operate the LRT system, then there will be an aggrieved resident bus operator, who will see the LRT system as a major abstraction from their basic revenue. For these operators, to then co-ordinate the bus services with the LRT, there must be raised the question of whether such action is anti-competitive in that it then potentially excludes other operators, and I believe that LRT could well bring about a rethinking of the present regulatory framework in which the bus industry operates. One must remember that in Tyne and Wear, the Metro was a brilliant concept of co-ordination which has been destroyed by the 1985 Transport Act and we now seem to have a tremendous waste of resources in the area with one of the resident operators, Go Ahead Northern, announcing autumn cutbacks, presumably to improve viability. Most of the co-ordination with the Metro was, of course, undertaken by Tyne and Wear PTE who, in their new form as Busways, find themselves in exactly the same position as any of the other operators running in the area.

A further aspect which will, no doubt, affect our future thinking is the matter of finite fuel resources. We have already seen the problems with fuel prices caused by the invasion of Kuwait by Iraq, and this must remind us that the fuel supply industry is very volatile. The dual mode trolleybus certainly could be an avenue for future consideration and, indeed, a demonstrator from Nancy came over to Britain a few years ago. This form of road transport gets away from the rigidity and inflexibility of fixed tracked vehicles and only needs overhead wiring for sections of roads where service frequencies are sufficiently high to justify the infrastructure. Over the last few years, signs of development of this form of transport in Britain seem to have ground, if not to a halt, to a very slow crawl. Now we have problems in the Middle East, I do see this as an area of probable development which seems greatly favoured against battery driven vehicles on the account of the weight penalties associated with current technology in that field. The normal trolleybus is possibly going to enjoy a revival, but I do feel that the dual mode vehicle, in spite of the capital cost of vehicles, will perhaps be favoured in the medium and long term and certainly as a less capital-intensive means of conserving fuel than light rapid transit.

## OTHER ISSUES

Deregulation does not seem to have stemmed the tide in reducing passengers, a feature of bus operation that has now been taking place for nearly 40 years. However, I do believe that with the freedom of choice being introduced for educational purposes, there will be a greater emphasis on the carriage of scholars to and from school - 'bussing' as the Americans call it. There is no doubt in my mind that for most local bus service operators, this increased schools travel will cause a greater peak vehicle requirement and for the smaller coach operator, such work will continue to offer a year-round revenue base on which to build their other activities, which are generally seasonally biased. The freedom of choice being introduced for education will, undoubtedly, more than compensate for any projections that exist for reducing school rolls. From a bus operator's point of view, the most economic way of carrying the children is to carry the largest number at any one time and, in acknowledging the British objection to standing on vehicles, I believe this ensures a rosy future for the large double decker in this country as the most fuel efficient vehicle that takes up the least road space. There will, of course, be exceptions and as people look to Europe, there will be those who advocate the use of the articulated single decker. However in my view, the costs associated with this in altering street furniture, together with the British dislike of standing and the total reconstruction of many bus depots that will be required to both park and service such vehicles, offers a bleak future in the UK for the articulated bus.

Finally, as somebody who has been brought up on the operational side of a bus company, I wonder who will be running the bus undertakings of tomorrow. Will it be the transport man, or will it be somebody from the professions or industry? It does seem that currently there is a trend away from the transport professional; since whilst the bus industry has to operate commercially, there are difficulties in paying salaries to transport orientated managing directors who are then supported by specialists, particularly in the finance and personnel fields where (especially for accountants) salaries commanded tend to be on the increase, relative to other disciplines. Much was said in the build-up to the 1985 Transport Act about improved safety standards and, indeed, measures were taken to ensure that these steps were acknowledged and implemented, at least on paper. Because of this, much of the responsibility for safety in the bus fleet lies in the hands of the fleet engineer or engineering director, and yet how many current managing directors of bus companies are engineers by background? If one goes back to the days when the bus industry was expanding, one finds that many of the erstwhile general managers were from an engineering discipline and maybe their day will come again as increasing importance is attached to their activities.

In this article I have put forward a few random thoughts and pointers for the future as I see it, but I emphasize that I cannot claim to have any better foresight than any other reader of **Transport Management**. There is no doubt that a lot of change in the medium term will depend on our political masters, both at home and at Brussels, who will inevitably keep public transport high on their agenda. With the throttling of cities by traffic, and the move towards a green environment, I feel that as time passes, bus operators are less and less going to be able to 'do their own thing' and that the freedom at present provided by deregulation will, in due course, appear as a temporary phenomenon.

# 3 Changing to contract distribution

*Article by D. Buck*
*National Carriers Contract Services (NCCS)*
*June 1988 issue*

## INTRODUCTION

As recently as the 1960s most third party transport and distribution services on offer to clients were based on some form of general haulage. Development of more specialized services since that time has been rapid.

Contract hire was one of the first of these specialized services and grew in importance during the 1970s. In a contract hire arrangement, the client is provided with vehicles by the third party operator, who will usually be responsible also for maintenance of the vehicles. Some forms of contract hire also make the third party operator responsible for the provision of drivers, although their work will be organized by the client. Contract hire therefore, means that the control of transport and distribution remains with the client, as in an entirely own-account operation. So the main benefit of contract hire to the client is often purely financial in nature, with no large outflows of capital being required for fleet purchase.

More recent developments in specialist services have looked towards giving the third party operator more control over transport and distribution work, so that the expertise of the operator can be exploited to the full and greater overall efficiency achieved. Foremost amongst these developments has been contract distribution.

33

The key feature of contract distribution is that the third party will operate and control both the vehicle fleet and warehousing facilities. In some cases, moreover, the contract distributor will also manage the holding of inventory in the warehouses, necessitating the installation of sophisticated computer systems linking client and distributor.

Differences in arrangement between client and distributor are bound to occur, reflecting important differences in distribution requirement. It follows that there can be no singular definition of contract distribution and one of the crucial distinctions to be made is between dedicated and shared contract distribution. An example of the former is the NCCS operation for Harris Queensway, where vehicles and warehouses are dedicated to the one operation. By contrast, in a shared operation, a distribution network will be developed for joint use by a number of clients. SPD provides a good example of a shared contract distribution operation.

Having set the broader context for contract distribution, the remainder of this article is dedicated to an examination of a series of questions. These are:
* Who are the contract distributors?
* What has been their success as providers of distribution services?
* Why do clients change to contract distribution?
* How should a client go about selecting a contract distributor?

## WHO ARE THE CONTRACT DISTRIBUTORS?

Increasing competition has meant that the providers of distribution services must regularly appraise and revise the portfolio of services on offer to clients. Current and projected levels of growth are a particular stimulus to changing services. Contract hire has levelled off in growth terms with the annual rate of growth not expected to exceed 5 per cent. The distribution market on the other hand is experiencing growth in excess of 10 per cent per annum. A number of contract hire companies have therefore expanded to offer contract distribution as part of their portfolio. These companies see the move into dedicated distribution as a natural next step to ensure growth and profitability.

Companies that have emerged from the contract hire market and which are now actively chasing dedicated distribution business include TNT, Transfleet and Wincanton. Table I shows estimates of their revenues earned from dedicated contract distribution, using market intelligence reports as source material.

## TABLE 1
## CONTRACT HIRE COMPANIES ACTIVE IN CONTRACT DISTRIBUTION

| Company | Total Revenue (£m) | Estimated Dedicated Distribution Revenue |
|---|---|---|
| TNT | 81.0 | 27.5 |
| Wincanton | 62.1 | 15.5 |
| Systemline | 9.1 | 9.1 |
| Transfleet | 54.0 | 6.5 |
| Mitchell Cotts | 42.3 | 5.5 |

Not all providers of contract distribution, however, have come to the market via the contract hire route. A number of companies have established a contract distribution operation without using contract hire as a stepping stone. Nevertheless, they offer a comprehensive range of dedicated services, and will distribute a wide variety of products. Table 2 shows the major companies with estimates of revenue earned from contract distribution.

## TABLE 2
## MAJOR CONTRACT DISTRIBUTORS CARRYING A VARIETY OF PRODUCTS ON DEDICATED CONTRACT

| Company | Total Revenue (£m) | Estimated Dedicated Distribution Revenue |
|---|---|---|
| NCCS | 70.0 | 70.0 |
| NFC Distn. Group | 150.0 | 65.0 |
| TDG | 481.5 | 48.0 |
| Lowfield | 23.5 | 17.8 |
| UTD | 22.0 | 12.0 |

The third broad category of contract distributor contains those that specialize in particular market sectors, or who offer only common user (or shared) distribution. Table 3 lists companies active in this work.

TABLE 3
COMPANIES OFFERING SPECIALIST AND/OR SHARED
CONTRACT DISTRIBUTION SERVICES

| Company | Total Revenue (£m) | Type of Operation |
|---|---|---|
| SPD | 107.0 | Common User/Shared |
| Glass Glover | 84.1 | Fresh Food |
| Hunter Saphir | 64.6 | Fresh Food |
| United Biscuits | 39.1 | Food-Own Account + 3rd Party |
| Express Dairy | 23.5 | Food-Own Account + 3rd Party |
| TLT | 23.2 | Food-Own Account + 3rd Party |
| Christian Salvesen | 22.5 | Frozen Food |
| McGregor Cory | 20.0 | Common User/Shared |
| Robsons | 19.0 | Dedicated Haulage * |
| NFT | 15.8 | Food-Common User |
| Swifts | 10.0 | Dedicated Haulage * |
| Booker Distribution | 8.3 | Food-Common User |
| Butlers | 8.0 | Warehousing + Haulage |
| Bucks | 8.0 | Dedicated Haulage * |
| Bonds | 5.3 | Common User/Shared |

* Companies which are dedicated specialists either by products sector or region of operation.

36

# THIRD PARTY PENETRATION OF DISTRIBUTION MARKET

No analysis of the market place would be complete without some indication of the market share held by third party operators. However, this is a difficult undertaking because available statistics often do not tell the whole story. The following examination of market shares relies almost exclusively on surveys carried out for the Institute of Physical Distribution Management (now the Institute of Logistics and Distribution Management) in 1984 and 1985, together with government statistics showing industrial output.

These sources broadly indicate that over £24 billion was spent annually on distribution services in the mid-1980s. Approximately 27 per cent of this total (i.e. about £6.5 billion) was spent with third party operators of all kinds, ranging from general hauliers to contract hauliers.

A further important fact emerging from the surveys is that expenditure on all forms of distribution (i.e. third party and own-account) measured as a percentage of sales value is diminishing, as illustrated in Table 4.

TABLE 4
EXPENDITURE ON DISTRIBUTION AS A PERCENTAGE
OF SALES VALUE
1980 TO 1985

| Year | 1980 | 1983 | 1984 | 1985 |
|---|---|---|---|---|
| Average of sales | 17.0 | 12.3 | 11.6 | 10.6 |

Two main factors account for the reducing percentage expenditure on distribution shown in Table 4; the rising value of goods being distributed and improved distribution efficiency. It could be argued that the substitution of third party services for own-account operation is an important factor in improving distribution efficiency. Expenditure on third party carriers increased from 22 per cent of total distribution expenditure in 1984, to 27 per cent in 1985.

Some attempt can also be made to show how separate parts of the distribution process are represented by third party operation. Not unexpectedly, third party transport has the greatest penetration and although its market share increased from 40 per cent in 1984 to 47 per cent in 1985, growth in this area now appears to be slowing down. Third party storage has taken longer to gain favour but now shows the greatest potential and expanded from 14 per cent in 1984 to 18 per cent in 1985.

It is also possible to obtain some indication of third party penetration by market sector. Table 5 shows the sectors where third party operations of all kinds have achieved the greatest penetration.

TABLE 5

PERCENTAGE EXPENDITURE, BY MARKET SECTOR, ON 3RD PARTY DISTRIBUTION SERVICES

| Market Sector Expenditure | Percentage on 3rd party |
|---|---|
| Food, Drink and Tobacco | 29 |
| Distributive Trades | 25 |
| Chemical and Allied Products | 21 |
| Electrical Engineering | 13 |
| Textiles, Clothing etc. | 12 |
| Others | 14 |

The dominance of the food, drink and tobacco sector is particularly noteworthy. Major grocery multiples have been amongst the most innovative of the users of distribution services and third party operators have enjoyed a close relationship with most of the multiples for a considerable period of time.


## REASONS FOR CHANGING TO CONTRACT DISTRIBUTION

The reasons for moving to a third party operator from own-account distribution are numerous, but rarely will there be one single reason for the change. More often than not, a client will choose contract distribution because of a combination of circumstances and it is often difficult to rank by importance the different factors taken into account by a client. The following factors are therefore not necessarily listed according to their order of importance when client companies make their decisions.

38

## Concentrating on mainstream business

It is a compelling argument that companies should concentrate on doing what they do best. Manufacturers are in business to manufacture, retailers to retail. So the distribution of products should be managed by specialists in distribution. Otherwise there is the risk that the manufacturer, say, will be so preoccupied with the intricacies of manufacturing that he will fail to give sufficient time to the development of distribution services, leading to falling levels of customer service and declining competitiveness.

## Changes in market for the client

Business expansion/growth: a company may, for a variety of reasons, wish to keep a newly acquired subsidiary separate from its established business. This will mean keeping distribution systems separate as well, and a contract distribution operation may then be essential.

Business retraction: When a company suffers a reverse in business fortunes, its priority will be to use its capital either to re-establish itself in existing markets or develop new ones. Essential capital can be released for this purpose if the company divests itself of an own-account operation and changes to contract distribution. A recent example is provided by the home computer market, where a decline in sales forced some manufacturers to concentrate production on the Continent rather than having several manufacturing bases in the UK and other European countries. Distribution in the UK is now largely carried out under contract.

New product launch/test market: Some companies wish to isolate the sales and distribution function for certain product lines, for monitoring purposes. Argos, for example, requires its toys to be distributed quite separately from the rest of its product ranges and this work is carried out by NCCS under a distribution contract.

## Changes in distribution activity

Demographic criteria: It has become recognized as good marketing practice to ally distribution activity to areas of demand rather than supply. Producers' distribution systems, therefore, have had to become more flexible to meet changing patterns of wealth, population and other factors affecting demand for products. For many producers it has been an attractive option to switch to contract distribution using a national operator with depots throughout the

UK. This has saved the producer having to invest periodically in expensive depot relocation.

Industrial relations criteria: It is not unusual to find that, over time, restrictive working practices develop within own-account operations. Common examples of restrictive practices are overmanning or limits on daily workloads. Some companies find that a switch to a contractor is often the only effective way of returning to realistic working practices in distribution.

Technology criteria: As distribution specialists, third party contractors will usually be up to date with the latest technological developments affecting distribution. Their readiness to innovate, particularly in the field of information technology, can lead to advances in operational efficiency which ultimately benefits clients. For example, NCCS drivers delivering to Argos stores carry a floppy disc to update the stock files on the shop computer. This innovation has helped make delivery notes redundant.

**Financial changes**

Tax criteria: Recent changes in taxation, and especially the abolition of 100 per cent first year allowances on vehicle acquisition, have made own-account distribution less attractive than previously. However, it may be advantageous for some clients to set up a joint venture distribution company with the contract distributor. In this way the client can purchase the vehicles and enjoy wider tax advantages while the expertise of the contract distributor is used to manage the joint venture company.

Financial position of client company: Joint ventures (see above) are a useful way for high profit companies to enjoy tax benefits and the advantage of specialist distribution expertise. Less profitable companies might prefer simply to contract out their distribution since it requires no capital outlay. Contract distributors will, of course, need to be sure that distribution service payments can be made by a less profitable company. However, it is by no means inevitable that a contract distributor would turn down the offer of work from a potential client going through a temporary business trough.

## SELECTING A THIRD PARTY OPERATOR

Changing to contract distribution needs careful consideration and takes time. Frequently the lead-time between initial contract with a prospective client and the start of the contract distribution operation is between 12 and 24 months.

Of course not all companies moving to contract distribution will necessarily give all of their business to a third party or indeed if they do move to third party, necessarily give it to just one operator. Depending on the size of distribution expenditure some companies will "put their eggs into several baskets" and some will retain some of their distribution 'in-house' - this is a very good way to monitor performance.

Assuming that a decision has been made to change to third party contract distribution, it is essential to consider how selection of the right company should be made. There are numerous avenues but the most common are:

- By invitation through media, (advertising/direct mail), word of mouth and reputation.
- Through management consultants i.e. using independent experts.
- By formal tender.

Having agreed to the method of selection, it is then necessary to assess the shortlisted third party operators against a set of performance criteria, before coming to a final decision. The following criteria should be used as a basis for measurement:

- Product
- Implementation
- Price and Service
- Place
- Operational Support
- People.

Obviously some of the above criteria are more important to a company than others. However, all should play a significant part within the selection process.

**Product**

The product of a third party operator is complex because it embraces a wide variety of functions and activities. The distribution product may be defined in logistics terminology as 'the process of strategically managing the movement and storage of materials, parts and finished inventory from suppliers, through the firm and on to the client'.

Consequently any break in the distribution process may mean that a company will be unable to market and sell its goods and services successfully. Many companies are rightly examining more closely the total distribution function and not just the individual elements in isolation. But most companies are not looking broadly enough at where the distribution chain should begin, or at how and who should be controlling and implementing it. In other words, perhaps distribution should be examined within the broader aspects of management and perhaps it should be controlled by the marketing function within a company. The importance of distribution management as a means of maintaining and improving corporate profitability has never been greater than it is today, and it is essential for a company to choose an appropriate distribution strategy.

In many modern economies, the combined effects of recession, inflation and technological change have produced an environment in which the options for a corporate strategy are considerably constrained. Yet, for many companies, these same conditions have provided an opportunity for development. In particular, many improvements in performance have occurred through revisions to distribution strategy.

A professional third party operator will have the resources to offer a full distribution package to the client companies. Elements of the package would include warehousing, drivers, operating managers and staff, materials handling equipment, computer systems, stock control, order processing, management information technology, high purchasing power, flexibility, a track record of practical experience and, not least, a substantial fleet of vehicles and trailers.

But one of the secrets of success for a top third party operator is to anticipate the trends and requirements of a fast changing distribution market. One of these, and perhaps the most significant, will be stock ownership. The time is fast approaching when third party operators will not only be responsible for warehousing and movement of stock but will also legally own it. The client will retain control over buying decisions and be responsible for negotiations with manufacturers on, for example, quality, price, discounts. This trend is a direct result of retailers' efforts to reduce the level of stock.

The benefits to retailers of transferring stock ownership are an improved balance sheet, greatly improved cash flow (retailers pay for the stock as it is drawn off) and the incentive for the third party operator to maintain stock holdings at the lowest possible operational level. Adopting the kanban (or just-in-time) method of supply is likely to be of increasing importance in reaching lower levels of stock-holding and the contract distributors have been busy evaluating the method and its implications for clients.

## Implementation

The process by which the third party operator builds his distribution product is complex. He has to create relationships embracing trust, confidence, expertise and professionalism with the potential client.

Although some elements of distribution operations (e.g. customer service performance) can be measured, many others are qualitative and difficult to measure because distribution is, first and foremost, a service. The method of selling a distribution service therefore has to be on a face-to-face basis. The operator also needs to maintain relationships with the client and dialogue has to be open and forthright. He is, in effect, entering into a partnership and both sides have a full part to play.

It is also necessary for the operator to communicate at all levels within the client's company. The decision within a client company to switch to contract distribution is usually a board decision. But once the contract is settled the operator will need to start a dialogue with other parts of the company, especially those previously responsible for operating the distribution system. He will also have to talk to the client's client who, after all, will be at the receiving end of the new distribution service.

For some larger contracts it is quite usual for operator and client to consider a joint company approach. In this way the client retains full control over how the operator performs on his behalf.

This joint venture approach is becoming increasingly popular. Both parties are equally committed to tackling immediate or potential problems together, and benefit from the future success of the new company.

## Price and service

Price plays an important part in business decisions and more often than not provides the initial comparison between a third party distribution operator and the prospective client's own cost assessment of present 'in-house' operations. As a guideline, third party distribution operators are usually cheaper than own-account, and this is because they are distribution specialists and therefore more efficient. However, any comparison must also take account of the greater flexibility that a contract distribution package can bring to distribution operations.

The aim of the contractor is to produce a number of options which can be examined by the client. Different options will incorporate different levels of service and price, so the prospective client has a unique opportunity to choose which option best suits his needs. Many operators will even offer an open book accounting system which allows the client to scrutinize and discuss all the price elements for the different options. This approach also ensures that the terms of the contract are fair.

## Place

A good third party operator should be national. This is mainly because a national service can readily incorporate the local and regional needs of clients requiring a more limited service. The national operator is therefore able to offer the most comprehensive service to clients. Indeed, it is often a major marketing requirement of contract distributors to meet the needs of prospective clients, irrespective of UK distribution area.

Furthermore, industry sector is another important consideration when selecting a distribution contractor. Third party operators are often closely identified with particular industry sectors, ranging across the spectrum of retailing and manufacturing activities. Industry sector will, of course, be a vital factor determining where distribution activities take place. Some sectors will require high street delivery, others will send their goods to factories or warehouses. The distribution environment, by industry sector, can therefore vary enormously. It also follows that it is wise for a potential client to ensure that a contract distributor has substantial experience in, say, high street deliveries before entrusting him with this kind of work.

## Operational support

The initial sale of the distribution service designed for a client is just the beginning. The after-sales service is invariably more important. This involves the third party operator placing great emphasis on understanding each client's objectives and reacting accordingly.

It is preferable that all clients should have a contract manager who is responsible for representing their distribution interests and to ensure communication and understanding between client and operator. In addition, clients of any size should ideally enjoy direct access to a Board member belonging to the operator.

There are six important points which should be observed when operational support is provided to the client after the initial sale has been made. They are:

1. Regular communication with the client.
2. Regular reporting to the client.
3. Monitoring performance.
4. Regular strategic reviews (internal and external) with the client.
5. Awareness of the need to change as market conditions change.
6. Willingness to update the distribution system.

## People

People are the greatest asset of any company and central to business success. Communication between staff in the client company and their colleagues in the contract distribution company is therefore an essential consideration.

A third party operator should be organized to promote communication with the client. Individual members of staff should be given responsibility for one or more clients business. Staff must be seen as an extension to the client and, indeed, almost part of the client's staff. For example, drivers would usually wear the client's uniform not that of the contract distributor.

Moreover, the successful third party operator should place great emphasis on training and manpower development. His staff should be motivated by internal communication, good salaries and, perhaps, incentives based on productivity and performance improvement.

The National Freight Consortium, of which NCCS is part, would appear to have got it right through privatization and employee ownership. Employee ownership in the NFC has brought with it a new style of participative management and a greater commitment by everyone to their work. The NFC's unique partnership with its staff has brought financial reward to both the company and to the individual shareholders. Some 70 per cent of the total workforce are shareholders.

## SUMMARY

* Third party distribution services of all kinds are increasing in popularity and now hold about 27 per cent of the total distribution market, by value.

* An increasingly important element of third party distribution services is storage. More clients now require storage management performed by specialists along with more established transport work.

* Greatest third party penetration is in the food, drink and tobacco sector, followed by the distributive trades.

* An increasingly popular form of third party operation is contract distribution. Many contract hire companies now offer contract distribution as part of their services portfolio, while other companies have been established to operate solely as contract distributors.

* There is usually a combination of factors which motivate a client to select a third party operator to manage distribution services. Numbered among the factors are a wish to concentrate on mainstream business, changes in market for the client, changes in distribution activity and financial changes.

* It is important for prospective clients to undertake a systematic examination of contract distributors to assess their suitability for the work on offer. There are a number of important criteria against which the examination should be made, including the range of distribution services available, plans for the implementation of the chosen distribution package and subsequent distribution support for the client company in a changing environment.

# 4 The liberalization of road haulage in the European Community

*Paper presented to the Leicester Centre by*
*Mrs N. Chattle*
*Department of Transport*
*April/May 1990 issue*

## INTRODUCTION

People sometimes give the impression that the formation of the European Single Market will be an overnight process. They imagine they will go to bed on 31 December 1992 and wake up to a startlingly different world. In fact the Single Market is being pieced together all the time at a startling pace.

Many of the important building blocks of a Single European Market were already set in place in the Treaty of Rome in 1957 - provisions on competition, FTPS, right of establishment, state aids etc. But some do not apply directly, e.g., FTPS, and need specific regulations in order to apply in the field of transport.

There was an important EC Judgment in 1985 which found the European Council at fault in not applying FTPS "within reasonable time". However, the agreement reached on the SE Act in 1985 and the setting of the target of a single market by the end of 1992 gave the whole process the necessary impetus. Since then some 300 single market measures have been agreed, including a record 68 under Spanish Presidency in the first six months of 1989. Now more than half the 1992 legislative programme is complete. Some may not greatly interest you e.g. the Directive on trade in fresh and deep-frozen bovine semen - but some important ones are very relevant to transport.

# GROWTH OF ROAD HAULAGE IN THE COMMUNITY

When road haulage permits were first used bilaterally, this undoubtedly helped trade. But demand for permits from UK hauliers always tended to outstrip supply, ie, artificially imposed quotas proved insufficient.

The issue of such quotas is clearly against the spirit of the Treaty, which promotes free movement of people and goods. Consequently, an involved system of annual bilateral negotiations between governments to raise quotas has to be evolved. There is always more demand from our hauliers than from the other side of the Channel, e.g., German hauliers easily cross land frontiers with the Netherlands, Belgium, Luxembourg, France, Switzerland, Austria, Denmark, Czechoslovakia, etc.

Nevertheless, there has been increasing success in raising quotas for the UK. For example in 1970 the total of the UK's bilateral quotas with different EC Member States, was only 20,000 permits. By 1989 they had risen to 220,000, ie, an eleven-fold increase.

Besides bilateral permit arrangements, the Community also issues multilateral permits. In 1973, when the UK first joined there was a tiny allocation of just 99 permits. Increases since then mean that the UK's total allocation is now 1,770 permits - a 17 or 18 fold increase.

Nevertheless, we still have not reached the position where the supply of permits meets natural demand. We have had to apply a rationing system for bilateral permits which we only ended in the spring of last year. We still have to ration Community permits.

Growth in road haulage to mainland Europe since 1973 has been steadily upwards, despite the recession in business during 1980. This reflects the gradual strengthening of trading links with other EC countries since the UK joined. This growth has been shared fairly equally between powered vehicles and unaccompanied trailers, which have both doubled in volume over the last ten years.


## LIBERALIZATION

Liberalization has for many years been the Government's watchword. From the time when the Department first started negotiating bilateral agreement in the late 1960s, it was always seeking maximum liberalization whether Labour or the Conservatives were in power.

48

Even so, it took long and hard negotiations before the EC Transport Council finally agreed in June 1988 to liberalize the EC international road haulage market by the end of 1992. All quotas and permits will be abolished from that date and in the interim the level of bilateral quotas (where they still exist) is intended to be increased in line with trade and traffic.

So prospects are for permits to be increasingly available between now and 1992. From 1993 all permits, multilateral and bilateral, will disappear in the EC and hauliers will no longer obtain loads for some countries before knowing whether they have permits to deliver them. They will no longer have to pay for cumbersome bureaucracy - a cost necessarily passed on to customers.

From 1993, the Community system will be governed solely by qualitative criteria governing access to market (as the UK's has been since 1968). The regulations on these criteria were adopted a few months ago. Hauliers will probably need a piece of paper/licence to show that they fulfil these criteria. They will also have to ensure that the wording of the regulation is such, that the piece of paper cannot become in any way a 'permit' subject again to any kind of quantitative controls.

The Government believes that British hauliers are well placed to benefit from the single market. Growth in the UK's road haulage trade with other Member States is expected to continue up to and beyond 1992. UK hauliers are better placed than most to benefit from growth in the new freedom of wider markets because of the twenty years' experience they have had of free competition. Undoubtedly some Member States are fearful of what will happen to their hauliers. We should be able to understand this, since before 1968 UK operators were similarly fearful that increased competition arising from 1968 deregulation would lead to inadequate prices and profits and consequently, to an excessive rate of bankruptcy, and declining standards of vehicle operation and safety. Such fears proved groundless as none of this happened. Instead, a marked feature of the UK domestic road haulage industry is its stability and continuity. The total number of operators peaked at around 140,000 between 1972-1975 and today remains very steady at about 130,000. Bankruptcies which were most likely to reach high levels during recession even in the bad year of 1983, were only about 1 per cent of the total number of operators.

It should be said that the standard of vehicle maintenance in the UK also improved significantly in the early 1970s, following deregulation. The failure rate in annual vehicle tests fell from 30 per cent in 1969/70 to 19 per cent in 1975/76 and has remained fairly constant at around 20 per cent. Since 1967 there has been a 60 per cent fall in the involvement rate of heavy goods vehicles in accidents.

## CABOTAGE

The liberalization of the Communities' international road haulage market is now going full steam ahead for 1 January 1993. But there is a need to go further. Indeed the EC is obliged by Treaty and the single market to go further - and free our hauliers to pick up and deliver loads anywhere within the Community. In other words they want to see domestic markets fully opened up to non-resident hauliers, otherwise known as cabotage.

Cabotage proposals are on the table in virtually every sector. However, until the end of last year none had actually been agreed. The first real breakthrough came in December. The EC Ministers agreed on a transitional phase, in opening up cabotage, starting in July 1990 and lasting until the end of 1992, when it is to be replaced by a definitive cabotage regime. The transitional phase involves a cabotage quota for each country, but the final 1993 regime will need to be unrestricted. We hope the transitional system will allay existing fears on cabotage. The DTp fully understands these fears, but does not believe UK hauliers have anything to fear. The fact that the UK road haulage industry has been deregulated for 20 years, means it is far more competitive and able to meet the challenge than competitors abroad, who still operate in a highly regulated environment. Moreover, the fact that we have far fewer lorries from other Member States transiting the UK than say Germany, means there are far fewer lorries for other Member States' hauliers to pick up domestic loads here than UK hauliers (and others) will have in France or Germany. A study commissioned by the Department and undertaken by the Polytechnic of Central London confirms this fact. We confidently expect British hauliers to obtain a good share of cabotage loads in other Member States, so reducing the wasteful cost of empty running.

## HARMONIZATION OF MARKET CONDITIONS

Free competition in 1992 is all very well but will it be fair competition? British hauliers already point to the relatively high rates of VED, together, of course, with road tolls in some other Member States, who themselves impose lower rates of excise duty on their vehicles so that British hauliers effectively pay twice over. The UK Government wants to see the Community take action to minimize the extent to which British hauliers and exporters are placed at a competitive disadvantage by tax regimes. This means that other Member States should be required to increase their road taxes in order at least to recoup their own infrastructure costs. Our Government has long argued in the Community for this important principle and has won support from other Member States.

Indeed, the Commission is now recommending a system of infrastructure cost coverage based on gross vehicle weight and axle configuration very similar to the UK's. The Commission's proposals also include a provision prohibiting any reduction in VED to prevent present differences in international taxation from growing wider. The UK Government endorses these proposals: if acted upon they would represent another important step forward. There are further proposals being considered to base tax levels on track costs in countries used by lorries. Such a system - known as territoriality - would undoubtedly be very complex and needs a good deal of further consideration.

Of course, harmonization concerns more than taxation and another important area is enforcement. Early last year an EC Directive designed to achieve a simpler and adequate standard of enforcement of drivers' hours regulations came into force. It provides for minimum levels of checking at the roadside and at operator's premises and for co-operation between Member States over cross-border offences. Governments are also committed to ensuring lorries are not loaded beyond levels they are approved to carry. It is in everyone's interest to see that lorries wherever they are in EC, meet required safety and other standards - accidents cause costly delays as well as needless suffering. The UK has already embarked upon a widespread weighbridge programme and we are aiming to provide 85 weighbridge sites by the early 1990s; 63 have already been built. The 1989/90 target is 115,000 weighings, including 14,300 foreign lorries.


## OTHER FACTORS AFFECTING ROAD HAULAGE

Besides liberalization and harmonization what else is happening towards 1992 in the field of road transport? The Government fully recognizes the need for improved roads enabling lorries to travel quickly and safely, avoiding congested areas in our towns and helping hauliers to keep costs down. The real level of capital expenditure on trunk roads in the last 10 years has been increased by some 30 per cent with roughly 870 miles of new trunk road being provided. Bypasses have been the focus of attention since they speed traffic round centres of population rather than through them and improve the environment for residents. England's motorway and trunk road programme is now running at about £12 billion and is due to add over 2,700 miles of new or widened roads to the trunk road network. Over the next three years we will be spending 50 per cent more in real terms than in the previous three years 1987-90. The Government is keen to secure the benefits which the private sector can bring in terms of finance, innovation, enterprise and management efficiency, while itself contributing with large public infrastructure programmes.

However, better roads are of limited help if it still takes hours to get through Dover! Fortunately, Customs and Excise is working hard to speed things up. The introduction of a single administrative document and fast-lane clearance system with direct trader input, so as to obtain clearance in advance, are considerable breakthroughs. Doubtless, as we approach 1992, computer clearance and electronic data input will become increasingly important.

## THE CHANNEL TUNNEL

1993 is not only the first year of the economic Single Market, it is also due to see the physical link from the UK to Europe by Channel Tunnel established. This will provide new competitive opportunities for rail freight straight through to the heart of the European markets. In addition, Euro-Tunnel will also offer a fast frequent, all-weather shuttle service for road freight. Indeed together with ferries and air transport, four modes of cross-channel fre ght transport are available. This reflects the keystone of the Government's transport policies - encouraging choice and healthy competition to the benefit of the transport users.

## CONCLUSIONS

The years between now and 1992, will see considerable changes. However, these changes will be greater for the transport operators of the other Member States. In many areas the Commission's proposals are similar to conditions already prevailing in the UK. In other areas, change will be of direct benefit to the customers. There will, for instance, be a new Community drivers' licence covering both private and vocational driving which is to be introduced in 1991. This in itself, like European passports, should speed up necessary checks by being immediately recognisable throughout the EC.

The 1992 process has now really gathered momentum and is irreversible. It offers new and exciting challenges, new opportunities and new risks. Many UK companies are already ahead with their 1992 plans and they are the ones that will flourish.

# 5  Environmental costs of road goods vehicles

*Article by C. Sharp*
*University of Leicester*
*December 1974 issue*

It is not surprising that the country in which concern about the environmental costs resulting from the operation of goods vehicles has been expressed most strongly is Britain. We have come to rely more than most other countries on road transport as the main means of carrying inland flows of freight traffic. In 1971 77.1 per cent of goods traffic (measured in tonne kilometres) according to one estimate was carried by road. Comparable figures for other European countries were:

| | |
|---|---|
| France | = 36.9% (1970) |
| W. Germany | = 25.6% |
| USSR | = 7.1% |

(These figures reflect not only a slower rate of decline in the proportion of goods carried by rail in the Continental countries compared with Britain, but also the much greater importance in these countries of inland waterways). Although the total number of lorries in Britain of more than 1.5 tons unladen weight only increased by 5.5 per cent between 1960 and 1970 there was a much bigger increase in the number of lorries in the heaviest weight categories. The total fleet of goods vehicles of 8 tons unladen weight or more increased by 567 per cent between 1956 and 1968. Britain not only has more lorries but has been relatively slow in developing a network of motorways, and still has many very heavily trafficked roads which pass through the centres of small towns and villages. We also have a number of large conurbations where major roads must cut through the built-up environment.

This article is based on a study of the environmental costs of the operation of goods vehicles which was supported by the Road Haulage Association and the Freight Transport Association, and which attempted to examine ways in which these social costs could be reduced. The major problems which were encountered in making the study were:

(i)   The identification of the nature of the environmental costs which result from the operation of lorries, and their relationship to the total environ mental costs caused by traffic flows.
(ii)  The examination of the possibilities of changing the technology of lorries and their operation in ways which would reduce environmental costs.
(iii) The investigation of other possible methods (besides those relating to vehicle technology) of reducing environmental costs.
(iv)  The very difficult problem of evaluating the benefits which might result from reducing environmental costs, and comparing these with the costs involved.

The main components of the total environmental costs which are caused by lorries are noise, air pollution, roadwear, accident involvement, effects on roadside buildings, (either by direct contact or through vibration), 'visual intrusion', and delays caused to other road users. Noise is one of the most serious of the social costs imposed by lorries. The present legal maxima (measured in specified test conditions) are 92 dB(A) for the heaviest vehicles and 89 dB(A) for those with engines rated at less than 200 BHP. Peak noise levels can be reduced to about 86-89 dB(A) by the encapsulation of existing engines. More drastic noise reductions to about 80 dB(A), (which, it has been suggested would be an 'acceptable' peak noise level) would involve a major redesigning of engines with slower engine speeds, smaller bore cylinders (and more cylinders where power must be maintained), and possibly the use of turbochargers. Government sponsored research on the production of a 'quiet lorry' is in progress. Air pollution is a much less serious problem for diesel-engined lorries as their emissions are generally less harmful than those from petrol engines. The emission of black smoke, or unburnt particles of carbon, is controlled by government regulation. Black smoke emission

(which is unpleasant, though not harmful to health) is a sign of bad maintenance and should normally be avoidable. But methods of reducing smoke
levels, such as advancing injection timing, may increase the output of more
dangerous emissions such as oxides of nitrogen. Advancing injection timing
will also tend to increase noise.

It is debatable whether road wear is an environmental cost in quite the
same way as noise or air pollution. It can be identified and is borne mainly by
highway authorities, rather than by the general public. There is controversy
about the exact nature of the relationship between axle loads and road wear,
but there is no doubt that the heavier vehicles are responsible for a very
considerable part of road wear. Calculation made in 'Living with the Lorry'
study suggested that, although lorries as a whole paid more in taxes than their
share of road construction and maintenance costs, the burden was not fairly
distributed between the lighter and heavier vehicles. The replacement of
vehicle licence duty, which varies with unladen weight, by a tax which was
related to axle load and gross vehicle weight would compel operators to pay
directly for the road wear caused by their vehicles.

The degree to which lorries are involved in road accidents, and the extent
to which they may be to blame for the accidents in which they are involved
are both controversial and complex issues. Measured in terms of accident
involvement per million vehicle miles travelled, lorries have a fairly good
record. For accidents of all severities the figure for lorries of over 1.5 tons
unladen weight in 1970 was 241. Equivalent figures for some other types of
vehicles (per hundred million miles travelled in 1970) were:

| | |
|---|---|
| Motorcycles | 2,311 |
| Cars and taxis | 261 |
| Bus and coach | 858 |

On the other hand, accidents in which lorries are involved, particularly those
also involving other road vehicles, result in a relatively high proportion of
deaths. One study showed that out of 1,888 car occupants killed in road
accidents of all kinds, 403 were killed in those involving lorries of over 3 tons
ULW and 46 in accidents involving goods vehicles of 1.5 - B3 tons ULW.
Possible measures to reduce the incidence or severity of lorry-involved
accidents include better and clearer rear lighting (to prevent cars hitting the
rears of slow-moving lorries at night); redesigning the backs of lorries to
prevent under-run accidents (in which projecting parts of the lorry or its load
hit a car windscreen); improvements to braking and regular medical checks
on drivers. There are, at present, no available statistics which can be used to

57

compare the accident involvement of medium-heavy (16-24 ton GVW) lorries with that of heavy lorries (of 28-32 tons GVW).

Vibration caused by lorries may be unpleasant but is unlikely to cause structural damage to normal buildings. Heavy traffic could, however, cause structural damage to old buildings. The effects of vibration can be reduced by improving vehicle suspension, by restrictions on maximum axle loads, and by maintaining a smooth road surface. Delays to other road users can be reduced by increasing the power to weight ratio of lorries so that they will be able to travel up hills or away from halts at intersections more quickly. Here again, however, there may be corresponding environmental or other losses such as increased noise levels or worse fuel consumption figures. It is difficult to think of any way in which lorries might be made more visually attractive, though some people believe that more smaller lorries would be less offensive than a smaller number of larger ones.

There are three other main measures, apart from changes in vehicle technology, which might be adopted in order to reduce the environmental costs caused by the operation of goods vehicles. These are the transfer of traffic to some other mode of transport; an attempt to reduce the demand for transport; and measures to move lorries from roads where they inflict high environmental costs on the community to roads outside built-up areas.

The only alternative method of transporting goods inside Britain which is immediately available is rail. The present canal system in Britain is quite unsuitable for carrying large scale traffic flows. There is nothing peculiar about the geography of Britain which makes the construction of modern canals impossible, and inland waterways in many continental countries carry very considerable traffic flows. There may be a case, as argued in the Inland Waterways publication "Barges or Juggernauts" for investigating the costs and benefits of constructing a new major inland waterway. But at present we have little idea whether such a project would prove worthwhile when all the economic and environmental factors were taken into consideration. It seems unlikely that any major new waterway will be constructed in the next few years.

The idea that the environmental costs of road goods transport can be removed or greatly reduced by transferring traffic to rail has received much popular support. At the end of 1971 there were only 11,643 route miles of rail track open to carry traffic, and only 607 access or egress points for goods traffic. The vast majority of factories, warehouses, quarries, building sites, shops and other premises which send out or receive goods traffic do not have a direct connection to the rail system. It is therefore literally impossible to transfer most traffic from an all-road to an all-rail haul. The most that can be done is to take traffic by road to rail depots, use rail for the trunk haul, and then deliver the goods by road from the destination goods station. This process happens already, and the freightliner service was specifically developed to carry large flows of traffic which can be brought into the terminals by road. But the scope for such transfers must be limited. Although locomotives may be able to pull impressively large loads, the number of goods trains which can be run on any trunk route could not be expanded very greatly, particular¹y if it is planned to share the rail lines with more and faster passenger trains. Many hauls in Britain are too short to make transfer to rail for the trunk a practical possibility. (The average length of haul for road-borne goods traffic in 1971 was estimated to be 29 miles.) The environmental advantages of road to road-rail-road transfers are not so self-evident as is sometimes supposed. Since rail depots are often in the centre of built-up areas, the latter may involve more running of goods vehicles on urban roads than the former. The building of new railways (as illustrated by the current controversy over the rail link to the Channel Tunnel) may involve environmental costs just as much as does new road construction. The railways may be able to make some increased contribution to the carriage of freight in Britain but their role in solving the environmental problems of goods transport has been greatly exaggerated by those who are looking for a cheap and easy solution, or who still have a nostalgic and sometimes almost mystical attraction to trains.

The environmental costs of road goods transport could, undoubtedly, be greatly reduced if the demand for freight transport was cut. It is difficult to see how this can be done in the short run unless the people of Britain are prepared to accept a drastic reduction in living standards. In the past the demand for freight transport has been highly correlated with the size of the nation's gross domestic product. There is some evidence that this relationship may be changing (because service industries or manufacturing industries which do not generate a large demand for transport have become more important), but future economic growth must involve some increase in the demand for freight transport. In the long run the dispersion of industry and centres of population which has been taking place for the last fifty years or so, could be reversed, and people and industry concentrated in a few densely-built large cities. This would reduce the demand for freight transport but might produce other social and environmental costs which would be even less acceptable than those created by goods vehicles. It does seem reasonable to argue, though, that more attention should be paid to the transport needs of new industrial developments, and their environmental implications, in the future.

The most promising way of reducing freight transport environmental costs in the next few years appears to be through finding routes for lorries

59

where they will not affect people in their homes or in urban streets. The scope for doing this by forcing goods vehicles to use "designated routes" is very limited, unless this is linked with some new road provision. Lorries do not generally use congested urban roads when alternatives are available, and closing roads to lorries may merely divert them to other roads which are even more environmentally unsuitable. The local authorities in Canterbury and in Exeter have both recently produced schemes for excluding heavy goods vehicles from their streets, but in both cases their proposals were overruled by the Department of the Environment because the alternative routes were worse, or in the case of Exeter, virtually non-existent. Some towns would undoubtedly gain if they could remove streams of through goods traffic, but this could bring economic ruin to other parts of the country which were served by these vehicles. There are many villages and small and medium towns where through-flows of heavy traffic could be removed altogether by the construction of a by-pass or a new through road.

It is, of course, true that new road construction itself involves environmental costs, but it may nevertheless be the best available solution. Some opposition to new road building has concentrated on the environmental losses and ignored the possibly more substantial environmental benefits which might result where traffic is removed from built-up to uninhabited areas. It is interesting to notice that the postponement of the construction of the M69 motorway, which would have linked the M6 near Coventry to the M1 near Leicester, and which would remove heavy streams of through traffic from the A46 and A47 roads (which pass through a number of towns and villages) had led to much protest and the formation of an "M69 Now" group. The inhabitants of built-up areas on the existing trunk roads are naturally very disappointed at being condemned to suffering from the costs of through-traffic for several years to come. The assumption by some environmental groups that any new motorway must do more harm than good to the environment is by no means always justified.

The problem of heavy traffic flows in many large conurbations is more intractable since it may be impossible to find any routes or to provide new roads, which would be outside the built environment. The social and economic costs of some proposed new urban motorways may prove to be prohibitive. Nevertheless, there may be some gains in providing through-routes for heavy traffic which will concentrate the flow as much as possible in the least environmentally sensitive area. To some extent this may involve making generous compensation to those whose homes or businesses would be most adversely affected. There is at present no formal way of allowing for environmental costs and benefits when appraising new road schemes, and there is some evidence to suggest that in the past, savings in motorists' and other travellers' time may have carried too much importance relative to environmental factors.

One very important benefit of road construction is that total flows of through-traffic, not only those of heavy lorries, may be removed from places where people work and live. Although lorries may be the most widely disliked component of traffic flows, it is the environmental costs of the total traffic flows to which most people object. Studies of three "High Streets" in Putney, Newbury and Camberley were made recently by TRRL teams. These showed that the main complaints were against traffic as a whole. Thus in Putney (which has the largest flow of goods vehicles of the three High Streets) the leading three complaints were "Too much traffic" (26.9 per cent), "Generally awful/terrible" (24.2 per cent) and "Traffic causes difficulty in crossing the street" (17.5 per cent). Only 8.3 per cent of respondents mentioned the problem of noise.

The final, and in some ways most difficult problem is to find some method of evaluating the costs and benefits of measures designed to reduce the environmental costs of road goods transport. While there is no doubt that most people would like to see these environmental costs reduced it is far from certain what they are prepared to pay to achieve this end. Discussion of the social costs of transport sometimes seems to be based on the assumption that environmental benefits are infinitely valuable. This, of course, is not true. No-one can prove conclusively that human happiness will be increased if a 2 dB(A) reduction in high Street traffic noise is obtained at the cost of a 1 per cent increase in food prices. Unfortunately it is very difficult to put both environmental and "economic" costs into the common currency of money. The problem can be illustrated by considering the value of the "benefits" which would follow from a reduction in the noise level of heavy lorries. Lorry and other traffic noise does not cause direct physiological damage (except, possibly to the hearing of lorry drivers) but is a subjective nuisance. Reactions to noise vary greatly; some people may be sensitive to relatively low noise levels while others can put up with much louder sounds. Even the dB(A) scale is not a completely objective measurement since certain frequencies which are considered to be particularly unpleasant for human ears are weighted most heavily. Aircraft noise is measured on a different scale which is not directly translatable into the dB(A) scale.

Evidence about what people are prepared to pay to enjoy noise reductions is very scanty and gives no clear set of figures. Research carried out for the Roskill Commission during its investigation of the alternative sites for a third London airport showed that equivalent levels of aircraft noise nuisance depressed house prices near Heathrow less than it did those near to Gatwick. It also showed that the percentage depression of house prices for any given noise nuisance level (measured by the "Noise and Number Index") was greater for more expensive houses. A survey of the effect of traffic noise on house prices on an estate of virtually identical houses in north Birmingham actually showed that prices were higher on the noisy main road than they were on quiet side streets. A great deal more evidence is required before reliable estimates can be made of the average value of the benefits of reducing environmental costs such as noise. Another difficulty is that what people are willing to pay to have a nuisance reduced or removed may be less than the compensation which they would require to be prepared to put up with the environmental cost. As Mishan has argued, the compensation level may often be a more appropriate measurement of the value of reductions in environmental costs.

There is a strong desire in Britain to reduce the impact of the unwanted side-products of the operation of goods vehicles. How much the community is willing to pay for any given environmental benefit is at present very uncertain. The most hopeful methods of reducing goods transport environmental costs in the next few years appear to be by improving technology, and by a combination of new road construction and the use of designated routes for heavy goods vehicles. The social costs caused by lorries are, however, only one part of the environmental costs of total traffic flows.

# 6 The economic costs of smoke emission control

*Article by D.G. Rhys*
*University of Wales*
*June 1975 issue*

The motor car has become one of the favourite targets for the odium of environmentalists, conservationists, and the consumer's "safety-first" lobby. It is incontestable that the car's internal combustion engine does produce noxious gas emissions which can be deemed harmful to humans. The use of the car in large numbers, by the large part of the population which has shown itself willing and able to purchase one, is regarded by some people as destroying our leisure habitats because of the improved ease of access given by the car. In addition, it makes travel to work unpleasant by causing congestion. The situation in the centre of urban areas where noxious gases are emitted in large quantities by cars, and other vehicles, stuck in traffic jams, does give a strong case to the environmentalist lobby interested in clean air and general amenity.

Unfortunately, however, one must conclude that the attack on the car is in danger of being overdone. If the economic and financial costs following from a complete victory by the "guardians" of our environment and energy sources were fully understood by the general public, who after all will have to pay the bill, then the environmentalists, consumer interests and conservationists might find that their arguments and actions would provoke a more antagonistic response. In short, the expenditure of vast amounts of scarce resources, which after a certain point will only have a marginal effect on the environment, should at least be questioned. As an indication of the expenditure which the British car-owning public may be faced with in the long term, it is instructive to look at the present state of the game in the USA.

The Federal government's proposed standards for 1975-76 for gas emission control called for a 98 per cent reduction from uncontrolled levels by hydrocarbon emission, 96 per cent of carbon monoxide, and 93 per cent of nitrous oxides. In practical terms this means that the "air" emitted by car exhausts would be about twice as pure as that breathed daily in an industrialized town or city. Most pollution is caused by the general industrial activities of mankind, only some 6 per cent being attributable to the car[1]. It must also be remembered that nature itself is a polluter; pine trees emit more hydrocarbon than all the cars in the USA combined, a similar picture emerges in the case of the other gases. Nevertheless attention can and must be paid to man's activities, including his use of the car, as this is something which can be controlled, often relatively cheaply. It is the pursuit of perfection which appears prodigal of resources.

Much of the interest in car emissions in the US and elsewhere stems from the peculiar phenomenon of the Los Angeles smog, a phenomenon which has been directly linked to car exhausts. However the true scientific knowledge is scanty; for why does Tokyo, apparently suffering from the same problem, have the smog at night time[2]? Furthermore Santiago in Chile, with a small car density, suffers from the same problem. In other words, the anti-pollution lobby's attack on the car is based on an inference which can be severely questioned as to its validity. Nevertheless, the "special" conditions of Los Angeles are leading to a world-wide revision of smoke emission standards and vast expenditures on attempts to develop new types of engine and/or equipment to clean-up existing engines. This chain of causation does appear to have more than a hint of activity being based on a panic reaction rather than on logical analysis.

Many attempts have been made to supersede the internal combustion engine, but always the economics of the new product have proved inferior. However, the failure to produce a conventional engine capable of meeting the Federal pollution standards has, at least, given a fresh opportunity to new forms of propulsion to make a bid to become the main automative power source. The electric car, the gas turbine, the Wankel rotary engine, the Stirling external combustion engine, are all being pursued, but in all cases the material costs, tooling costs and engineering costs are higher than those for conventional engines. For particular uses - electric milk floats which are used on a limited daily mileage, gas turbine engined lorries for use at 40 tons gross plus (another problem for the environmentalists) - the alternative motor power packs are promising. In terms of universal usage therefore, only the Wankel may succeed. At present electric storage batteries are very heavy, an experimental British bus using this power source weighs 13 tons gross compared with eight tons gross for a diesel engined equivalent, and the operative mileage is limited to around 40 miles before recharging is necessary. Overall the Wankel powered car may weigh from 600 to 1,000 lbs less than a conventional car, a saving of $600 to $1,000. However, the Wankel internal combustion engine is as "dirty" as the conventional engine, its smaller size simply allowing easier installation of smoke emission equipment. Furthermore, we will later see why the Wankel may not gain the approval of the conservationist lobby because of its prodigal fuel consumption, a factor reinforced by the traumatic increase in oil prices in 1973-74. Be that as it may, the fact remains that in 1967 GMC spent $3 million on unconventional engine research; by 1972 the figure was $36 million, with $92 million being spent between 1970-72. Between 1967-72 Ford spent $50 million, and in 1973 the Company spent $24.5 million. These expenditures[3] are a direct function of the need to bring the internal combustion engine to a very high level of cleanliness.

Even apart from the costs spent on developing new types of engine, the anti-pollution process still results in the expenditure of huge totals of real resources. It appears likely from car manufacturers' estimates that the 1975-76 emission standards will cost the car buyer $500 more per car in initial costs and another $1,500 for maintenance specific to the smoke emission system over its lifetime, although "discounting" procedures would produce a somewhat lower net present value figure and the ten year period over which the latter figure is based seems to overestimate the economic lifetime of an American car - but not by as much as popular mythology concerning American replacement cycles would indicate. In 1973 extra costs were already being experienced; they were about $40 for first costs and $80 annually. In addition, the 1973 smoke emission standards were costing the car user a 20 per cent decrease in fuel economy which would increase to 35 per cent if the proposed 1975-76 standards reached the US statute books. According to oil industry estimates, made in early 1973, this increased fuel consumption would alone require the US to increase oil imports from $5 billion in 1970 to $30 billion by 1985. Clearly, what is good for the environmentalists is not always good for the conservationists, and indeed following the increased price of oil these figures must be increased at least five-fold. Therefore smoke emission standards can have a severe balance of payments effect, and everything that follows from that, especially in the UK.

Most estimates stem from the US Inter-Industry Emission Control (IIEC) programme which is made up of car makers and oil producers. Clearly this organization has a vested interest, but no one else has tried to quantify the costs of pollution control and until they do, these are the "best" indictors we have. However, the above figures are agreed by a variety of sources including the US government.

In addition, systems able to meet the proposed emission control standards will require lead-free fuels, at a cost in terms of early 1973 oil prices of $8 billion to the oil industry and ultimately to the consumer. Such fuel costs about four cents per gallon more than ordinary petrol, so the US consumer will be paying more per gallon as well as receiving 35 per cent less economy!

1973 model cars achieved 80 per cent, 70 per cent and 50 per cent reductions in hydrocarbons, carbon monoxide, and nitrous oxides respectively. The cost difference per car in terms of first costs and maintenance between the Inter-Industry Emission Control's proposals of 90 per cent, 89 per cent and 77 per cent, and the Government's 1975-76 standards of 98 per cent, 96 per cent and 93 per cent therefore appear to be difficult to justify on an incremental cost-benefit basis. That is, the attempt to attain perfection runs into the law of diminishing returns, the increased "output" is small in terms of the increased "inputs" or "costs" needed to achieve this improvement. It is almost certainly true that the resources involved could be spent elsewhere, even in terms of pollution control, say in the greater use of water purification plants, or alternatively on research into motor vehicle accident causation. The diversion of those resources to house building, schools and hospitals would also be justified in terms of the private and social rates of return.

The cars needed to meet the Federal standards require additional equipment which is both complex and expensive and leads to a diminution in economy and performance. As yet no catalytic convertor (an exhaust cleaning catalyst) meets the government's 50,000 mile durability requirement; for instance Ford has spent $400 million in trying to do so. Furthermore, it now appears likely that the catalyst creates more lethal fumes than they eliminate. The convertors create other problems, for instance by promoting the conversion of sulphur dioxide to sulphuric acid. America's National Academy of Sciences has branded the catalyst as most disadvantageous in terms of initial cost, fuel economy, maintenance costs and durability. Hence the industry's renewed interest in new types of engine which may not need the same emission equipment. A further hidden cost to the motorist would be the cost of replacing convertors stolen for the platinum they contain.

The "energy crisis", i.e. the psychological impact of the oil price increase on the US motorist who feels that it indicates the relative scarcity and drying up of oil supplies, by producing a consumer swing to small cars, may have had some good. That is until the American car buyer turned to smaller piston engines in their cars, the conversion of large US engines, even if possible, may only have been successful with a Wankel engine. The smaller Wankel allows bonnet space for the required special equipment. However, the Wankel has a fuel economy 20 per cent inferior to conventional engines; this must be added to the 35 per cent reduction already specified. So what price the supposed oil shortage with US cars operating at 4 mpg? The switch to smaller engines allows the existing piston engine to be converted to cleaner operation.

Another costly problem is that, despite all this special equipment, car engines do not meet Federal standards during the first 30 seconds of operation following a cold start. To overcome this a special petrol is required, on top of the need to incur costs by developing and using lead free petrol. As a result 15 per cent of today's oil would have to be removed from petrol blends and re-processed. Losses to petrol volume compared with present procedures would amount to 150 million barrels a year by 1980 according to the Union Oil Company, and 250 million extra barrels a year would have to be imported to meet demands. In addition, the amortization of new and extra refinery capacity would be about $2 billion a year. Clearly the impact of pollution control on society is going to be tremendous in terms of resources used.

The size of the diminishing returns can be seen if we use water pollution as an example. To achieve 95 per cent pollutant removal would cost approximately $60 billion over a 20 year period. The water so produced would be fit for human consumption. However, to remove the extra 5 per cent would, it is estimated, cost $340 billion. This would provide absolutely pure water in its natural state, a degree of perfection only normally reached by that part of the water stock earmarked for human consumption. If it achieves the Federal standards, the car would function as an air purifier, as the air emitting from a car exhaust would be purer than urban air. Congestion in the High Street would have some social benefit, and deaths in closed garages would be eliminated. To achieve the IIEC's original standards would have an initial cost of $250 per car; i.e. to achieve an overall pollutant level some 5 per cent below Federal proposals would only cost half as much. The cost of achieving this 5 per cent would divert resources away from other private and social objectives. Clearly this American situation may not be repeated entirely in Europe but something very similar may emerge, and if so the public should be made aware of what is really being proposed and what is at stake.

The consumer will have to pay the costs involved in achieving this "last" 5 per cent, but is he or she being asked whether he or she wants this level of perfection? Clearly some would argue that the entire removal of the car's noxious gases - even if it means removing the car - is worth any sum it may

67

require. But in a world of scarce resources and competing wants, such a view is of doubtful validity. Even the "guardians of society" may prefer to resort to cost-benefit studies to substantiate their own preferences and to give their value judgments a seemingly scientific backing of "objective" facts and analysis. It would be difficult to substantiate the view that the resources needed to eliminate the "final" 5 per cent could not be better spent elsewhere, say on houses, schools, urban renewal or the complete removal of the pollution and squalor left by the Industrial Revolution, which is far worse than anything the car is responsible for.

As regards conservation and environment generally, is the car being unfairly pilloried? Is it the car or man's insistence on living in cities and travelling in large numbers, to and from work, at the same time as all his fellows which is at the root cause of congestion in towns? Does not the car give the vast body of the population[4] the means for ease of movement quite unparalleled in human experience, or is the majority of car owners to be priced out of the market and confined to the neighbourhood of their homes, unless prepared to face the joys of bus or train travel - wife, children, pushchair, shopping bag and all? It must be remembered that the railways cannot cope with a diversion of more than 8 per cent of road traffic without further substantial net investment. Would it not be more equitable to spend the resources on roads to provide for the transport mode which people demonstrate that they want? What is the environmental advantage or moral justification of imposing further noise and nuisance on people living alongside the railway tracks at Paddington in preference to those living alongside the Hammersmith flyover?

Congestion and pollution in its entirety is no creation of the car. "The inconvenience caused by the blocking of traffic in London streets, and the need for improved passenger transport between its central and suburban districts, are matters which closely touch both the convenience and personal comfort of each inhabitant living in or adjacent to the Metropolis" was an observation made in 1905 and referred to the problems caused by horsedrawn vehicles and pedestrians[5]. "In 1900 the USA had 20 million horses. One city estimated that its 15,000 horses produced enough manure in the course of a year to breed 16 billion germ carrying flies. But that was not the reason why America graduated from the horse to the automobile". (Economist, May 19, 1973). Car demand is largely a function of the level of personal incomes and car prices; car usage is largely determined by convenience. If road pricing is used to combat congestion then the motorist may return to the bus, but the level of car demand is unlikely to change much. Few motorists buy cars to replace bus journeys, the motives underlying car purchase are more deeply based than that. So although the need to bring motorists face to face with the full social and private costs of car usage is a legitimate economic goal if we wish to optimize the use of society's scarce resources, the hysteria generated by exhaust emissions has a much more questionable economic base.

As indicated, the law of diminishing returns seems to suggest that the goal of perfection will result in a misallocation of resources. Indeed, the possibility of a world energy crisis may lead to a substantial long term rise in the relative price of oil and petrol, in addition to what may be the short-term rise in 1973-74, perhaps enough to make the petrol engine redundant. In short, the electric, gas, steam, and even the oil-using gas turbine, could come into their own, and the emission problems associated with these power forms are less severe. However, the energy crisis is the conservationist's chance to appear in the forefront of public debate. Nevertheless, it must be remembered that the American oil shortage, which triggered-off the energy scare, is due to special factors, and is mainly a problem of economics. Therefore, just because the Americans are faced with a structural problem in their energy sector is no reason for the rest of the world to feel that global shortages are imminent. The 1973-74 price rises are due not to relative real scarcities but to the cartelization of what was a much freer market. The price mechanism and technological change will solve much of the long term problem if problem there be[6] while with the present well-head price being seventy (70) times its marginal cost the life-time of the cartel will be limited and a future oil glut a real probability.

The car has perhaps become too easy to attack. The real environmental damage to South Wales and Lancashire was due not to the car but is attributable to side effects of the industrial revolution of the past century. However the more time the mass media's "Problem Makers" spend on the "evils" of the car, the less attention is paid to the much worse pollution and squalor caused by coal mining, chemical and fertiliser production, waste disposal and so on. Rather than attack the car in terms of its social consequences, other issues may be worthier of attention. For instance, the seemingly ethically neutral "Town and Country Planning" acts, framed and supported by the middle class, in fact make it harder for the poorer members of society, living in decaying urban and rural surroundings, to purchase a semi with a garden. High house prices stem partly from high land prices which, in turn, is a function of the artificial land scarcity caused by building-land restrictions. There are those who, while very concerned with footpaths and the rights of the rambler, and ever ready to attack the social effects of the car, fail to see the normative aspects of green belt legislation - i.e. to preserve green fields but price the low income groups out of the housing market. There is a danger that the car will again become the preserve of the middle class with many potential customers being priced out of the market and forced back to the "advantages" of public transport. If we add to the costs already considered those stemming from improving the safety features of cars, many of which are necessary and overdue, the motoring bill becomes even greater. However, some developments in safety seem hasty and ill-considered. There is little sense in building a car like a tank, and able to withstand the impact of another car, when evidence stemming from the Birmingham Accident Hospital indicates that collisions between cars and lorries were the commonest cause of death for car occupants on motorways and link roads, accounting for as much as 40 per cent of fatalities. In other words, would some of the resources expended on developing safety vehicles be better spent on improving the safety of lorries and improving road lighting?

The environmentalists attack the car, the conservationists attack its thirst for oil, the consumer interests see it as a 20th century successor to Malthusian war, pestilence and famine in its destruction of human life. The car makers are responding to all three and are spending scarce resources in trying to placate them. However, the question must be asked as to whether too much is being spent. After all, the cost of seeking perfection in emission control may be the opportunity foregone for cleaning-up all derelict landscapes in the UK. This is the type of choice which has to be made. The environmentalist's anti-polluter has a valid point to make, but by overstating it, society may be condemned to misallocating scarce resources. The consumer movement wants a safe car built like a tank which would burn even more fuel because of its very weight, but other approaches such as the compulsory use of seat-belts for all car occupants and the judicious use of body strengthening members may be sufficient. A car totally safe from the effects of impact by another car is still vulnerable to a truck or bus. This paper in no way questions that greater pollution control and car safety, or a tackling of the congestion problem in town and country, are laudable objectives, but it does attempt to show that an obsession with these objectives is in danger of diverting attention and resources away from other areas; away from projects which at the margin would prove to have a greater return, that is, they would be more worthwhile.

A decision by the US Federal government's Environmental Protection Agency in June 1973 only reinforced this point. The EPA announced that nitrogen dioxide is not a widespread air pollution problem after all, and that a 93 per cent reduction of oxides of nitrogen in car exhausts is not necessary. This negated the billions of pounds manufacturers have been spending world-wide to meet the proposed 1976 emission standards. Due to shortcomings in the method of measurement the EPA admitted that the problem has been overstated. Manufacturers who have tooled up with millions of pounds worth of platinum exhaust catalysts might have to forget it for a least a decade. If so, then to this must be added the resources wasted in gearing-up for increased platinum production. If the US government accepts this latest advice from its own agency, then part of the problem of increased fuel consumption will be alleviated, as will many problems facing car importers in trying to meet the U.S. standards. It could be, therefore, that the argument propounded in this paper is at least partly understood by the law makers, an argument which is reinforced by the recent oil price increases, and which has manifested itself in the appearance of the 50p gallon in early 1974.

In precise terms our conclusions must be as follows. It is likely that the "exaggerated" energy crisis of 1973-74, which followed the Middle East war of October 1973, has changed society's objectives. The fixation with both smoke emission control and safety vehicles has been replaced by a need to conserve fuel supplies. As we have shown the "overkill" control of smoke emission, plus the thinking on safety vehicles which was leading to the production of cars weighing almost two tons in the USA, would result in a very significant increase in the use of society's scarce energy and raw material supplies. Consequently, it is unlikely that in a society concerned with energy conservation that ultra stringent gas emission and safety vehicle legislation will be enacted. It is always dangerous to predict long-term changes from what has, after all, been a short-term concern with energy supplies, especially as this concern goes against the long-term energy environment of the post-war period i.e. cheap oil in abundant quantities. However, even if the Middle-East oil cartel is short-lived and the relative price of oil returns to levels similar to those experienced in the past, some long-term effects are likely on the motor industry; after all, the Suez Crisis of 1956 not only created a short-term British demand for cheap "Bubble cars", it also sired the long-lived British Leyland "Mini". Design parameters now being laid-down call for light weight, long-lived high quality cars with low wind resistance, all helping the efficiency of what will be car engines of already high thermal efficiency i.e. low petrol consumption. The results of this design and engineering exercise would be on the market for many years to come. Sources independent of the car manufacturing interests already claim that existing European car engines can be easily and cheaply modified to improve fuel efficiency by up to 20 per cent. The post-war obsession with speed and high performance has led to a secular deterioration in the fuel efficiency of car engines. The re-emergence of fuel economy as a real marketing strategy could quickly reverse this trend[7] If thermal efficiency does indeed become the main objective of engine development, relatively clean exhausts will automatically result, from power sources consuming 25 per cent less petrol per horse power per hour than at present. Speed limits could help this process but only at a cost. In a modern complex industrial society "time" is one of our scarcest resources, therefore society must decide whether it can afford to travel more slowly, the "cost" of which must be set against the "benefits" from reduced energy consumption, fewer accidents, and so on.

Another result of a society elevating resource conservation to a high priority would be to produce long-lived motor cars which the car buyer would replace less often. A social decision to "outlaw" the wastes incurred in making a car that is shoddy, quickly deteriorating and therefore scrapped relatively quickly will conserve resources both in terms of maintenance and in reducing the annual production levels of motor cars. It must be remembered however that a high scrapping rate may be a function not of physical deterioration but of the economics of the car market. In a market with high per capita incomes but low new-car prices, it may be cheaper to purchase another car even a second-hand one, than to save one's car from the scrap heap by expending resources on major overhauls. Firstly, a labour-intensive overhaul is likely to be expensive and secondly, the low prices in the car market would mean that it would be unlikely that the motorist would benefit from his expenditure when he came to sell his vehicle. Therefore, it is only if the purchase price of cars increases relative to "other things", or if the "income effect" of higher running costs means that a car has to be depreciated over a longer period because of financial reasons, or raw materials take on prices that reflect new social attitudes to scarcity, that longer replacement cycles may emerge.

Alternatively the production of long-lived cars, in long production runs, may change the customers attitude to the car i.e. to come to regard it as something which "need" only be changed less frequently. Legislatively, an annual excise licence which declines in value with the age of the car would help such a process along. The use of long-lived cars could give the mass manufacturer a new business in overhauling his products. Such a situation is common-place with the small makers of quality cars and commercial vehicles. For example, the Oshkosh concern in the USA rebuilds its customers' lorries on its production lines at two-thirds the cost of new. It must be remembered that the modern car is a compromise between the cost-accountant, the designer and the engineer. Therefore, "high quality" and "high-technology" may often be sacrificed to the dictates of penny-pinching and styling. This contrasts with the heavy commercial vehicle sector where the engineer, more loosely constrained by the accountant, is able to produce a "tool for the job". The position of the stylist in the C.V. sector is minor, therefore the engineer has free rein, within the bounds of commercial viability, to produce a long-lived efficient product.

All this illustrates that with other objectives suddenly appearing, the use of resources to produce "100 per cent" gas emission and accident control is likely to be misplaced. The "energy crisis"[8] only serves to highlight this by showing how resources could perhaps be spent with better purpose even within the narrow automative world, leave alone outside. The final word is to reiterate that cleaning-up the car, or, say, to remove lead from petrol, is an objective to be applauded on the grounds of social cost-benefit analysis, but it is the attempt to reach technical perfection which must be questioned on the grounds of a "waste" of scarce economic resources which could be better used in the pursuit of other private and social objectives.

## NOTES AND REFERENCES

1. For instance the costs imposed on British society are: from the coalfire costs are £400 million a year, from industry £120 million, and with £35 million worth of damage ascribed to motor vehicle emissions. (Programmes Analysis Unit, An Economic and Technical Appraisal of Air Pollution in the UK, HMSO., 1972).

2. The Los Angeles smog is believed to be caused by the interaction of sunlight on car exhaust fumes.

3. In other directions GMC has spent £200 million on exhaust related R. & D.; in 1973 another £150 million, about one-tenth of total UK manufac turing investment.

4. The 1971 figure of 32 cars per 1,000 people must mean that over 50 per cent of the population has access to car transport when family size is taken into consideration.

5. Meik and Beer's evidence to the Royal Commission on London Traffic 1903-4.

6. In 1947 there were 22 years known reserves of oil; in 1955 the figure was 33; in 1960 it was 37 years; in 1965 it was 30 years, and in 1971, it was 34 years. (See "Is There a World Energy Crisis?" by C.Robinson and E.M. Cook, National Westminster Bank Quarterly Review, May 1973).

7. Under touring conditions the 1974 1½ litre family saloon is hard put to return 30 m.p.g. while to its 1946 equivalent 40 m.p.g. was common place.

8. It is interesting to note that even at 50p a gallon, in real terms petrol was still cheaper in 1974 than it was in late 1956 to mid 1957.

# 7 Motorways: Safe or sorry?

*Article by R. Diment*
*British Road Federation*
*February 1988 issue*

A whole generation has grown up in Britain's motorway age. December of this year will mark the 30th anniversary of the opening of the eight-mile long Preston By-pass which was Britain's first length of motorway. November 1959 saw the opening of the first 73 mile stretch of the M1 London-Birmingham motorway. Since then there have been regular opportunities for Transport Ministers, and the occasional Prime Minister, to cut a piece of ribbon, say how much the Government is investing in the road system, and declare open the country's latest length of motorway. The network now stretches over some 1,850 miles, a further 120 miles are under construction or planned. Today most, though not all, major centres of population lie fairly close to an access point to the motorway system.

Few could dispute the importance of the motorways to Britain's transport. Motorway traffic has grown from nothing 30 years ago to 26.2 billion miles in 1986, with an estimated growth of 12 per cent in 1987. Today motorways carry about 15 per cent of all traffic and about 30 per cent of heavy goods vehicle traffic. Table 1 charts the growth of the network and the volume of traffic using it.

Recently there has been considerable debate about the safety of our motorways. Everytime there is a motorway accident the issue is brought sharply into focus, particularly if the speed and volume of motorway traffic is likely to have contributed to the accident.

It is appropriate to look briefly at the history of the motorway in Britain. Amazingly, the first call for a motorway, specially designed for high speed and for heavy motor traffic with limited access, was made in 1923. A group led by the then Lord Montagu proposed a route from London to Liverpool via Birmingham and Salford, with a spur at the northern end from Golborne near St. Helens around the north of Manchester to Bolton, Bury and Oldham. The Montagu scheme was far sighted; at that time the total number of motor vehicles in Britain had only just exceeded one million, and barely one third of those were cars. Unsurprisingly the idea came to nothing.

Throughout the 1920s traffic grew, by 1930 the number of vehicles had grown to 2.3 million, and the number of accidents also rose, the number of fatalities from, road accidents reaching 7,305 in 1930. It was during the 1930s that the real pressure for motorways in Britain began. Had the war not started, it is likely that Britain's first motorways could have appeared in the early 1940s. In 1937 the County Surveyor for Lancashire had proposed a North-South Motorway through the County and the following year Blackpool Council was considering building a Ring Road to motorway standard. As it was it took the rising traffic of the 1950s to start the programme.

TABLE 1
GROWTH OF THE MOTORWAY NETWORK AND TRAFFIC

| | Length of network (miles) | Motorway traffic (million vehicle miles) | % of all traffic |
|---|---|---|---|
| 1960 | 95 | 500 | 0.7 |
| 1965 | 347 | 2300 | 2.3 |
| 1970 | 635 | 6100 | 4.5 |
| 1975 | 1200 | 13100 | 8.5 |
| 1980 | 1588 | 17100 | 11.1 |
| 1985 | 1763 | 23500 | 13.4 |
| 1987 | 1848 | 29300[1] | 15.0[1] |

[1] BRF estimate

At that time, faster journey times were the main justification for the new roads. They offered the prospect of inter-urban journeys at average speeds

76

closer to 60mph than 30mph, with significant savings in operating costs for industry and the private motorist.

Supporters of the motorways also knew there would be safety benefits. Several reasons were cited. As pedestrians and pedal cyclists would not be allowed on the motorway, the possibility of pedestrian/vehicle and pedal cycle/vehicle accidents would be virtually eliminated. In the late 1950s pedestrian and cyclist made up 50 per cent of fatalities and about 40 per cent of injuries from road accidents.

## TABLE 2
### INJURY ACCIDENTS PER HUNDRED MILLION VEHICLE MILES

|      | All roads | motorways |
| ---- | --------- | --------- |
| 1966 | 262       | 47        |
| 1970 | 201       | 34        |
| 1975 | 185       | 27        |
| 1980 | 160       | 24        |
| 1985 | 138       | 19        |

As the design of the motorway would be to a much higher standard than other roads there would be safety benefits for the road user. Smoother curves would give longer sight lines. Junctions would be few. There would be no access from roadside premises, always potential danger spots. Right hand turns, across the opposing traffic flow would be eliminated. The provision of dual carriageways would reduce the number of head-on collisions. Thus the motorway could result in a very significant reduction in the number of accidents, particularly when the motorway by-passes a built-up area where pedestrians and cyclists are particularly vulnerable.

A study made early in the motorway age by Lancashire County Council showed that before the M6 was opened through the county the average rate of injury accidents was 3.56 per million vehicle miles, whilst on the Preston By-pass (opened December 1958) the figure was 0.3, on the Lancaster By-pass (opened April 1960) 0.47 and on the length from the Cheshire boundary to Preston (opened July 1963) 0.26.

Similar figures can be shown for the M1 in 1962. At that time injury accidents for the whole road system were running at 4.37 per million vehicle miles, but at 0.89 for the M1. The difference for fatalities was less dramatic but still quite apparent, with rates of 0.085 per million vehicles miles generally and 0.046 on the M1.

In 1970 at the request of the British Road Federation the Road Research Laboratory estimated savings of casualties due to the provision of motorways in Great Britain. The calculation rested on the assumption that if the motorways were not there the traffic now using them would have to use the ordinary rural 'A' roads instead. After allowing for the motorway 'generating' an additional 20 per cent of traffic, the study estimated that 110 lives and 3,500 injuries had been saved in 1966 and 120 lives and 4,400 injuries in 1968.

Despite the volume of traffic tripling over the 30 years since the first motorways were opened, the total number of road casualties has fallen, with the result that accident rates for all roads have been steadily falling as shown in Table 2. Throughout this period the motorways have maintained a consistently lower rate than the average. The reductions have come about for many reasons, better braking, more vigorous testing and stronger bodies of vehicles; increasing moves in urban areas to separate people and traffic; improved education of road users, but as the figures show the higher the standard of the road the safer it is likely to be.

The fact remains, however, that motorways are only relatively safer than other roads. In 1986 there were more than 5,000 accidents on motorways. This was only 2 per cent of the total but enough to result in 248 deaths and 8,000 injuries. Measures to reduce this appalling figure are urgently needed. Better driver education and improved vehicles are undoubtedly one element. Another must be to alleviate the rapidly increasing congestion on the motorway system. The Department of Transport recommendations on the number of carriageways on the motorway depend on the forecast of the average annual daily traffic flow using the motorways in the 15th year after the motorway is opened. The current standards are:

| | |
|---|---|
| 2-lane motorway | 28,000 to 54,000 |
| 3-lane motorway | 50,000 to 79,000 |
| 4-lane motorway | 77,000 and above |

Although no upper standard for four-lane motorways is shown, statements by Government Ministers have suggested the 118,000 is probably the maximum. Unfortunately, many of Britain's motorways carry traffic well in excess of these levels. For example, on the M25 all sections except for those in Kent carry flows above the design level, some sections to the west of London are carrying 50 per cent more than their design capacity. Sections of the M1, M4, M6 and M62 are in a similar position causing severe congestion, particularly in the peak periods, which results in increasing numbers of accidents. Current Government plans for road improvements over the next decade are only going to have a marginal effect on relieving motorway congestion. Even with the opening of the M40 extension from Oxford to Birmingham to provide a second motorway link between the south east and the west Midlands, the southern section of the M1 will be carrying over 140,000 vehicles per day. This is significantly above the maximum design flow for a three - or even a four-lane motorway. The Government is coming under increasing pressure to commit itself to a major motorway building programme in the 1990s. The British Road Federation has shown that a second orbital route around London, a second motorway from the West Midlands to the North West and the upgrading of the A1 throughout its length from London to Newcastle will be needed by the late 1990s. The BRF programme has gained widespread support from industry, trade unions, local authorities, politicians and members of the public. The pressure for action will continue to grow until the Government realizes that economic growth, which it wishes to take credit for, also causes traffic growth, for which it must take responsibility.

Another major area of motorway safety concerns repairs. Contraflow and cones are no longer just matters for groans from the presenters on Radio Four's Today programme; they are causing major disruption. However, we must accept that motorway repairs are here to stay and for the next four or five years, whilst the backlog of repairs that was allowed to build up in the late 1970s and early 1980s is cleared, there will be 80 miles or so of repairs to be undertaken each year. For various reasons the bulk of these will take place in the spring, summer and early autumn. Part of the problem is the sheer volume of traffic, if the motorway is straining to carry 80,000 or more vehicles on three normal lanes, queues will quickly build up if only two narrow lanes are available . Good signing and better traffic management is helping, but concern exists about the ability of plastic cones to separate opposing flows of traffic even when a mandatory speed limit of 40 or 50 mph is imposed. Alternatives exist which are cheap and flexible. Research has been done into concrete barriers which would deflect vehicles back into the line of traffic. Unfortunately, the 'not invented here' syndrome seems to apply and so far the Department of Transport seems wedded firmly to the cone.

One recent move by the Department to be welcomed warmly, is the adoption of higher specifications for the foundations and surface layers for future motorways. These should have a life of 40 years without needing major reconstruction, a considerable improvement on the current 25 years.

Although the improvements needed to ensure further reductions in motorway accident rates will be costly, there is no doubt that the investment will be worthwhile. In addition to the incalculate cost of pain and suffering, the cost of road accidents runs to about £3,000 million a year.

The Government is willing to take credit for the economic growth that results in rising traffic. It must also take responsibility for alleviating the less pleasant side effects. Only then will it be truly possible to say that our motorways are safe.

# 8 Computers in transport: Routing and scheduling of road transport vehicles

*Paper presented to the Annual Conference by*
*S. Jones*
*English Electric-Leo-Marconi Computers Limited*
*July 1966 issue*

Computers today are being put to an ever-growing number of uses in all sections of the transport industry - road, rail, sea and air. In the road transport field alone they are being used to control traffic signals, analyze vehicle census figures and forecast future traffic generation, to calculate servicing and replacement timetables, and to plan vehicle routes and schedules. It is with this last application, and with the fields which the ability to plan vehicle routes opens up, that this paper is concerned.

The importance of route-planning lies in the fact that the costs of distribution depend on the number and type of vehicles employed, and this in turn is largely determined by the route-plans to which vehicles are des patched. The circumstances of the last few years - the increasing competitiveness of retailing, complexity of distribution, and shortage and cost of manpower - have lent urgency to the search for ways of improving the efficiency of road transport and reducing the enormous costs involved.

Experience in implementing the computer routing and scheduling programmes developed in the last four years shows clearly that they can assist in this search in several types of transport operation. The range of problems in which programmes have already been successfully used includes daily planning for delivery of goods ordered until 12 noon the previous day, scheduling of vehicle fleets for one, two and four weeks, dealing with fleets ranging in size from as few as five vehicles to as many as 700, evaluating alternative depot sites and measuring the effect of changing such constraints as the number and capacity of the vehicles and the length of the driver's working day.

The plans produced in these applications do not necessarily, or even probably, constitute ideal solutions to the various routing or scheduling problems considered by themselves; any such solution would require a prohibitively expensive amount of computing time. But the plans are probably very near optional in terms of the total of transport and computer costs. They have been accepted by the management concerned as being satisfactory and practical; when compared with manual plans they have been at least as economical and have commonly saved upwards of 10 per cent of the vehicle requirement. In many cases this would alone outweigh the computer cost. In some cases, particularly those where the delivery requirements are subject to frequent change, no practicable manual solution could have been found in the time available.

Before proceeding to describe the computer programmes, the types of problem to which they are applicable, and the advantages to be gained from them, it is necessary to emphasize that these programmes are planning and not simulation tools; the point is fundamental. Vehicle fleets are normally operated under an agreement between management and men about acceptable standards of performance. In some cases this agreement is specified in detail and may be based on thorough time-study investigations. In others there is no formal contract whatsoever, but there is a general agreement that some things are reasonable and others are not.

The situation is inevitable in transport because the problems of supervision are practically insuperable. In these circumstances the driver acts as a control system. The incidence of random factors is not allowed to upset overall performance except in extreme cases. In general the impact of these factors is taken into account in establishing the standards of performance. The driver performs to a target -set for him by management within the context of whatever agreement exists - and adjusts his rate of working accordingly. If he does better than expected, there is always a handy transport cafe. If he does worse, usually he manages to speed up either driving or deliveries, or occasionally takes a bit longer than expected. Given a plan which really demands too much, or which he thinks demands too much, he will just bring work back on some excuse or other.

In this situation it is the task of management to devise plans which exploit the agreement to the limit in obtaining work from drivers. It is not necessary for a computer programme, any more than for a manual planning system, to simulate the occurrence or effect of the random factors inherent in transport operation. The plans can be generated as if the situation were deterministic. The random factors which upset plans are extreme circumstances such as breakdowns, fog and ice. These factors seriously affect any planning system. However, since it is generally accepted that it is better to plan journeys than not, it must be assumed that the incidence of such factors does not destroy the value of journey planning and the same applies to routing or scheduling by computer.

It is necessary to distinguish two main types of route-planning problems, for which two completely different types of programme have been developed. The first is to plan economical routes in circumstances where a number of services - a collection, a delivery, or both - are required at various points at specific times; this we refer to in my company as Van Scheduling. The second, which we believe to be the more common problem in the final stage of distribution, is that of planning the best use of vehicles when time constraints are less rigorous, and the main objective is therefore to reduce vehicle travelling time. The programmes designed to solve this type of problem are those we refer to as Vehicle Routing programmes. In practice, of course, the problems are rarely so simple and readily distinguishable. A scheduling programme whose overriding object is to have vehicles at the right place at the right time will have the minimization of travelling time as one of its secondary objectives; while a routing programme primarily concerned to minimize vehicle mileage will frequently have to comply with a number of time restrictions as well. A decision has to be made about which is the dominant consideration, and which type of programme is therefore appropriate. The decision will depend on a number of factors including extent of the delivery area and the number, severity, and likely effect of the time constraints.

A classic example of a route-planning problem dominated by time requirements is that facing the Director of the London Postal Region of the Post Office. The Inner Area of the London Postal Region is divided under the control of nine District Postmasters and two Divisional Controllers. Each of these eleven controls has its own fleet of mail vans. Additionally, there is a separate fleet, known as the Centrally Controlled Service (CCS), which caters for the bulk conveyance of mails, mainly between District offices and the railway termini, and provides support for the local fleets. A Van Scheduling Programme has now been devised to schedule services for the CCS fleet.

The fleet consists of 689 vehicles stationed at five garages and driven on a three-shift rota, by 1,230 men. The fleet performs about 30,000 services (i.e. individual loaded trips) each week and covers some 250,000 miles mainly within a five-mile radius of King's Cross. The services are strictly

83

timed because of the need to meet trains and to schedule sorting office work. Each service consists of a start and finish time and place and many also have a number of timed intermediate calls. The number of terminal points is 360. Of the 30,000 services, about 88 per cent are scheduled against known commitments while the remainder are performed on ad hoc demand. Ad hoc services vary from 350 to 1,000 per day; changes to scheduled services, consequent on alterations in requirements or to railway timetables, vary from about 50 in most weeks to as many as 1,300 in a single week. The services which may be allocated to an individual driver are restricted by the statutory limitations on hours, by agreements with the drivers' union about such matters as attendance times and places, duty rotas, mealbreaks, overtime, etc., and by exceptionally complicated requirements in scheduling the location and duration of mealbreaks. Meals come within four categories and must be scheduled to be taken at a canteen. There are 18 canteens and each may have different opening hours for each meal category.

Scheduling is carried out manually by clerks in the Transport Branch of the Director's Office. The task is so complex that a full-scale manual overhaul would be out of date in respect of amendments before it could be implemented. The tendency, therefore, is to amend existing schedules piecemeal rather than attempt any overall rearrangement of services. The manual system is not capable of providing management easily and regularly with the information needed for adequate control of the fleet. Because of the constant state of change, major effort is needed to establish the extent of idle time and the points in time and place at which it occurs. Without a full-scale rescheduling, it is not possible to assess the effects of changes in requirements, timetables, staff conditions and economic factors on the location of sorting offices, garages and canteens.

A team formed to consider whether a computer could be used to produce drivers' schedules, fleet statistics and management control information decided that the scope for economy lay in:

(i)   reducing idle time at the end of services;
(ii)  reducing empty running time between services;
(iii) reducing clerical costs by producing for each driver an accurately timed and detailed schedule of all loaded and empty journeys showing the statutory and privileged breaks in duties and the times and places where they should be taken;
(iv)  the use that could be made of better management information.

It is not possible to detail in a paper such as this the lengthy process of sorting out this immense and complex problem and refining the programme to the point at which a satisfactory compromise was reached between the quality of the solution and the amount of computing time needed to reach it; in this case about 15 minutes per day. It must suffice to say that the approach adopted was to match services to van schedules on the basis of the lowest cost of idle time and empty running time combined, according to their relative costs. This rule results in the accumulation of periods of both busy and idle time. While it might not always be desirable to accumulate periods of idle time, it was done in this case to allow meals to be taken and assistance to be given with the unscheduled ad hoc work. Wherever a driver's schedule includes a period of idle time sufficiently long to be of use, an instruction is printed on the schedule that he should either phone or attend the control point where ad hoc services are allocated. The availability and location of vehicles with usable idle time is also printed out for management. The vehicle requirement is minimized by a rule which ensures that no service is assigned to a new vehicle unless the programme is unable to find a vehicle already on duty available to perform it.

The programmes are now complete and operational and at the time of writing negotiations are in train with the union representing the drivers to introduce the system. It can be said with confidence that the savings resulting from the system have made the exercise worth while. The combination of factors present in this Post Office transport operation appears to be unique, but we trust that some part at least of the experience gained in implementing this programme will be relevant to the solution of other problems in the transport field. As mentioned earlier in the paper, the main objective of both Van Scheduling and Vehicle Routing programmes is to plan routes with a minimum number of vehicles. The reason for this is that at least 75 per cent of the cost of running a delivery vehicle is incurred simply by having a vehicle and driver available for work; no more than 25 per cent is attributable to the actual mileage run or volume of goods delivered. The requirement to save vehicles may be interpreted as a requirement to make the most valuable use of vehicle time. The aim of a Van Scheduling programme, such as that described above, is to satisfy this requirement by reducing idle time and empty running time. In transport operations where vehicles are despatched from a depot to make deliveries to a number of recipients during the same journey there is, of course, no empty running time until the vehicle has made its last call, nor does management wish or anticipate that the vehicle day shall include any idle time in excess of that required for prescribed rests and meals.

In this type of operation the scope for improving vehicle utilisation lies in reducing:

1. Travelling time between calls, i.e. vehicle mileage.
2. Wasted time, i.e. the amount by which the total of all the separate times needed for travelling between calls, parking, delivering goods, completing paper work, etc., falls short of the time which the vehicle and driver could reasonably work.

The system by which the computer seeks to reduce mileage is by linking points according to how much mileage the linkage saves. Hence the method is commonly called the savings technique. The theory behind it is as follows:

Consider a depot and delivery points A, B and C, distant a, b and c respectively from the depot. The distance between the delivery points A and B is ab.

If deliveries were made to A and B on separate journeys the total distance travelled would be 2a+2b.

If deliveries to A and B were combined into the same journey, the distance travelled would be a+ab+b.

The distance saving achieved by linking A and B, written S(AB), would be S(AB) = 2a+2b - (a+ab = b) = a+b-ab.
The savings property is additive.
Thus the distance travelled in visiting A, B and C in the same journey is a+ab+bc+c,

and S(ABC)     = 2a+2b+2c - (a+ab+bc+c)
               = a+2b+c - ab - bc
but S(AB)      = a+b - ab
and S(BC)      = b+c - bc
Therefore, S(ABC) = S(AB)+S(BC)

Thus, if linkages are made between places in order of saving, an attempt is being made to improve the result as rapidly as possible.

This may seem at first sight to be only a more precise description of the aims and methods of an intelligent an experienced transport manager or routing clerk. But in fact the way manual routes are constructed is normally that the delivery area is divided into smaller areas, and orders for each sub-area are put into the appropriate pigeon-hole as they are received. When enough orders have accumulated in one pigeon-hole to make a reasonable day's work for a truck, this constitutes a load. If the orders for one area do not constitute a full load or loads, they are combined with orders for adjacent areas. The practical justification for this system is that it is the only way a human being can begin to sort out hundreds of different orders and organize a reasonable distribution of work. The theoretical justification, if one were sought, would be that points were being linked according to how close they are to each other. Superficially, this is by no means contrary to commonsense.

The effect of applying this rule can be illustrated by linking together 48 points in the distance matrix in the AA book in journeys starting and finishing in London and containing not more than four points per journey. The effect of this is that the more isolated places tend to be assigned last, and the total mileage required to visit all the points is 7,150; The result of solving the same problem by applying the savings criterion, shows that the mileage is reduced to 6,251, a saving of between 12 per cent and 13 per cent.

If, instead of being limited to four calls, each journey had been limited by time, this saving could have been translated into a saving of vehicles. The second source of saving, in addition to reduction of mileage, is in making better use of available time by more accurate planning. In Britain a driver may not work, by law, for more than 11 hours in association with his vehicle in one day. The journey planners, in order to ensure that they stay within the law, only plan to utilize the vehicles on average for 10 hours a day but the computer, because it calculates more precisely the total of all the individual driving and unloading times, can plan to utilize the vehicles on average for 10½ hours a day, this extra half hour can be put to more productive use.

Alternatively, if within the overall objective of reducing mileage there is a requirement that some calls are made at -or before or after - certain specified times, the programme can calculate taking the start of the vehicle day as the base time, whether a point can be fitted into a route without violating a time restriction. If the working day at the depot is longer than the maximum permitted vehicle day, it can move the vehicle day back or forward, within this limit and indicate that a vehicle should leave earlier or later than usual.

A good example of the development of a vehicle routing programme for day-to-day operational planning is the work we have carried out with Schweppes (Home) Limited. Although the results of the various stages of the work to date have all been published and are no doubt familiar to many people in the transport field, a brief recapitulation of the progress to date and the facilities to be included in the system now being planned for a large branch, affords a good guide to the range of practical problems which a programme can be designed to contend with. All the work so far has been carried out in a fairly small and efficient depot at Romford delivering to 100-250 customers per day (out of a total of approximately 3,500) in an area covering East London and most of Essex. Orders are accepted up to about midday the day before delivery. The Schweppes fleet comprises nine 6-ton vehicles; two or three 8-ton vehicles can be hired from a contractor when demand is heavy.

The first experiment was to use the computer to replan all the deliveries made on two days to test whether it would produce reasonably practical routes, whether the figures for average speeds and unloading times produced reasonable results and whether any restrictions other than those we had allowed for would have to be taken into account. After some modifications, the computer was used to plan routes in parallel with the manual system for several consecutive days. The most important and encouraging single result was that effectively one vehicle out of ten could have been saved by the routing programme on each of the days planned. The third stage was to set up a Telex link from the depot to a computer bureau, transmit daily the details of deliveries required the following day (order number, customer location, and weight of goods ordered) together with any time or geographical restrictions on delivery, and details of the vehicles available (number and capacity) and use the programme to plan the deliveries. The vehicles were despatched by this method on nine days with no difficulties arising. Only one route was substantially altered by the Depot Manager, and on this occasion it appeared that it was permissible to make one journey longer than the parameters given to the computer allowed. As a result of these successful experiments, a computer system is to be applied to a much larger depot on a regular basis later this year. This larger depot appears to be less efficient and to offer scope for proportionately greater cost savings. However, if the transport cost saving is no greater than the 10 per cent achieved at Romford the net saving after taking the computer system costs into account will still be 5 per cent of the total.

As a result of improvements to the programme and further work study by Schweppes, the new system will include two improvements over that used at Romford. Firstly, it will utilize three different average speeds for country, suburban and town travel, and will allow still lower speeds to be specified for any areas of particular congestion; secondly, the permanent information about each customer will include both the appropriate early closing day and a choice of one or two out of a total of seventeen different time bands when deliveries may be made during the day. This is designed to cater for all the known time restrictions on deliveries to customers who include for instance, public houses only open between 10 a.m. and 3 p.m., off licences which close at 2 o'clock, firms which either close for lunch or are too busy serving lunches to accept deliveries, firms to which deliveries are restricted by police waiting restrictions, and so on. This, to date, is the most advanced stage of implementation of the programme as an operational tool, though work we have done for Shell-Mex and BP Limited with a different version of the programme is not far behind. Tankers were despatched from one of their distribution depots by computer on two days last week. A full comparative analysis of performance is not yet available but the exercise again demonstrated the practicability of the system and we believe that it will also prove to have despatched the fleet more efficiently.

These demonstrations of the programme's practicability lend confidence to its use as a planning tool. If the results it produces in a current situation are realistic and efficient, it is reasonable to believe that its evaluation of the effect of changing, let us say, the depot location, the number or size or performance of the vehicles, or the hours of work, is equally reliable. Work of this type is more advanced and a number of examples can be given.

In one organization, goods were despatched as parcels either by rail or by road haulage contractors. It was proposed that the company should establish its own delivery fleet in the belief that this would halve the costs of distribution. The routing programme showed that this costs saving could only be achieved by holding up some deliveries for up to seven days in order to combine calls in to reasonably economical routes. To have used a company fleet to carry out the company's policy of despatching all orders within 24 hours would have cost as much as the existing method; the proposal to establish their own fleet was therefore turned down.

The five major banking companies in Britain are rapidly establishing the processing of current accounts and cheques by computer. The cheques are despatched from the branches to the computer centres by post, arriving the next morning and leaving the computers unemployed overnight. A proposal has therefore been made that they should join together to arrange for a system to collect cheques from branches in the evenings after the close of business so that the computers can start work on them overnight. In order to assess the cost of this proposal and find out whether it was likely to be profitable, the vehicle routing programme is being utilized to find out the number of vehicles that would be required to collect an adequate number of cheques under different circumstances from the branches in the Greater London area where there are in total some 1,700 branches of these five banks. This work is proceeding rapidly and smoothly. An alternative manual system would take years to prepare and assess and it would not be possible to test the effects of alterations in the methods of collection, as it is by computer. Another major company has been using the programme to decide between alternative possible sites for the establishment of a depot to distribute their consumer goods to shops to the South-West of England and South Wales. This work has been sufficiently successful and instructive for the company to be proceeding to evaluate their total requirement for depots in Great Britain for the 1970s.

In one city the programme has been applied to the planning of the collection of refuse in bulk from factories, blocks of flats, shops, etc. Collection of refuse in bulk is basically much cheaper than collection in small bins but the situation has been reached where extension of the service required replanning and reallocation of the routes which was becoming increasingly difficult. The first application of the programme has shown that there need be no difficulties about this in future and also that according to the generally accepted standards of performance, the present vehicles are working to only 75 per cent of their capacity, which had not been realized.

In another company, the programme is currently being modified to enable it to plan calling schedules for van salesmen visiting customers at different specified intervals - commonly either once a week or once a fortnight, but in some cases only once a month and in others twice or even three times per week.

The examples illustrate the variety of types of problem for which the routing programme can be used. The size of problem to which it can profitably be applied also varies widely. At present there is a limit of 1,000 on the number of call points which can be submitted to one run; larger problems than this would need to be subdivided. Routes can only be planned from one depot at a time. Allocation of customers to depots can be carried out by another type of programme, but not concurrently with detailed route-planning.

The lower limit to the size of problem for which use of a computer is worthwhile depends on several factors and is consequently harder to define. Implementation of a computer system is obviously cheaper if a standard programme is suitable than if a programme was to be tailor-made. The cost of using a computer system is lower if the company owns its own computer than if a data transmission link to a computer bureau has to be set up. Although the system of locating customers by map references reduces the problem of data collection as far as possible, the time and expense involved is never negligible. If the routing programme is used as part of an integrated order processing system, including credit checking, warehouse stock control, preparation of loading and/or packing summaries, delivery notes and or/ invoices, sales analysis, sales accounting, and distribution costing, then the cost of data collection is spread over a wider range of activities. The cost of planning a delivery schedule which changes every day is obviously greater than that of planning a long-term schedule which will continue to show savings for months or years after the plan has been made. As a very approximate guide, it appears unlikely that a depot despatching less than 15 vehicles would find it profitable to use a computer for daily routing, and the limit might be higher than this, depending on circumstances. For long-term planning on the other hand the limit might well be lower. The replanning of bulk refuse collection, mentioned earlier was deemed worthwhile - and, to take account of anticipated changes, even necessary - for a fleet of only five vehicles.

The computer is not a panacea for all problems, nor a substitute for experienced management. But as a long-term planning tool it can give intelligent and realistic answers to intelligent and precise questions; in daily operation it can deal efficiently with the bulk of the routine work, leaving management free to exercise discretion and experience on those problems which require it. It is a tool which has proved its value already in a variety of applications and which deserves serious consideration by all those concerned to improve the efficiency of their transport operation.

cost of maladjustment is spread over a wider range of activity. The cost of planning a delivery schedule which changes every day, is bound to be greater than that of planning a long-term schedule which will require to shift twenty four months or even after that has been made, once some very approximate ratio, it appears unlikely that a departmental manager less than a fortnight would find it profitable to use a computer for daily routine and the final might be higher than this, is possible on equipment once the cost of planning on the situation. The final table will be low as a percentage of profit ratios of action from 0.0 rather was deemed worthwhile, and to take account of minor and major changes, even necessary, in a fleet of only three vehicles.

The computer is not equipment for all problems, there is obviously an experienced management. For it is a foundation planning tool, it can give valuable information. It is able to answer to briefly the anticipate questions. Simply operation it can deal effectively with the bulk of the routine work leaving the management free to exercise discretion and experience on those problems which require it. It is a tool which has proved its value, its advantages clarity of implication, and which deserve serious consideration by all those concerned with improving the efficiency of the distribution operation.

# Section Two
# Rail Transport

The first five selections in this group focus on Britain's rail network since nationalization. The Modernization Plan of the mid 1950s and its impact on railway productivity provides the theme of the two opening chapters, by Sidebotham and Bryer respectively. These are followed by Green's chapter, which emphasized the achievements of British Rail in the late sixties and early seventies with respect to both passengers and freight. Next, with the advantage of hindsight, Asteris attempts to place the radical proposals of the Beeching Report in historical perspective by examining its background, nature and consequences. Chapter 13 shifts the focus of attention by considering how a privatized railway system could be achieved.

The contribution by Ekins deals with that most romantic of trains - the Orient Express. Once it was the prestigious means of reaching cities such as Vienna and Constantinople: in its present form, this luxurious conveyance is desired primarily for the sheer pleasure of the journey itself.

Undoubtedly, the building of the Channel Tunnel constitutes one of the greatest transport infrastructure projects this century. Proposals to construct a fixed link were first presented in 1802. Harrison brings the story up-to-date with a description of the rail-only Eurotunnel. This private sector venture is scheduled to commence services in June 1993, thereby linking the United Kingdom to the European rail network for the first time.

Finally, Meads deals with a very important form of the iron way - the underground railway. He traces the history of Londons' system, including the building of the Heathrow extension and the Jubilee Line.

# 9  British Railways and the Modernization Plan

*Paper presented to the Manchester Centre by*
*K. Sidebotham*
*British Railways*
*January 1959 issue*

## INTRODUCTION

It may seem out of place to speak of the history of railways when talking about modernization, but it is only by examination of past events that the present state of affairs and future plans can be seen in their true perspective. Moreover, since the paper is being presented to the Manchester Branch of the IOTA, it would seem appropriate to mention that Liverpool Road Station, Manchester was one of the termini of the Liverpool and Manchester Railway opened in 1829, in connection with which George Stevenson and Henry Booth won the prize of £500, offered by the Directors of the Company for the famous "Rocket" locomotive.   George Stevenson had already achieved success with his locomotive designed and built for the Stockton and Darlington Railway in 1825.

It is of interest to note that at the opening of the Liverpool and Manchester Railway Mr Huskisson, President of the Board of Trade, was killed accidentally when, not realizing the speed of which a steam locomotive was capable, he attempted to step across the railway track in the path of the "Rocket" to greet the Duke of Wellington, with whom he had previously had a disagreement.

## SUBSEQUENT DEVELOPMENT

As is well known, the railways, in the mid-19th century, proved so great a success financially that in 1840 an Act of Parliament was passed to limit railway dividends to 40 per cent per annum. During these years of prosperity many new lines sprang up and public opinion became so alarmed at the powerful influence that railways could exert collectively on the growing industrial life of the Country, that every effort was made to keep the companies in small independent competitive units. Any attempt on the part of the railways to amalgamate was regarded with suspicion - so much so that one of the principal functions of the Railway and Canal Commission (forerunner and father of the present Transport Tribunal) was to examine any intended amalgamation with a view to seeing how it could be avoided. The Railway and Canal Traffic Act of 1854, which established the Railway and Canal Commission, also embodied certain clauses which prohibited the exercise of what was known as "undue preference", i.e. the favouring of one trader, either by rate or service, more than other traders forwarding the same type of traffic. These restrictive clauses were later to prove one of the burdens under which the railways laboured, but to which their future road competitors were not subject.

After World War 1, however, the economic position changed. Already, ex-army transport on the roads was providing the first chill wind of the competition which was later to strip the railways of much of their more lucrative traffic and it was apparent that amalgamation had become a national necessity. The Railways Act of 1921 rationalized many existing companies into the four well known main line companies with which we were all familiar prior to 1947 - LMS, LNE, GW and SR.

The Act also provided for the formulation of a system of Freight and Passenger charges which, introduced in 1928, aimed to earn the railways a standard net revenue of about £45 million per annum, a figure based on the 1913 level of total railway revenue, modified in the light of the post-war variation in the value of money, together with an allowance for the economies which it was thought would accrue through amalgamation.

The late Lord Stamp referred to economic planning by a rather apt metaphor, saying it was rather like trying to play a game of billiards on a rolling ship; as soon as the balls had been lined up on the table for a shot, the ship rolled and the pattern changed. So it was with the railways. Increasing road competition prevented the standard of net revenue ever being earned and the annual earnings of the railways fell progressively below the target, until, in the late 1930s, the revenue earned was in the region of £26 million. It was this state of affairs which inspired Lord Stamp to launch his "Square Deal" campaign on behalf of the LMS Railway, of which he was Chairman.

On the outbreak of hostilities in 1939, the Government once more assumed control of the Railways as they had done in 1914, and the revenue which would have been earned by carrying troops and war materials, had the railways continued to operate as profit making organizations, was in the region of £96 million per annum - or nearly double the standard net revenue.

## NATIONALIZATION

When the railways were nationalized under the Transport Act 1947, their assets had depreciated very considerably during the preceding eight years. The low revenue earned in the late 1930s had necessitated the most stringent economies. Much of the maintenance of the permanent way and works had been reduced to the minimum, with consequent considerable deterioration; whilst during the  war years all effort was concentrated on keeping the railways operationally effective in the face of enemy action, an atmosphere hardly conducive to even the barest maintenance over and above that concerned directly with the movement of traffic.

Between 1938 and 1953 there was a steady running down of railway assets and it has been estimated that the deterioration between these years was something like a quarter of the capital value of the whole system. This deterioration has only been met by continuing to use equipment which was either obsolete or past the end of its useful life.

The years immediately following nationalization proved little better from the railway's point of view, as restrictions on expenditure still prevailed. Government policy, coupled with the shortage of railway funds, still limited all expenditure over and above current operational maintenance, and it was not until the advent of the Modernization Plan in 1955 that it was decided - not before time it will now be appreciated - to expend some £1,200 million in modernizing the railway system - over a period of ten to fifteen years.

## OUTLINE OF THE MODERNIZATION PLAN

The Plan - the expenditure is controlled by a Planning Committee set up by the British Transport Commission and comprises Headquarters and Regional Officers working in conjunction with the Regional General Managers - is now well under way and it may be of interest to know how the sum involved is to be devoted:

                                                        **£millions**

1.     The modernization of track and signalling including extension of colour light signalling and introduction of automatic train control. The modernization of the track is particularly important if high speeds are to be achieved. Already, many miles of long section flat bottom rails have replaced the old fashioned but familiar bullheaded rail, which was secured to the sleepers with chairs. Speeds up to 90 mph are envisaged for the Midland Section of the LM Region...                                     210

2.     Replacement of steam by multi-unit diesel and electric traction, involving the electrification of many miles of route.Examples are Euston to Liverpool and Manchester, Kings Cross to Leeds and York and Liverpool Street to Ipswich and Harwich. Instead of DC formerly employed in connection with electrified railways in this country 25 KV 50 cycle AC has been adopted with many advantages...........          345

3.     Replacement of obsolete rolling stock by modern passenger diesel and electric trains ...            285

4.    Re-modelling of freight services, the fitting of continuous braking to all freight wagons, thus speeding
up freight trains to passenger train standard. The
number of marshalling yards is to be reduced and
they will be modernized. Goods depots will be re-
sited and modernized and mechanical handling methods introduced. A "North Circular route" is envisaged from Whitemoor in the Eastern Counties to
destinations south of London, via Oxford and Reading to avoid the congestion encountered in working
through London. The accent so far as goods and
parcels terminal working is concerned will be on
concentration depots between which high speed
services will operate.....................          365

5.    Sundry items, including staff welfare, improvement
in office mechanization and development and
research.................                                35
                                                        ─────
                                                        £1,240


Over one-third of the £1,200 millions programme is either in hand or authorized and items of expenditure so far authorized include:

    £92     Millions for electrification;
    £33½    Millions for  diesel main line
            and shunting engines;
    £32½    Millions for multi-unit trains;
    £46     Millions for major works such as track signalling.

Concrete evidence of the initial stages of the plan is to be seen in the introduction of:

a.    The following Manchester and District Diesel services:
<u>February 1956</u>  The Bury-Bacup line was completely dieselized and the number of passengers carried and the receipts earned trebled.
<u>October 1956</u>  The partial dieselization of the Manchester (London Road) to Macclesfield and to Buxton lines with an increase of 33 and one third per cent in passengers and receipts in the former case and one-half per cent in the latter.
<u>June 1957</u>  Manchester (London Road) ER to Marple, Macclesfield and Hayfield.

This year Manchester-Oldham-Rochdale diesels have been introduced with a 20 minute interval service between Manchester and Oldham and 40 minute service between Oldham and Rochdale and Oldham and Royton. This has also proved to be very popular.

Schemes in hand but not yet completed include those for NE Lancashire, Leeds to Liverpool, Manchester to Liverpool and Manchester to Chester.

b.    Electrification of the Manchester-London line.
The electrification of the line from Manchester to Crewe via Styal, which is the first stage.  Progress is evident for passengers travelling from London Road to the South.


## RE-ORGANIZATION

Concurrently with the Modernization Plan, the central control from a relatively remote headquarters has been broken down to - on the LM Region - six traffic divisions with a local Divisional Traffic Manager, having a much greater autonomy than has previously been conferred at other than headquarters level.  On the Divisional Traffic Manager's organization will be concentrated the major aspects of the production of the commodity the railways have to sell, i.e. the service of transport, involving the operation of the railway, as well as selling service which, of course, includes the formulation and quotation of freight rates under the new charging scheme.  The Divisional Traffic Manager's organizations are not intended to detract from, but rather to strengthen the District Goods and Passengers' Managers, who will obtain rapid decisions on day to day matters locally.

Earlier in this talk you will recollect the severe restrictions under which the Railways laboured under the mid-19th Century Road and Canal Traffic Acts. These have very largely been removed, in theory at any rate, by the Transport Act 1953, which gives the railways much greater freedom in competitive charging and permits the quotation of rates at a much lower percentage below what is now known as Maximum Rates than was hitherto possible without recourse to the Transport Tribunal.

The Modernization Plan, coupled with the re-organization of the railways will lead, it is hoped, to a "railway renaissance". Whilst many uneconomic branch lines and services are being pruned, much greater weight will be thrown on providing efficient long distance and suburban services at prices which will be truly competitive for a standard of service which will rival that on any transport system in the world today.

# 10 Productivity in British Railways

*Paper presented to the Annual Conference by*
*W. J. Bryer*
*British Railways*
*July 1963 issue*

Productivity means many things to many people but in essence it is really making the most effective use of men and materials. The choice of subject for your Conference is particularly appropriate to the railway section of the transport industry at the present time as the recently published "Re-shaping Plan" lays so much emphasis on increased productivity.

On British Railways the search for higher productivity takes many forms; there are obvious ones like Work Study. Tonight I will only mention that Work Study and O & M Techniques have been used in railway work only in the recent past; they are now firmly established and expanding. The cover goes much further than the shop floor or factory type of work and includes carriage cleaning, marshalling yards, station working, cartage work and the host of routine maintenance jobs that is so much a part of the work of the Civil, Signal, and Electrical and Maintenance Engineers.

But many less obvious techniques are doing a very similar job. Every time a signal, a pair of points, a bridge requires renewing, these techniques go into action. Constant examination of train working, of staffing, of the possibilities of concentrating and rationalizing the work takes place. The methods used are not those commonly regarded as Work Study, although, as with sanity and insanity, the dividing line is often thin and always invisible.

I would like to expand upon one technique which is rather special in the transport world, and use it for the theme of this paper, namely "Planning for Maximum Utilization" and in particular in the field of Railway Operating.

Running a railway has appealed to small, and somewhat larger boys, ever since there were railways. Everybody knows how to do it, of course, but as we today know very much to our cost, if you are to stay in business, running a railway is certainly not as simple as dealing with a train set on the floor. One of the best ways of keeping the cost down and hence improving the net revenue is to plan for maximum utilization.

I will not pretend that railway operating is an exact science. I will not be afraid to admit that the tail can wag the dog; that you may produce brilliant utilization but perhaps be running trains when nobody wants to use them or by giving an inferior service to the consumer, so a compromise is sometimes inevitable; but a great deal can be done.

This is a comprehensive subject. How can we break it down? I think you can say that planning should be aimed at four sectors:

1. Track and Signalling.
2. Motive Power.
3. Rolling Stock.
4. The Timetable.

To a large extent these are not separate considerations but very much inter-department. If you insist on a certain timetable you must have the other three to make it work. To touch briefly on each sector then.

## TRACK AND SIGNALLING

Some 20 per cent of our annual costs go in track and signalling. Obviously the track did not spring up overnight and it is not changed rapidly either. Many of our track facilities were originally designed for traffic and conditions that no longer exist. Changed methods of train working have rendered redundant much that was provided for a purely steam-hauled railway. New works are a comparative rarity today, the great era of planning and building new railways being over, though one does get the new diesel depot or the new marshalling yard; but most of the planning work is either directed towards simplifying the track or towards making the best use of it. The first where density is lower than the track capacity and the second where, perhaps by closing other lines or running more and faster trains, capacity limits density.

To a very great extent the signalling imposed on the track is the limiting factor, but we cannot ignore speed restrictions through turnouts and around curves, the holding capacity of reception, loop and platform lines, or the actual existence or otherwise of them.

Signalling has a dual function, namely preventing accidents and keeping the traffic moving. The first does not concern us today. The second can only do this job properly when allied to an efficient track layout. Often the two do not occur naturally together but modern signalling is often the means of improving the productivity of deficiencies in layout. In particular the introduction of reversible working, and centralization of control will get more trains through a bottleneck, will help to make the best use of the layout. By reversible working I mean where running lines are signalled and used in both directions and the new type of panel signal boxes concentrating the work of a whole series of orthodox boxes over many route miles are typical of centralization of control. Now signalling is like any other product, you can have nearly any amount you like and the quality can vary enormously but you do not get anything for nothing; and here an inter-dependence with the timetable comes in. Very often by suitable train planning, new works expenditure can be avoided.

I will leave you to think over one or two contentious points:

i)   Modern signalling does not necessarily produce greater utilization of other assets.

ii)  To what extent should one place the safety element (with its high cost) against maximum flexibility of movement (and hence aid utilization)?

iii) To what extent should one provide track and signalling for the occasional emergency, i.e. derailment, engine failure, etc.

## MOTIVE POWER

To say that locomotives and the men who drive and maintain them cost a lot of money is to state the obvious; to add that the current book value of locomotives on British Railways is in the region of £250 million is to underline it.

Here again the timetable tends to be the generating force, for normally the planned working of engines and men follows it. It is clear that if the timetable is planned with economy of motive power in mind, higher productivity in this field is easier to achieve. But even if this has not or cannot be done, ingenuity will help.

In its simplest form this consists of optimizing the possible ways of fitting engine and crew workings to the demands of the timetable. "Simplest" must not be taken too literally; the vast number of such possibilities apart, regard has to be paid to the suitability of the locomotive for the work in question, spacing of watering points, the running distance between refuelling, servicing and maintenance, and route restrictions. With the crew, the agreement with the Trade Unions and road knowledge comes in. As modernization brings power capable of longer running in service, so synchronization of man and machine becomes more and more difficult. In the case of the now common diesel or electric multiple unit train the engine and coaches are one. This itself simplifies many problems of railway working, but also produces others, for the "personal needs" of the two do not always coincide and the engine part cannot be used to haul a freight train during any unproductive time.

Inevitably the question of productivity in this field encroaches upon others. It becomes clear that if a certain service ran at a different time  an engine or set of men could be saved; that a very small acceleration of a schedule can have a very large effect on power provision. It is not long before the geographical location of motive power depots (or even their existence at all) must be questioned. The problem here is not to search for new ways of increasing productivity - but rather how to contain them to practical limits with the time and staff available. Do not let us forget though how valuable is the prize. The cost of one diesel locomotive standing idle in traffic for an hour is around £300. This is a real loss, expenditure with no return at all.

## ROLLING STOCK

Most of my remarks on motive power apply equally to passenger coaches. In addition there is the special problem of peak traffic, for at these times there is a tendency for the extra locomotives required to be drawn from freight workings, the holiday time producing little freight traffic, or line capacity preventing its movement. We cannot tonight consider peaks as such, nor what measures can be adopted to flatten them. When all is done there will always be peaks, be they only for an hour or so a day. Once again skilled planning can give us coach working at its cheapest and best.

Freight Rolling Stock presents an entirely different picture. It is rarely possible to plan the actual working of the individual vehicle, and the demand fluctuates widely. The problem here is to devise means which will throw up wagons where they are required with the minimum of empty haulage, and to keep the fleet down by improving the loading, and reducing journey and turnround time. A problem then of distribution and utilization. It is because so high a proportion of freight traffic is loaded and unloaded by the customer that persuasion in the form of education, exhortation and demurrage is necessary. The difficulties of distribution stem from the difficulties of location. We are experimenting with "Continuous Progress Control" which keeps a check on the location and state of all wagons, in terminals, private sidings, in marshalling yards and running in trains. There are difficulties and there are costs, but let us not underestimate the savings to be achieved by better distribution and better utilization. For more Railway capital is accounted for by freight rolling stock than any other type of vehicle.

Again I pose questions, relevant to Motive Power and Rolling Stock:

i) Any specialization tends to reduce utilization. Modern developments have brought us multiple units and diesel locomotives not all capable of coupled control, Pullman diesels, special freight vehicles, and the problem of train heating with electrification. How do you measure and justify any loss of utilization by a commercial yardstick of attracting traffic?

ii) Any unrealiability of timekeeping reduces the scope of maximum utili zation by requiring a greater safety margin for turn-rounds. How much margin is it <u>prudent</u> to provide? How much margin is it <u>economic</u> to provide? And are the two incompatible?

## TIMETABLE

And so we come to the Timetable. I have already pointed out a paradox. The timetable can have a good or bad effect on full utilization but the quest for the latter can also influence the timetable. The more that work can be planned in advance the less one suffers from the inefficiency of improvization. It must be an efficient timetable, however, realistic, accurate and comprehensive. It must neither expect too little, nor demand too much. If it can be planned to give maximum utilization of track, signalling, motive power and rolling stock, so much the better. It cannot always be so planned, mainly because of commercial needs.

There are certain fundamentals to be observed if the timetable is to aid utilization. First, one should aim at reducing the speed differential between the slowest and the fastest train. The nearer you get to all trains running at the same speed the nearer you get to optimum line occupation. Where severe speed differences are unavoidable, the grouping of trains in speed blocks will bring better utilization than random scheduling. One of the surest ways to pull down good line occupation is to force an ultra-high speed train through a mass of slow trains. As well as the clear line needed ahead a vacuum is created behind. Second, plan your engine and coach workings at the same time, with particular reference to turn-rounds. A good example of carrying this through is the regular interval service. Apart from the commercial value of such a service, economy in power and rolling stock will follow provided the terminals can be chosen such that the running time leaves sufficient turnround time related to one hour or a multiple. Perversely enough, an interval service often prevents train grouping, and is apt to destroy margins for freight trains which existed before. Clearly, if the speed of freight trains can be raised relative to passenger trains the difficulty is reduced. Such an acceleration will bring other benefits as stops for water and crew relief can be reduced or eliminated, and obviously the faster the train the better the transit and the fewer are the locomotives, wagons and men required to run the service.

A timetable is an intricate product requiring a long manufacturing process. Because it is intricate, if you modify a small part, the resultant modifications can be formidable. The cries of the works manager and the production engineer cannot go unheeded and so there is the danger that before long the finished article may be marketed in time, but be sadly lacking in design and workmanship. This will be inevitable if you keep patching up to meet the needs of a constantly changing world, and so there is nothing for it but to have regular and drastic redesign in the drawing office, so that it comes off the production line inspected, incorporating the most modern techniques, and above all, at a cost allowing profit on the open market.

Public attention has been focused very largely on what might be called the negative aspects of the "Re-shaping Plan", yet if railways are to remain competitive it is the positive side which is so important. It is with approaches such as I have just described that the main body of railway officers are concerning themselves. Here is where the really big economies can be made.

People talk about the "Admin Ratio". It would be interesting to study the "Planning Ratio", for there must be a point where the time and money expended on planning railway work gives optimum results in terms of productivity.

Productivity in British Railways. This is very much more than I have mentioned. I have merely skimmed over part of one section of a large and complicated industry and I am very conscious of it. That the other sections, the goods and passenger stations, the offices, the maintenance and repair depots, the methods of renewing way and works, have productivity problems you can well imagine. That they are being grappled with I must ask you to believe. That it is worth grappling with I am sure you are convinced.

# 11   British Rail in the 1970s

*Paper presented to the Annual Conference by*
*C.E.W. Green*
*British Rail*
*June 1973 issue*

## THE FUTURE OF THE RAILWAY

### Size of industry

Few travellers out for a rail trip appreciate the sheer size of the business that is speeding them on their way. This very size and complexity, however, is a significant factor in any discussion on the future role of rail in this country. With a work force of around 250,000 British Railways is frequently termed a "labour intensive" industry. It is often forgotten that with a turnover of £650 million per annum and assets almost twice this value, it is also one of Britain's most capital-hungry industries.

Moreover, when considering the future of British Rail we are talking not only about one of the world's most intensive railway systems - we are considering the largest shipping and hovercraft ferry services in Britain, a major hotel owner, one of the largest mass-catering businesses in Britain, one of the top ten property owners and - dare one mention it - a road fleet owner second only to the GPO.

Our first question must be to challenge the need for this giant transport industry. If an advanced nation such as the United States has virtually managed to live without railways for a generation, why not Britain? Enormous improvements have been made to Britain's own road and air communications and new transport solutions are increasingly available.

The theme of this paper is to suggest that Britain is unlikely to adopt the American approach in the next decade. Far from being the twilight era of the railways, the 1970s are likely to be seen by future transport historians as a critical transitional period. The role of railways will certainly be more selective and specialized, but it will play an increasingly dominating role in particular fields. The 1970s is proving to be an era not only of technical break-through but also of political, social and economic re-orientation.

The obvious disadvantages of rail transport are the high fixed costs and an inflexibility to meet rapidly changing markets. The problems of the post-war period have largely arisen from the inability of the system to adjust itself to new markets and competition quickly and cheaply, to attract the enormous capital reinvestment needed to realize the full value of rail, and to adjust the size of the system to its new role. New towns, oil terminals and airports are being built, and connecting them to rail is a slow and costly investment when a mile of basic single track costs around £50,000 before any allowance is made for earthworks, junctions, bridges and stations. This is, of course, in strong contrast to the bus operator and road haulier who can usually adapt their routes at very short notice at little cost.

The advantages of rail are the tremendous capacity they offer for heavy traffic volumes. Units of 1,000 tons or more can be run at 75mph at 5 minute headways in a highly regulated way maximizing the use of track, equipment and staff. Moreover, whilst the road industry argues over 11-ton axle weights, the railway already operates a 25-ton axle-load using 100-ton wagons. There is no other proven system which can convey 600 passengers at 100mph every 3 minutes or, indeed, 1,000 commuters at 90 second intervals on suburban routes. These advantages of high capacity and speed are also very suitable for adaptation to automation. As the environment is becoming an increasingly public concern, it is also worth noting the more efficient land-use of a railway system as illustrated by the Euston-Manchester main line which is calculated to have the equivalent capacity of an 18-lane motorway. Indeed, the ability to operate railways electrically is likely to become a major advantage as the world enters a period of oil shortage.

The new role for rail is based on developing the very advantages we have discussed. The 1960s saw a necessary pruning of those areas where railways no longer had a useful role to play such as the rural branch line and the wayside goods station. Between 1948 and 1965, for example, the number of terminals fell by 50 per cent and marshalling yards by 66 per cent. The new role for rail lies in developing high capacity trunk routes - Super Highways - offering the maximum possible speed, headway and load factors. These highways may be the glamorous intercity routes or the unsung commuter routes feeding major conurbations. They may carry spectacular new block freight trains or an improved wagonload business. The important point is that it will be a specialist solution rather than an attempt at total transport. Major investment is increasingly being concentrated on to the fields where rail has the most to offer - mass transit schemes for cities, high speed inter/city services and block freight trains. The car, bus and lorry are no longer "the competition" but seen as partners conveying passengers and freight to concentrated railheads.

The inevitable question will be asked about the viability of the network and the 1968 Transport Act does, of course, require the Railways Board to break even taking "one year with another". This was achieved in 1969 and 1970 when profits of £15 million and £8 million were achieved, but this performance has not been maintained.

It is becoming clear that a rail system cannot be solely judged on traditional accountancy lines. No attempt is made to operate the nation's system of highways, buses, lorries and cars on a single balance sheet, nor is there any public demand for such an accountancy approach to a necessity of civilized living. The railway is, moreover, heavily dependent on political and economic changes which can drastically affect its fortunes. The recent recession in the coal and steel industry has had a crippling effect on an industry which relies on coal and steel for 74 per cent of its freight tonnage. Investment in vital new track, locomotives, wagons, electrification, etc., is understandably dependent on the availability of Treasury funds in any given year.

No European country makes its railway system "pay" in the narrow sense, although it is often forgotten that Britain is nearer to doing so than any other country with French and German railways netting deficits ten times greater than our own. European countries have, for a long time, been aware that railways do "pay" many times over in the wider social and economic terms. They make life safer, simpler and cleaner by keeping heavy passenger and freight traffic away from roads, houses and city centres and this cannot be calculated in traditional book-keeping terms. The best example I can give to illustrate the point is the new Victoria tube across London. This has run at a loss in the accountant's book from the day it opened, yet is equivalent in capacity to a 14-lane motorway from Victoria through Buckingham Palace, Green Park and Oxford Circus. Can there be any doubt where the true profit lies in social and economic terms?

I believe that there has been a remarkable swing of public opinion in the last two years away from the "make 'em pay or close 'em" approach to the more sophisticated belief that railways have an essential but specialized role to play in civilized living which cannot be fully accounted for in a balance sheet.

111

In the second part of the paper we shall be taking a closer look at these specific roles.

## THE NEW RAILWAY

### The freight business

In 1971 the passenger business overtook the freight for the first time by earning 54 per cent of total revenue. The freight business is far from declining, however, although it has become far more specialist. Over half the freight tonnage now moves in block trains - the vast majority beginning or ending in private sidings. This means the minimum of shunting and marshalling and increasingly, the capital investment in new private sidings and wagon fleets is being shared by the customer, which, of course, helps to spread railway investment over more projects.

Classic examples of such developments are the oil and car companies. Almost every oil company in Britain has signed medium-term contracts with British Rail guaranteeing large tonnages to rail in "block trains" of privately owned 100-ton wagons. This keeps vast fleets of oil tankers and their inflammable cargoes off the road and gives rail an ideal new traffic to replace dwindling coal receipts. New and partly completed cars now move in block trainloads with some famous manufacturers giving a near 100 per cent handover to rail. A conveyor belt of block trains links Linwood to Coventry and Halewood to Belgium.

The block trainload business is a growth story and at the present expansion rate it will increasingly dominate the rail scene. Other examples are, of course, cement, chemicals, steel and aggregates. The latter is the current boom market and involves meeting the insatiable appetite for road building materials and industrial ingredients such as limestone and china clay. Simple new railheads are opening throughout the country and this promises to be more than a short-term boom. The coal industry remains rail's ideal traffic and despite a steady decline, still accounts for about 50 per cent of the freight business. New fears of a world oil crisis may influence new investment in giant coal-fired power stations such as Rugeley, Buildwas and Ratcliffe-on-Soar. If they do, rail is uniquely equipped to handle the growth with its Merry-Go-Round services. These are continuously coupled trains of around 36 hopper wagons which can be loaded and unloaded without any need for the train to stop. This allows up to four round trips per wagon between coalfield and power station instead of the average of one trip per 11 days achieved in the old wagonload system. Ratcliffe Power Station, for example, is fed by 24 1,000-ton trains every day, the equivalent of about 700 lorry loads. About 80 per cent of Britain's coal passes by rail.

The most spectacular development has, of course, been the freightliner container train and ship. This now offers a complete network of terminals and services across Britain and through to Europe. The terminals are open to any haulier wishing to use rail for the trunk route. Intending developments include the daily flow of half-finished Ford cars from Liverpool to Belgium via the Sealink container ships and the growing 'deep sea' flows to docks such as Tilbury, Southampton and Greenock.

The freight business must not be left without mention of the wagonload side. For many years there has been doubt on the net value to the system of retaining an individual wagon system. A series of in-depth studies have shown once and for all that a well organized wagonload system is essential to the network and great emphasis is now being laid on developing and improving the system.

The keystone is TOPS - a real-time computer system which will control the movement of every wagon and locomotive in Britain by 1978, enabling a revolutionary minute-by-minute control to be maintained. This will at last give the reliability and control that has been demanded by the customer and a big saving in the wagon fleet and locomotives through more efficient handling.

The future for freight on rail looked bleak ten years ago. Today, whilst only 23 per cent of Britain's freight moves by rail compared to 49 per cent in France, there is every sign of a real growth.

**The passenger business**

The passenger business has been the star performer in recent years due to the many break-throughs that have been achieved. Not only has revenue grown rapidly, but until the recent recession/inflation, passenger journeys have been increasing at a steady 5 per cent per annum. Traditionally the passenger business is divided between the local London services, local provincial and intercity.

**London area**

The London area is at once the safest and most difficult business. 80 per cent of Londoners arrive by public transport - and most include a rail journey. In the peak a train is arriving at a London terminal every 18 seconds. It is the ultimate example of rail's indispensability and yet it involves various problems of train operation and, above all, capital investment. A major Government investment programme is under way to electrify the remaining commuter routes into the capital (e.g. Hitchin-King's Cross), to re-equip the Southern Region suburban fleet with ultra-modern rolling stock, and to invest in new continuously welded track, power signalling and stations. This illustrates both the public need for a system that will never break even and the railway's reliance on Government investment.

**Provincial local services**

These services are all grant-aided and include four Passenger Transport Authority areas such as the West Midlands where bus and rail services are fully co-ordinated and it is likely that further PTAs will be formed shortly. It is in these areas that major railway developments can be expected. All four PTAs have announced plans for major new rail schemes aimed at bringing more commuters into their cities by rail. Merseyside is building a new loop-railway, SELNEC a tunnel under the city linking up all its suburban routes, Newcastle a new loop railway and the West Midlands an upgraded high-capacity link between Redditch, Birmingham and Sutton Coldfield.

Outside the PTA areas there are 139 local services throughout the country with few major investment schemes. There is, however, good evidence that the new Non-Metropolitan Counties will be taking rail investment very seriously and in the East Midlands, for example, Derby, Leicester and Nottingham are currently evaluating upgrading existing commuter services and building about a dozen new stations.

**InterCity**

The greatest investment and growth has occurred in the InterCity business where passenger travel has steadily grown despite competing motorways and airlines. Even on short distances such as London-Birmingham, rail's share of the market has risen from 15 per cent to over 40 per cent since electrification, whilst on the ideal 2½ hour London-Liverpool run the figure is near 80 per cent. InterCity has set itself high standards and is a high cost product - but by any standards is also a profitable one.

The recent investment in new stations, track, signalling and rolling stock has brought Britain to the top of Europe's league table in frequency, comfort and speed. Nowhere else in Europe can one find a 30 minute 100mph express service such as Birmingham enjoys. Nowhere else can one find a growth in

114

train services to a point where Birmingham has 33 per cent more trains to London in 1973 than when electrified in 1967. There are more catering services in Britain than in any other country and the standard of general Inter-City comfort is outstanding. It is now the policy to offer fully air-conditioned travel to every second class and first class passenger at no extra charge.

InterCity has not reached its ultimate development. It has rather begun an entry into a new technical era after half-a-century of slow progress. Who would have thought ten years ago that rail speeds could be pushed up to 100mph standard on most of our main lines, yet alone increased by another 50 per cent by the end of the decade and possibly tripled by the end of the century? The strategy is to complete the 100mph all air-conditioned railway in the mid-1970s and then move into a 125mph speed band by about 1976 based on the high speed diesel. This will become the standard train, appearing first on the East Coast and Bristol/South Wales routes.

Thereafter the Advanced Passenger Train with its tilt mechanism and 155mph potential will appear in electric form on the Euston mainline and will ultimately be mass produced in both electric and gas-turbine form as the standard InterCity train of the 1980s. The increase in speed will result in the doubling of passenger journeys on some routes as traditional time barriers are broken. Glasgow will become four hours from London instead of the present six hours; Manchester will be as close in time as Wolverhampton is at present. Birmingham will be little more than one hour.

The full potential for the APT, however, is linked to the Channel Tunnel. Phasing Britain into Europe's railway network and major traffic developments will result. An APT on a new railway from London could reach Paris in 2 hours 45 mins compared to the present 6 hours 45 mins and would raise rail's market share from about 30 per cent to 70 per cent.

Other developments include a new breed of station - Parkways. The latest opened on 7th May 1973, "Alfreton and Mansfield Parkway", is designed as a totally new railhead for a catchment area of a quarter million. The car is welcomed with a 280 space free car park and it is strategically situated next to M1 Exit 28. Many more of these new railheads are likely to appear on existing routes as InterCity adapts itself to new markets and the car.

Earlier main line electrification now seems likely and first thoughts on a London-Edinburgh scheme have been announced, just as the London-Glasglow electrification nears completion. It is a sobering thought that the entire Crewe-Glasgow section has been electrified for less than the cost of the 'Spaghetti Junction' road interchange at Birmingham.

# CONCLUSION

The future of rail in Britain is surely ensured by the technical developments of the 1970s and the growing conviction that only a rail solution can solve the problems that man is creating for himself both in and around our cities. Let us hope that rail, road and air will be used in a more sensible partnership in the 1980s and that more effort will be diverted from the accountant's book-keeping to the needs and wishes of a population which is daily finding easy travel a pre-requisite to a civilized life. In the words of our Chairman, the Rt. Hon. Richard Marsh, "The choice is too often seen as between road and rail, buses or cars, when what we should be talking about is the priority given by the Government to total transport investment".

# 12 The Beeching Report in retrospect

*Article by M. Asteris*
*Portsmouth Polytechnic*
*October 1988 issue*

## INTRODUCTION

This year marks the twenty-fifth anniversary of "The Reshaping of British Railways", the most famous transport report of the post-war era. Officially, it was the creation of the British Railways Board; in fact, it was widely known that the driving force behind it was a new personality on the railway scene - Dr Richard Beeching. For this reason the 1963 blueprint for change has always been known as the 'Beeching Report'. The document constitutes an important landmark in transport history because its radical and highly controversial proposals were rapidly implemented. In many respects, when the Beeching plan was published, the railway network still reflected the demand patterns of its Victorian heyday. By the early 1970s, in contrast, a leaner but more competitive system had emerged.

Anniversaries are occasions for reflection, so perhaps the time is ripe to re-evaluate the Beeching Report. Accordingly, this article looks at the Report in terms of its background, nature and consequences. Such a re-evaluation inevitably involves hindsight. In this case, the perspective of the 1980s highlights that the Beeching plan was directed at achieving a swift improvement in efficiency. In recent years such exercises have become almost commonplace in British Industry, but in 1963 Dr Beeching's approach appeared both novel and traumatic.

## THE BACKGROUND

The construction of an extensive railway system was one of the greatest achievements of Victorian Britain. By the late nineteenth century the permanent way had achieved a near monopoly of inland transport over all but the shortest of routes. To ensure that the railway companies did not abuse their dominant position, charges were subject to tight regulation, with the result that often they failed to reflect costs. Cross subsidization - profitable traffic paying for the unprofitable - became a prominent feature of the network. Moreover, inter-company competition encouraged the provision of additional services to customers (for example, the use of wagons for storage) at little or no charge. Even so, distortions in pricing policy raised few eyebrows while the individual companies earned large profits.

### The inter-war years

For the railways, the First World War constituted a watershed because after it their monopoly position crumbled away and they experienced a permanent fall in traffic. Primarily, the railways were in decline because of competition from road transport. In 1914 there were less than 400,000 motor vehicles on Britain's roads; of these 132,000 were private cars. By 1939 the number of vehicles had exceeded three million, some two million of which were private cars.

During the twenties and thirties the flexible pricing policies adopted by road vehicle operators deprived the railways of a great deal of profitable traffic. Railway charges were rigid and publicised so road transport could undercut on the more valuable custom, leaving the less desirable parts of the market to the permanent way. At the same time, the steep decline in mineral traffic, caused by the fall in production of coal and steel, implied a shrinkage in that part of the freight market where the comparative advantage of the railways was at its greatest.

The Railways Act of 1921 had amalgamated 121 companies into four large systems, each of which had a territorial monopoly. The railways were thus privately owned but non-competitive, an arrangement which produced little in the way of commercial dynamism. This was unfortunate because by the 1930s the railway companies needed to take three-pronged action if they were to keep abreast of changing circumstances. First, adopt more aggressive pricing policies, so as to staunch the haemorrhage of lucrative business to road transport. Secondly, prune under-utilized capacity because this was expensive to maintain and contributed little to revenue. Thirdly, invest in new equipment so as to offer a more efficient service. In practice, railway management failed to shed its monopoly mentality: the costing of services remained poor, route mileage did not alter significantly, and there was little attempt at modernization. Ultimately, growing competition from road transport was certain to compel a more assertive stance on the part of the railways, but the urgent needs of the Second World War intervened to postpone change. Indeed, until the early 1950s, the railways enjoyed something of an Indian summer in terms of the demand for their services since petrol rationing and a shortage of motor vehicles restricted the use of road transport.

**Nationalization and after**

Nationalization of the network in 1948 notwithstanding, as more normal conditions returned in the mid-1950s the pre-war problems of the railways re-emerged with a vengeance. In particular, the lack of investment during the war years was all too apparent from the exhausted state of equipment owned by British Railways. The Modernization Plan of 1955 was an attempt to remedy the situation by an extensive investment programme spread over 15 years. During this period a great deal of new equipment was to be introduced so as to increase the efficiency of the network. The major ingredients of the scheme consisted of improvements in track and signalling; replacement of steam power by diesel and electric traction; and the renewal of stations and rolling stock. The Plan achieved a great deal in terms of changing the face of the railways. Regrettably, however, it displayed little appreciation of the rapidly changing transport environment and thus tended to be crudely based on the replacement of the existing capital stock, rather than on a careful assessment of which parts of the system justified modernization in terms of likely profitability.

By the early 1960s, despite the removal of most traditional restrictions on charges and the writing off of a great deal of accumulated debt, the financial position of the network was deteriorating rapidly in the face of increasing competition from road transport. Between 1952 and 1962 rail's share of passenger traffic fell from 21 per cent to only 13 per cent, though total numbers held up reasonably well. Freight fared notably badly over the same period; rail's share of the traffic shrank from 45 per cent to only 25 per cent, and there was a fall of over a quarter in the volume handled. Progress with Britain's motorway programme was a clear indication that competition was going to become far more intense with the passage of time. Drastic action was therefore required to adapt the iron way to an era in which it was no longer the dominant transport mode. The man chosen to make a cold assessment of the way forward was an executive from ICI, Dr Richard Beeching, who was appointed chairman-elect of the new British Railways Board in May 1961.

## THE BEECHING REPORT

In essence, Beeching's task was one which has become very familiar to the Britain of the 1980s - the trimming of a nationalized industry so as to place it on a sounder market footing. In order to achieve this objective he needed to know in some detail the costs associated with the provision of rail services. Unfortunately, the collection of railway data for planning purposes left much to be desired, so that railway management had only a vague impression of what particular activities were costing. Such a state of affairs appears astounding until one recalls that for much of railway history managers did not have to bother with improved costing because both government and people tended to interpret greater profitability as an abuse of monopoly power. This monopoly mentality still permeated the management of the industry at the start of the sixties. Beeching changed all that. New staff appointments were made in the Regions as well as at headquarters, and outdated conventions were abandoned. The railways were thereby provided with a management structure conducive to rapid change.

At the same time, Dr Beeching initiated a comprehensive series of traffic surveys to supplement existing information. The results were published as part of the 1963 Reshaping Report and revealed an astonishing state of affairs. One-half of the total route mileage carried more than 95 per cent of all the passengers and freight that went by rail. The remainder of the system was virtually redundant and the revenue derived from it fell far short of that required to pay for the maintenance of the track and signalling equipment, let alone the cost of running trains, depots and stations. Disparities in the flow of traffic through stations was even more pronounced: 50 per cent of them produced almost 98 per cent of total receipts. The fact that stations were situated at roughly 2½ mile intervals was an important factor leading to this skewed distribution. Once such dense provision had been necessary in order to avoid placing too great a strain on horses; but by 1963 beasts of burden were conspicuous by their absence from the vicinity of railway stations!

# Freight traffic

The movement of freight was still the principal activity of the railways in the sixties. The Report demonstrated, however, that of the main categories of such traffic only coal and goods carried by coaching train - largely mail and parcels - were profitable. Even in the case of coal, the return on turnover was very low for two reasons. First, in spite of its suitability for through-train working, approximately two-thirds of all coal handled moved by the wagon load. Secondly, by tradition, the collieries made extensive use of wagons for coal storage, but paid very little for the privilege.

Mineral traffic (other than coal) and general merchandise freight made substantial losses. Again, the reason was largely historical. During the nineteenth century the railway companies had been willing to carry small loads without imposing the full cost on the customer. Wagon-load traffic (with its associated high costs) thus became the major feature of the freight scene because customers lacked the financial incentive to provide fewer, but more substantial consignments. The railways were thus unable to exploit the low costs inherent in taking train loads of freight to specific destinations. At the same time, a huge wagon fleet, of around 900,000 units, was needed as a consequence of extremely poor utilization.

# Passenger services

Turning to passenger services, the Report established that while all three main groups - fast and semi-fast trains, suburban trains and stopping trains - lost money, they varied widely in terms of the extent to which they did so. Fast and semi-fast services were potentially profitable because they operated over densely-loaded routes. The provision of additional trains for holiday periods was, however, becoming increasingly uneconomic because of widespread car ownership. Indeed, by the end of the 1950s, 6,000 of the 18,500 coaches allocated to fast and semi-fast services were required on not more than eighteen occasions a year. The annual cost of providing these 6,000 coaches was £3.4 million but they earned a mere £0.5 million.

Suburban passenger services fell into two categories: those feeding London, which came close to covering their full costs; and those feeding other population centres, which were more serious loss makers.

Stopping trains were particularly uneconomic. They had developed at a time when the only alternative form of passenger transport was the horse-drawn vehicle. Subsequently, much of this market had been lost to the bus

121

and the private car but comprehensive rail services continued to operate despite poor patronage.

## The main proposals

Overall, the commercial picture revealed by the surveys indicated a system crying out for reform. The industry was involved in too many activities for which it was no longer suited, while at the same time failing to exploit what it did best. In this context, the Report emphasized that railways are distinguished by the provision of a specialized route system for their own exclusive use. This gives rise to high fixed costs. On the other hand, the document spelled out the benefits which could be derived from this high cost system.

"Firstly, it permits the running of high capacity trains, which themselves have very low movement costs per unit carried. Secondly, it permits dense flows of traffic and provided the flows are dense, the fixed costs per unit moved are low. Thirdly, it permits safe, reliable, scheduled movements at high speed". (Report, P4).

The recommendations for reshaping were directed towards exploiting these advantages by placing the railways on a more contemporary footing in terms of the route system, pattern of traffic, and mode of operation. More specifically, the assumption that the horse and cart was the sole means of feeding and distributing from the rail network was finally being challenged several decades after it had ceased to be valid. In summary, the main proposals, which emerged logically from the Reports' findings, were as follows:

a)  Closure of many uneconomic lines, services and stations to passenger and freight traffic. In total, it was suggested that roughly half of all passenger stations should be closed and 5,000 route miles of passenger services withdrawn entirely.

b)  Substantial reductions in both passenger and freight rolling stock. For example, some 350,000 freight wagons were to be scrapped in the three years following the publication of the report.

c)  More efficient handling of freight. The number of stations receiving coal was to be cut from 3,750 to a few hundred. Similarly, depots handling freight sundries were to be reduced from 500 to about 100. Meanwhile, considerable effort was to be put into developing through train-loads and liner-train (container) services.

d)  Selective improvement of intercity passenger services. The expectation was that if the whole plan were to be 'implemented with vigour' much of the railway deficit would be eliminated by 1970.

## Criticism of the report

Understandably, a nation which has a sentimental attachment to railways tended to greet the publication of the Reshaping Report with instinctive hostility, simply because it advocated contraction. More specifically, the basic economic foundations of the Plan were also questioned. Critics pointed out that, while a great deal of data was published for the first time, there were crucial deficiencies. As a result, where the report came down firmly in favour of closing unrenumerative passenger services, it was impossible to suggest an alternative when detailed information relating to the costs of stations, track or signalling was not available. Surprisingly, strenuous efforts to reduce costs by such relatively straightforward devices as reducing stations to unmanned halts and adopting far more economical methods of train control tended to be embraced only when the closure of a line was ultimatly refused. The Plan was also criticized for tending to assume that branch lines could be closed with few repercussions for the remainder of the system. In practice, if the feeder links were lost, then most of the traffic was likely to abandon the railways. Such points not withstanding, the data provided in the Report was sufficient to convey the message that, even on the most heroic assumptions, many services simply did not justify retention.

## THE CONSEQUENCES OF THE BEECHING REPORT

Transport history is littered with illustrations of bold initiatives which were quietly put to one side: the Beeching Report does not come into this category. The election of a Labour Government, in October 1964, prevented the full implementation of the pruning programme proposed in the Report, but the basic analysis was reluctantly accepted. Consequently, through Dr Beeching left the Railways Board in 1966, the task of cutting out dead wood in the system continued. As Table 1 illustrates, by the end of 1970 the total route open to traffic had fallen by over one-fifth; traction units and coaching vehicles by one-third; wagons, stations and staff by roughly one-half.

## TABLE 1
### BRITISH RAILWAYS:  PHYSICAL ASSETS AND STAFF
1964-1970
(thousands)

|  | 1964 | 1966 | 1968 | 1970 |
|---|---|---|---|---|
| Route kilometres | 25.7 | 22.1 | 20.1 | 19.0 |
| Traction units | 15.1 | 12.4 | 10.0 | 9.5 |
| Coaching vehicles | 37.4 | 29.9 | 26.8 | 25.2 |
| Wagons | 650.1 | 551.4 | 437.4 | 370.9 |
| Stations | 5.1 | 3.8 | 3.2 | 2.9 |
| Staff | 475.2(a) | 339.0 | 296.3 | 250.8 |

(a)   This figure, which is taken from the Reshaping Report, is for 1962.

Source:  Transport Statistics 1964 - 74 (HMSO:  London, 1975).

**Increased efficiency**

The Beeching axe was wielded so effectively that to this day the former chairman is remembered very largely for the negative accomplishment of lopping off a significant part of the rail network.  In practice, the overall achievement of the Beeching philosophy was far more fundamental.  By emphasising that the railways should concentrate on what they do best in the modern world, the approach secured a permanent improvement in efficiency. Table 2 demonstrates the extent of this change in quantitative terms.

The figures in this tabulation reveal that, despite the marked decline in all inputs shown in Table 1, traffic conveyed held up remarkably well.  In short, the productivity of the railways increased dramatically in the years immediately following the publication of the Reshaping Report, largely because its broad recommendations were being adhered to.  This productivity advance was not, of course, solely the result of a reduction in inputs; qualitative factors also played an important though less obvious role.  For example, during the second half of the sixties steam traction disappeared from the network and an improved signalling programme was announced. Changes of this kind made quicker and more reliable services possible.

## TABLE 2
### BRITISH RAILWAYS:  PASSENGER AND FREIGHT TRAFFIC
#### 1964-1970
#### (million)

|                     | 1964   | 1966   | 1968   | 1970   |
| ------------------- | ------ | ------ | ------ | ------ |
| Passenger kilometres | 31,984 | 29,697 | 28,703 | 30,408 |
| Passenger journeys  | 928    | 835    | 831    | 824    |
| Freight net tonne km | 26,248 | 24,184 | 24,025 | 26,807 |
| Freight tonnes      | 243    | 217    | 211    | 209    |

Source:  Transport Statistics 1964 - 74 (HMSO:  London, 1975)

Despite the very considerable efficiency improvements stemming from the Beeching regime, substantial deficits became a feature of the railway scene. Elimination of the losses would have required 'butchery' of an unacceptable magnitude: the Labour government of the late 1960s therefore fashioned an alternative in the form of a public service operating grant for unrenumerative routes judged to be socially necessary. In effect, it is this subsidy which has steadily reduced in the past few years. The diminution has now reached the point where InterCity will be expected to be self supporting, which implies that the Beeching proposition with respect to the potential profitability of fast passenger services is about to be put to the test.

## THE WAY AHEAD

The shedding of uneconomic freight business and the decline in the movement of traditional bulk commodities has resulted in British Rail becoming predominantly a passenger system. At the same time, greater efficiency and the sale of peripheral activities, including hotels and ferries, has permitted a decline in staff to around 160,000. This slimmed down BR is making strenuous efforts to serve the needs of its customers in a commercial way. The more tailored approach is in no small measure a legacy of the Beeching era though, this debt acknowledged, the contractive mood of a quarter of a century ago is not a feature of BR on the eve of the 1990s. Traffic is booming as a result of better services and rapid economic growth, few lines are threatened with closure and many new stations have been opened in recent years. Moreover, provided the opportunity is seized, the opening of the Channel Tunnel in 1993 will create a new transport dimension for BR. The fixed link will facilitate the dense flows of passenger and freight traffic over long distances to which - as the Beeching Report emphasized - rail is ideally suited. The growth of such cost-effective traffic will do much to improve British Rail's finances.

## CONCLUSIONS

The ultimate achievement of the Beeching years was the establishment and implementation of a set of realistic guidelines which enabled the railways to adapt to modern transport conditions. The Reshaping Report ended the policy drift that had characterized much of the period after 1918 and replaced it by an organized retreat towards those activities where the merits of the iron way predominate. The Plan appeared revolutionary because changes which should have occurred gradually from the twenties onwards were squeezed into the middle and late sixties. It thus fell to Dr Beeching to rescue the railways from the commercial cul-de-sac of their Victorian heritage. In return, they bestowed a form of immortality upon their former head, in the sense that when the post-war history of Britain's railways is recalled the name **Beeching** springs readily to mind.

# 13   The great rail sale

*Anonymous article*
*October 1989 issue*

By the time of the Tory Party conference in October, the government is expected to have formed a pretty firm view on how it would like to privatize British Rail - and it will be very much the job of new Transport Secretary Cecil Parkinson to prepare the ground for that decision.

In the wake of the recent series of strikes, there is little doubt that the Prime Minister would relish the prospect of breaking up the giant BR, and unleashing a set of inter-competitive forces. The trouble is that would be both potentially costly in terms of duplicated management and overhead costs - and would not necessarily achieve a great deal.

The constraint must be that, by its very nature, a railway is an effective monopoly. Even in those halcyon pre-nationalization days, there was little actual competition for traffic between the various companies. Many believe that 'within mode' competition on the railway system is not attainable and should not even be a goal. Highway and (for longer distances) air services provide more than enough intermodal competition.

Whatever the course of privatization, specific groups will in any case put specific pressures or constraints on the final outcome.

For instance, major customers of Railfreight, and passengers in provincial cities who benefit from good cross country links, will demand the retention of a national network. Another interested party, the European Community is likely to oppose any structure that dilutes links to outlying regions.

Moreover, without doubt, fares and service levels in and around London are and will remain a highly emotive political issue - not to mention the similarly emotive question of rural lines.

Despite the public stance that bus deregulation has been highly successful, Ministers and their advisers will be aware that bus service provision has suffered in many areas. Whilst bus passengers are of little importance politically, and can be effectively marginalized, the same cannot be said for rail users. Rail passengers are organized and will be able to make MPs' lives a misery, whilst the three passenger sectors neatly correlate with the main strands of Conservative support (i.e. suburbia, rural areas and the business community). The Government therefore cannot afford to 'get it wrong'.

Finally, both politicians and civil servants have become increasingly aware of rail's role in combatting traffic congestion. A structure which would exclude on grounds of 'unprofitability' consideration of new works that could relieve road problems is thus unlikely. Likewise, a structure that puts fares up and services down in the interests of profitability, as could occur in the South East - and thereby drives more traffic onto the roads - will be most unwelcome.

Given the above, it becomes clear why the privatization of BR has been one of the last to be examined. It is also clear that there will be no easy solution and that the solution must ensure the continuous operation of the working railway. Hence a scheme which allows a progressive and incremental movement towards privatization may be preferred.

Apart from the ideal of a total BR sale, a number of particular and individual sections of the railway have been discussed as candidates for sale as virtually self-contained elements - particularly the Fenchurch Street-Southend section - but the fate of these is uncertain.

Looking at rail schemes which involve an element of private sector investment in infrastructure, Manchester, the current system in the limelight, shows the outline costs involved -infrastructure at say between £60-£100 million, annual revenue at £6-£8 million and annual operating costs lying between £4 million and £6 million. Clearly, even in a situation where the majority of the infrastructure exists, the difference between revenue and operating costs is not sufficient to finance the net cost of the system.

However, this is not always so, as five major construction groups are keenly pursuing the construction of the link between the Channel Tunnel entrance and London, and another group is actually constructing a tunnel under the Channel for a company whose shares are now worth double their original price.

These examples serve to demonstrate what is already blatantly apparent: that the financial viability of the railway system varies enormously between the different parts of the system.

By international standards our railway is good: it offers a frequent, fast and effective service, but it is presently hoist by its own petard and is suffering from a surfeit of passengers. This, along with previous under-investment, has the combined effect of producing substantial public criticism.

In parallel with the growth in patronage, there have been major changes in the overall structure of the railway management - a major contributor to the increased efficiency which is becoming increasingly apparent.

The bottom line responsibility for the railways has been invested in the five business sectors, namely InterCity, Network SouthEast, Provincial, Freight and Parcels, which work in conjunction with the operating regions of Scottish, London Midland, Eastern, Western, Southern and the more recent Anglia.

Each sector is controlled by a Director - a principal Officer, though not actually a member of the Board - with a full bottom line responsibility to meet the guidelines laid down by the DTp. Each is supported by a small team.

Quite clearly, as they gain credibility, the sectors are acting more and more as genuine businesses and those who deal with them can see this emerging. Not only has the BRB set its operations into a series of bottom line businesses, but it is also 'hiving off' a number of subsidiary activities. Some have been sold - such as the hotels, ferries and most recently BREL; others have been formed into arm's length groups such as the light overhaul group, BRML, and the Freight Distribution Company. Containing the old Speedlink distribution sub-sector of Railfreight and Freightliners, this aims to promote a total transport package including rail and road haulage for the small load market. There are also the property and consultancy companies, and more recently, BR Light, set up to tender for the operation for the new breed of light railways.

The railway is thus moving towards a number of core sectors responsible for sales, marketing, purchase of rolling stock and some on-train catering, with a regional management responsible under contract to the sectors for running the train service, operation of terminals and day to day infrastructure maintenance. All other activities are placed with subsidiary organizations.

That the above structure is working can be seen from the figures, the Public Service Obligation grant in 1987/88 was £781 million, the similar figure for 1988/89 was £549 million. The InterCity, Freight and Parcels sectors were able to break even in 1988/89; Network SouthEast required support of only £141 million on its £805 million turnover and Provincial Sector £465 million support against a turnover of around £250 million - confirming the statement that the different elements of the rail network have variable viability.

Privatization of further elements of the existing operation is clearly possible. The first potential candidate must be newly formed BRML, followed by perhaps the maintenance of track, infrastructure and signalling on a simple contractual basis. Already, as at London Underground, there are moves towards privatized carriage cleaning. Following this, the remaining catering, security, architectural services and finally vehicle design could, if required, be moved into the private sector.

At the end of the day, though, it will be the core railway system which is the candidate for high-profile privatization: a very successful railway, which can play an increasingly vital role in the expansion of the UK economy.

There are, in fact, four main groups who have important views on what the privatization should achieve.

As well as the Government, these are the British Railway Board, the rail users, and would-be investors in a privatized railway system.

From the Government's point of view, privatization will be intended to harness the demonstrated advantages of a privately as opposed to publicly run organization, whilst maintaining, if possible, the existing railway, using private and a minimum of public capital expenditure.

The second group, the BRB - at least as a board - already believes it has created one of the most efficient railways in the world - and if they are required to privatize they would prefer to move as a whole to create BR plc.

The third group, the actual users, are perhaps those with most to lose and potentially to gain. Their very important objectives are primarily the continuation and improvement of the railway system at a price they can afford.

The final group, the would-be investors, will be looking for an environment in which profitable investment can sensibly be made in the railway sector.

Any privatization of British Railways must thus attempt to satisfy the following criteria:
- Widen competition and consumer choice;
- Be relatively simple, quick and cheap to implement;
- Reduce the need for public support;
- Serve existing demands and respond to future demands;
- Be sufficiently viable to attract the Private Sector in a   management role;
- Encourage the use of private finance for new infrastructure.

The recent proposed change in section 56 funding requirement appears to militate against this. Conversely relaxation of the 'Ryrie' guidelines should improve matters.

Apart from the disposal intact of a single BR plc, the problem of one company moving over the tracks of another is a major issue whichever scheme is adopted. This has been resolved within the existing operation by the dominant Sector in any particular situation being responsible for the complete range of infrastructure. The others use the infrastructure and meet their so-called 'bolt-on' costs. It is this use of the other companies' assets which is the major managerial issue in any solution apart from BR plc or a total regional breakdown.

The current movement patterns appear to be so contrary to the Regional solution that this non market-led option is rejected. It has therefore been assumed that the relationships currently existing between sectors can sensibly be extended into the private sector.

Thus, on the basis that the preferred option must serve the market and should be similar managerially to that operated today, it is suggested that the InterCity and Network SouthEast Sectors should be privatized virtually as today and that the Freight and Parcels Sectors should be incorporated to form a third company. The Provincial Sector should be further divided into smaller units to better relate to its markets. It is, however, proposed that all land and air ownership and rights be vested with a new statutory authority.

All the sectors would have the right to raise monies in the open market and to apply for funds under section 56 or similar. They would have the same interface solutions as today with all infrastructure vested with one particular company.

Whilst the Provincial Sector would have exactly the same conditions, it is proposed that the Express services be created in a similar fashion to Inter-City, but they be operated in two distinct groups, for Scotland, and England and Wales. It is suggested that the major conurbations be operated as single units (as they are today), although it makes considerable sense for several to be linked, i.e. Manchester and South Lancs, Tyne and Wear and Tees. This would give some twelve distinct urban groupings. It would be nice to think that these could be funded locally, but there is a move away from local government funding per se, so that the majority of support may well still come from Central sources. However, the important issue is to provide a viable unit - i.e. one which is sufficiently large to allow efficient networking. It remains an open question as to whether these urban systems could individually be so.

131

The third Provincial group incorporates the less busy rural lines and it is proposed that these be offered as small but viable groups - the lines in Devon and Cornwall, for example. Once again the current system of managerial responsibility within the Provincial Sector lends itself to the creation of these smaller operations, perhaps containing between three and ten routes. They would, if feasible, have a defined geographical coverage to allow effective networking (preferably having a single vehicle type) and would be of suitable size to relate completely to the local market requirements. In all, there would be around ten such groups in the UK. The majority would require financial support, and it should preferably relate to the total operation. At the point of sale, they would have specific rights, if required, to operate over the track of neighbouring operations.

This preferred option is unashamedly modelled on the existing managerial pattern - yet it frees the new companies to utilize private finance (and so move away from External Finance Limits) and, it is believed, to relate to and serve their markets better. It should have little disadvantageous impact on the current travelling public and should - if increased efficiencies and level of service follow from privatization - offer an improved and more cost effective service.

The proposed system must fight against the stagnation of the existing service: today's pattern of movement will change and the overall service must reflect this. It is hoped that the diseconomies of scale are minimized and that the proposed Provincial companies would allow efficient networking. The solution raises question marks over the newly privatized service groups - such as BRML (short runs are less cost effective than longer runs). However, it is likely that leasing and secondhand markets would play a much greater role. It is believed that if the 'rural' and 'urban' railways are to grow this can best be achieved by direct relation to the local market. It may be that local communities or even 'governments' take a share in the new provincial companies - which would surely be seen as an advantage.

Of course, it may be that in time, smaller railway companies merge and others are bought. Just look at what is happening in the bus industry now...

# 14 The Orient Express

*Article by S. Ekins*
*In two parts: June and September 1984 issues*

## PART 1

On October 4, 1883, a train the like of which Europeans had never seen before steamed away from the Gare de Strasbourg in Paris bound for a distant Romania. It consisted of a small but elegant 2.4.0 express engine, No. 505 of the Chemin de Fer de L'Est of France, a four wheeler luggage van, two enormous (by the standards of the day) and very luxurious sleeping cars, an equally large and magnificently appointed dining car with a smoking lounge and a four wheeled crew van bringing up the rear.

It was called the "Orient-Express" and it carried some forty passengers, mostly Very Important Persons invited by the man whose bold conception this was, Georges Nagelmackers of Belgium. The inaugural run made headlines all over the civilized world due to the writings of senior journalist Henri Stefan Opper de Blowitz, Paris Correspondent of the London Times, who sent frequent despatches as the great train journeyed eastwards. He spiced his writings with interviews conducted at the very highest level - with King Charles of Romania (who hosted all the "Orient-Express" travellers while the train waited) and with Sultan Abdul Hamid II, "Shadow of God on Earth", ruler of Turkey, whose country was the ultimate destination of the passengers.

In those days the train could proceed no further than Giurgiu, about 45 miles beyond Bucharest, where the rails reached the Danube. Passengers had to cross the river in a ferry, then board an inferior train for the run to Varna on the Black Sea coast of Bulgaria, where they joined a ship for an uncomfortable overnight voyage to Constantinople.

A few years later railway lines had been built from Bucharest to Constanza on the Romanian Black Sea coast, involving some spectacular bridges. This new line avoided change of train but slightly lengthened the sea journey to Turkey. Four nights were still required for the Paris to Constantinople run, three of them aboard the luxurious "Orient Express".

By the turn of the century, rails had reached Constantinople by way of Budapest, Belgrade, Nisch, over the scenic Dragoman Pass and through Sofia in Bulgaria. The journey time came down to three nights aboard, where it stayed right through the life of the "Orient Express" until its demise as an exclusive luxury train in September 1960.

Georges Nagelmackers had formed his Compagnie Internationale des Wagons-Lits et des Grands Express Europeens shortly before the inaugural "Orient Express" run, after years of planning and study of sleeping cars in America under Colonel William d'Alton Mann and George Mortimer Pullman. The company came under the patronage of the flamboyant King Leopold II of Belgium. Although in recent years the lavish sleeping cars have become familiar in their blue and gold, they were a mundane brown colour until 1919.

Nagelmackers was 38 when he succeeded with the "Orient Express". His father was a rich banker and both father and son had been involved with the expanding railway industry. In the late 1870s they had provided comparatively comfortable sleeping carriages for the P&O experimental boat trains to Brindisi but this proved a short lived operation (later to be revived, both to Marseilles and Brindisi).

An expansion of "Grands Express Europeens" began a few years after the "Orient Express" became not only an established international train, but the ultimate in prestige and chic. Luxury sleeping car trains began running from the Channel ports of Calais and Ostend, for the British were then the great travellers of Europe, their wealthy section of society capable of filling any de luxe train or palace hotel available, in contrast to other countries which possessed only a tiny percentage of rich people. The situation changed to some extent after the turn of the century, with relatively wealthy Americans, French and Germans making a fairly numerous addition to the British.

As for the peasants in the fields through which the "Orient Express" passed on its 1800 mile journey, they stared in awe at the magnificent rolling stock, knowing that they could never hope to ride such a train in their lifetimes.

The rich and famous, the artistocratic and powerful, rode the "Orient Express" to cities such as Vienna, Budapest and Bucharest, sometimes all the way to Constantinople. It was in the 1890s that the expression "The Train of Kings, the King of Trains" was coined. But the legends of spying and mystery, of murder and intrigue, did not begin to grow until the 1920s.

A great feat of railway engineering, begun in 1898 by a Hamburg firm of contractors and completed eight years later, was to affect the "Orient Express" and its offshoots. This was the Simplon Tunnel under the Alps, linking the Canton of the Valle with Italy. It was opened as a single line tunnel 12 miles, 537 yards in length (by far the longest tunnel in the world at that time) on May 30, 1906. It meant that Paris was much nearer to Milan and Venice, and the more southerly route offered an alternative journey to Constantinople. A new "Grand Express", the "Simplon Orient", was started late in 1906, joining a flood of new trains through the tunnel which soon became traffic choked. A second bore had to be constructed to provide a double track route, but the 1914-18 War interrupted work, especially on the Italian side, and it was not completed until the beginning of 1921. This was when the new "Simplon-Orient-Express" really came into its own.

Georges Nagelmackers died the year before the Simplon tunnel opened, and so missed seeing the new potential for his Trans Europe concept. The "Simplon Orient" only ran as far as Milan at first, later extending to Venice, and then in 1910 to Trieste. This was the time when British society was discovering the delights of Venice and the buying or renting of "palazzos" was in full swing. For such owners, the "Simplon Orient" was the **only** way of travelling to Venice, through sleeping cars awaited them at Calais Maritime for the run to Paris and eventual attachment to the main train.

It is this "Simplon Orient" of the period 1907 to 1914 which is partly emulated by the splendid 1982 venture, but it is fair to point out that the Edwardian train was never so grand nor so luxurious as the one which has been refurbished as the "Venice Simplon-Orient-Express" of today.

Those years were the heyday of the old "Orient Express" as it ran through a Europe still largely composed of Kingdoms mainly at peace. The equipment was the best in Europe and its clientele consisted of the most important and glittering travellers of the day. But judging by the fact that on average only two sleeping cars, a diner, and four wagons went through to Constantinople, the Turkish capital was not the main destination of the elite travellers of that Age.

The First World War brought a savage interruption to rail travel across Europe and in that War, Turkey was on the side of Germany so no link existed from France to Britain. One of the Wagon-Lit cars, Number 2419 from the

"Orient Express" was used for the German surrender at Compiegne in November 1918. The car remained as a monument and then was used again by Hitler for the French surrender in 1940. It was later taken back to Berlin but destroyed by an SS unit in 1945 to prevent it falling again into Allied hands.

Immediately after the First World War a massive revival of travel in Europe and to lands in the Middle East developed rapidly. It was decided to avoid Germany and Austria with the premier train running to Greece and Turkey, resulting in the construction of a magnificent new express which was to take the Simplon Tunnel route as the "Simplon-Orient-Express". The route was Paris (Lyon) to Vallorbe, Lausanne, Brigue, the Simplon Tunnel, Milan, Venice, Trieste, Belgrade, Nisch and Crveni Krst (for division), then one section to Sofia and Istanbul (as Constantinople had become), the other to Thessaloniki and Athens.

It ran as a through train only as far as Sofia at first, starting on April 15, 1919, but in 1921 it began operating right through to Istanbul as a genuine express. Taking only 56 hours from Paris (but still with the traditional three nights aboard the train) it was the fastest timing on the route and has never been surpassed. The "Simplon-Orient-Express" enjoyed 19 years of excellence, its equipment being steadily upgraded until its prestige was paramount. Some of the sleeping cars from the late 1920s and early 1930s, which are now refurbished and included in today's great train, represent the peak of the railway craftsman's art.

## PART 2

Despite all the literature about the "Orient Express" which appeared in the Twenties and Thirties, led by Maurice Dekobra with his "La Madone des Sleepings" of 1925, typical passengers were not spies or politicians steeped in Eastern European intrigues. King's Messengers and Royal Couriers there were, of course, on every run, but their numbers, supplemented by spies and arms merchants would not have kept the train (or trains including the Bucharest 'Orient') as profitable as economic history records it.

Britons filled their Calais section. They were officials and their families bound for Palestine (where the Mandate ran from 1919 to 1948), oil executives and their families heading for the British-owned fields of Iraq and particularly Abadan in Persia (Iran), wealthy tourists going to Egypt for the Winter months who wished to avoid the lengthy sea passage, society people travelling to Venice for holidays on the Lido or to take up residence in their 'palazzos', and -on the Athens section - officials with families and winter tourists going to Cyprus which was then a British possession. British theatrical touring companies, immensely popular in pre-war days in the Balkans, made dozens of journeys.

But the exceptional passenger and the dramatic circumstance always make news, and this, coupled with the inspiration of a luxury train crossing six frontiers, caused six major cinema films, nineteen books, and one piece of sheet music to be produced about the "Orient Express" variations during the period between the wars. The music was a foxtrot called "Orient Express" written in 1933.

Passengers travelling through Bulgaria were sometimes subjected to the vigorous and erratic driving of no less a person than His Majesty King Boris III. The King, a very keen railway enthusiast, enjoyed travelling on the footplate and taking over the controls. He visited England on one occasion and was given footplate facilities aboard the "Royal Scot" which he drove from Euston to Crewe, although on that occasion an inspector also travelled in the cab offering firm but respectful advice. It is difficult to restrain a headstrong King on a visit abroad; in his own country where he was an absolute Monarch it was impossible. He would board the engine of the "Simplon-Orient-Express" at Sofia and take complete control sometimes as far as Svilengrad, driving as hard as the locomotive would take it. On one occasion in 1934, when he was merely firing the engine, a blow-back from the fire enveloped the driver, burning his clothes and skin severely. King Boris took over and brought the train to a safe halt in a major station where he had the driver transferred to hospital. Without waiting for a relief driver and wanting to pick up time, the King drove the great express to the frontier, often exceeding 70 miles an hour on sections where 60 was a safe maximum.

During its glorious years, the "Simplon Orient" was steam hauled from Paris to the Swiss border, electric hauled through Switzerland and the Simplon Tunnel to Milan, then steam hauled to Venice and Trieste. Taking the devious route into Yugoslavia, Italian electric traction was used to Ljubljana, after which it was steam all the way to Istanbul.

The Second World War did appalling damage to the railways of Europe and to the stock of the Wagons-Lits Company. A somewhat less luxurious "Simplon-Orient-Express" was, however, brought back into service in December 1945, running only as far as Trieste. Slowly it began to recover its old route into the Balkans, but at that time Yugoslavia and Bulgaria were very much behind the 'Iron Curtain'. Many difficulties arose and it is reported that from time to time the best sleeping cars became detached and were not seen again for months! The authorities decided to use only the oldest cars for the service, a state of affairs which continued until 1952, when Yugoslavia was out of the Soviet 'camp'. Some twenty new sleepers, with a majority of second class berths, were built and with these, plus a few day coaches for sections of the run, the "Simplon Orient" continued as a semi-luxury through service until May 26, 1962.

It was replaced by a mundane train made up mostly of day coaches but with Paris-Istanbul sleepers attached twice a week and Athens sleepers three times a week. Of the former Calais section, only a composite day coach remained, worked to Paris in a boat train and then around the 'Petite Ceinture' to Paris (Lyon). It was called the "Direct Orient Express", its main customers being itinerant Turkish workers, back-packing tourists, and peasants. This survived, in its final form without a restaurant car of any kind, until May 1977.

There are now no through trains from Western Europe to Turkey or Greece. It is currently necessary for passengers to subject themselves to the crowded and somewhat uncomfortable long distance services available, from the "Simplon Express" from Paris onto the "Venezia Express" from Venice to Athens or the "Istanbul Express" from Ljublijana. But now in 1984, a "Grand Express Europeen" in the Nagelmackers style, rather more lavish in fact than that legendary Belgian would have dreamed of, begins a regular journey from the Channel to the Adriatic. The "Venice Simplon-Orient-Express", devised by American Mr James Sherwood who has spent many millions of pounds restoring the finest sleepers and diners, runs twice weekly from Boulogne to Paris, Milan and Venice with a London connection consisting of magnificent day Pullmans plus an additional weekly run Paris to Venice. The journey of 1,472 kilometres is covered in virtually the same time as the "Simplon Orient" in its heyday, while the three times weekly Paris to Milan run is over an hour quicker. One difference between the train of yesterday and the train of today is that many passengers will be taking the journey simply for the glory of the experience and will be quite reluctant to alight on reaching their destination.

# 15 Eurotunnel: The advantages

*Article by T. Harrison*
*Alistair Dicks & Associates*
*August 1987 issue*

The prospect of a fixed link across the Channel has intrigued engineers and politicians for almost two centuries. Two previous attempts have failed, most recently in 1974 when the British Government withdrew the financial support of the taxpayer.

Mindful of the hard lessons of the past, the current venture is to be privately financed. The scale of the financial package probably makes the Channel Tunnel the largest privately financed civil engineering project this century.

Eurotunnel, the joint Anglo-French owners and operators of the tunnel, won a 55 year Concession in January 1986. The company plans to start commercial operations in 1993, having seen completion of the actual tunnels two years earlier. A number of crucial objectives have already been achieved this year, including an agreement with the British and French national railways that will contribute a significant slice of expected revenues. The Hybrid Channel Tunnel Bill completed its lengthy Parliamentary voyage when it received the Royal Assent on 23 July, becoming the Channel Tunnel Act. The Treaty between Britain and France was ratified on 29 July, thus bringing into Operation the 55 year Concession to build and run the Tunnel and all the necessary powers to construct the tunnels and the related railway works in England.

"Channel Tunnel" is something of a misnomer because, in fact, three tunnels will be bored through the favourable stratum of chalk marl on average some 40m below the seabed. Two main running tunnels, 7.6m in diameter and 50km in length, will house rail tracks serving both road and rail traffic. Road traffic will be accommodated in huge shuttle trains, operated and owned by Eurotunnel, running between terminals near Folkestone and Calais and sharing paths through the Tunnel with through rail passenger and freight traffic. The running tunnels are to be set 30m apart, either side of a central service tunnel 4.8m in diameter. Connecting cross passages will link the three tunnels every 375m, providing access from the service tunnel for maintenance and the modestly-pressurized fresh air supply and to the service tunnel in case an emergency requires evacuation of trains by passengers. This is just one of the many safety features of the Eurotunnel scheme which have been endorsed by the Government's award of the Concession. It is interesting to note the incident free operation of similar but much less modern shuttle train tunnels through the Alps. Ultimate authority for safety in the Tunnel will rest with an independent Safety Commission reporting to the Intergovernmental Commission set up under the Treaty.

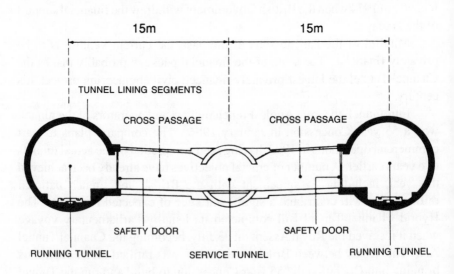

The Traffic Consultants' forecasts for the Tunnel have taken into account past trends in sea and air travel between Britain and the Continent, showing steady overall growth from the mid -1960s despite two oil crises and various other external sources of temporary stagnation. Uncertainty about the future growth of these markets is therefore more of a matter of 'when' rather than 'if'. Even with expected average annual growth rates significantly lower than the outturn over the last ten to fifteen years, the forecasts indicate passenger and freight markets doubling by early in the next century, only a quarter of the way through the 55 year Concession.

Eurotunnel's commercial task is to compete successfully in the various market sectors by offering service advantages to users. Users should benefit from the increased competition in the cross-Channel market in terms of increased choice of route and operator and downward pressure on tariffs. They will also appreciate fast, frequent and reliable crossings. But there is no room for complacency; the Concession does not guarantee income and there will be no support from taxpayers. Eurotunnel must attract customers to pay shareholders' dividends and repay bank loans, in addition to covering the relatively low system operating costs.

The traffic forecasts indicate a favourable response to both road and rail services. The shuttle system for road vehicles will operate at high frequencies and speeds. On opening, up to five tourist shuttles per hour in each direction at peak times will speed car and coach passengers between Folkestone and Sangette terminal areas. The entirely separate freight shuttles, accommodating 4.2m high trucks of gross weight up to 44 tonnes in each of 25 shuttle wagons will also be able to handle drawbar units. Reaching speeds up to 160kph, the journey between terminals will take about 35 minutes. There will be no need to book and the high service frequency should obviate the nerve-wracking and time-consuming business of "contingency time", built-in by drivers as insurance against unforeseen delays en route for a particular sailing, often booked in advance. The faster crossing, avoidance of check-in time requirements and contingency planning should appeal to users and reduce stress, particularly for the increasing majority of drivers already choosing the shorter Channel crossings. Additions to motorway networks on both sides of the Channel will ensure a choice also for users of longer routes. Customs clearance will adopt the free-exit approach, with both emigration and immigration taking place prior to the Tunnel transit. Clearance for trucks will take place at a new ICD in Ashford close to the Folkestone terminal (or at premises or other ICDs). An ICD will be located on the French terminal site.

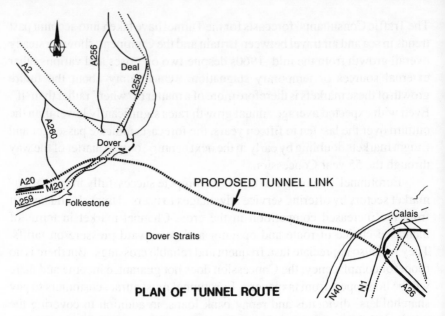

**PLAN OF TUNNEL ROUTE**

Through rail passenger services based on core services between a new international terminal at London Waterloo and Paris and Brussels will provide an attractive, competitive alternative to flying, with similar service times between city centres but without the need to travel to peripheral airport locations. BR and SNCF propose to extend services beyond these cities. In Britain, electrified routes from the north will by pass London via Kensington Olympia in all likelihood with Customs clearance on board trains, as required to be considered by the Channel Tunnel Act. In addition, sleeper and Motorail services are being assessed. Rail freight in wagons and containers (in trainload or wagonload form) will be able to avoid trans-shipment at ports and enjoy transit times into the heart of Europe which, for the first time, can be competitive with road haulage.

The first fixed transport link with the Continent is just six years away. It will not, of itself, transform travel patterns in Europe; the transport element of most journeys or commercial transactions is just a means to an end, the motivation for the journey being related to satisfying the demands for leisure, international trade and commerce. The Channel Tunnel will significantly enhance choice, quality and reliability for journeys to the Continent.

There is nothing new in seeking to improve cross-Channel transport services. What is unique to the Channel Tunnel is its constant availability, even in the face of difficult weather conditions in the Channel. It will help us become real Europeans; what that will mean ultimately in terms of travel patterns in a future Europe without frontiers - as a result of the European Single Market proposed for implementation by 1992 - depends on changes in perception and attitude. Existing relationships between European countries should ensure a growing cross-Channel market. The extent of additional travel created by changes in attitude is more speculative and, for Eurotunnel, will be the icing on a tasty cake.

# 16 Underground railway planning in London

*Paper presented to the London Centre by*
*R. Meads*
*London Transport*
*March 1979 issue*

The first underground railway was opened in January, 1863, between Paddington and Farringdon Street, but this 3/4 mile section of cut and cover railway was soon extended to Moorgate Street in the east, and from Edgware Road round to South Kensington and Westminster in the west.

The reason for this first section of underground railway was to improve communications and to prevent congestion in London Streets as the volume of road traffic increased, and there was a need to link the new main line terminuses. Parliament then recommended an extension of the underground to form a circuit around the central area. These reasons still form the main objectives of the underground system:

a) to carry passengers who would otherwise travel by road;
b) to act as an 'in town' distributor.

The first 'deep tube' lines were designed to perform a similar function, but instead of serving only the central area, they penetrated the heart of the City and the West End. Progress was rapid and by 1914 most of the present day underground system had been completed and linked with the sub-surface Metropolitan and District Railways.

One of the major problems today is that this system is now old and needs updating, even though a lot of money has already been spent on updating rolling stock, stations, lifts and escalators and other equipment.

During the 1920s and 30s, the underground system expanded outwards on a massive scale and was enlarged further by taking over what had been main line railway companies; service frequencies were increased and passengers given the benefit of through services direct to central London, although the West Ruislip and Epping extensions to the Central line were delayed by the Second World War and were not completed until the late 1940s.

The expansion of the system stimulated residential and other development in suburban areas and this is a valid point in the contemporary argument in favour of extending the system further, and it illustrates the close co-operation which exists between main line railways for the mutual development of the two systems. This is clearly vitally important. British Rail and London Transport must complement each other, although the present framework means that they are responsible to different political masters and have different financial responsibilities.


## THE VICTORIA LINE

The Victoria line has now been open for ten years and was first conceived in the 1940s by the London Railway Plan Working Party. It was not until 1968-69 that the main section from Walthamstow to Victoria was opened for traffic and marked an important change in underground railway planning.

The line had several objectives: first, it was designed to 'fill in' parts of the central area underground system by providing short cuts in the network; secondly, it was important to provide links between main line terminuses. (One of the heaviest peak loads on the Victoria line is carried north to Green Park, Piccadilly and Oxford Street, while on the opposite side of the central area, it provides an additional service for Euston complementary to the electrification of the North Western main line, completed in 1966.)

The third role for the Victoria line was to provide a much quicker route into the West End from Liverpool Street and suburban services from Chingford, Bishop's Stortford, Hertford and Enfield, already electrified.

A major extension to the tube system means consequential changes to the bus schedules by relaxing frequency of services on routes parallel to the new line, and re-structuring the route pattern to feed into the line at suitable interchange points. Like most major investments in public transport, the Victoria Line could not be self-supporting; the problem is not to cover day-to-day operating costs, but to provide a return on the massive investment of capital. Two independent economists, Foster and Beesley, quantified the various factors and demonstrated that there would be a substantial 'social rate of return' on the investment, but approval of the project was, in fact, given before the results of a 'cost/benefit' study were published.

# THE HEATHROW EXTENSION

The Heathrow Extension is the newest section of the underground system - the Piccadilly line from Hounslow West. It was confidently predicted in 1946 when the airport first opened that within six years it would be serviced by the underground but, in fact, it took over thirty years because of rival projects between BR and London Transport. The Heathrow Link Steering Group eventually opted in favour of London Transport's scheme, coupled with the active coach services to terminals at West London and Victoria.

Air passengers present special problems for the public transport operator in terms of facilities required to deal with currency exchange, travel information, transit tickets and the like. Over 27,000 people use the underground to and from Heathrow each day and 60 per cent are passengers; the rest are airport employees, spectators, business visitors, 'meeters and greeters', who bring receipts which more than cover the operating costs and interest on capital. Furthermore, the Heathrow Extension has generated new traffic over the whole underground system - most of it at off-peak times and against the peak flow.


# THE JUBILEE LINE

The first stage of the Jubilee line is due to open in the spring of 1979. Originally proposed as the Fleet Line, the section will enable two separate services to be provided from Stanmore to Charing Cross, and from Queen's Park to Elephant and Castle.

The main justification for the line is the relief of overcrowding it will bring to the heavily overloaded Bakerloo line. A few years ago this carried 24,000 passengers southbound in the morning peak hour when reasonable conditions were assessed as 18,000 passengers.

Stage 1 of the Jubilee line will provide further significant improvements in the service north of Baker Street. The line capacity of a tube railway is limited to about 30-32 trains per hour over the track section and the frequency over two divergent branches is obviously not more than half this, i.e. about a 4-minute peak service. With the opening of the Jubilee line, a peak frequency of 14 trains will be operated.

## STAGE II

Final authority for the construction of Stage II of the Jubilee line has yet to be given, although London Transport has the Parliamentary powers to construct it. The problem with this section - Charing Cross, Aldwych, Fenchurch Street - is that it will be extremely expensive and will not, in itself, bring major benefits. The reason for the high cost is tunnelling under the most heavily developed area of London and complicated station works at all station sites.

The benefits lie in providing a fast link between the City and the West End and in serving the only BR terminal, Fenchurch Street, not yet connected directly to the underground system. Also, it will provide relief from the over-crowding on the Central and District lines, though not where the section could most do with it between Mile End and Bank.

Stage II on its own is likely to have a rather poor cost/benefit ratio and proposals are now being developed for the Jubilee line to provide a major stimulus for re-development in the Docklands district. The Greater London Council (GLC) see a public commitment to attract large scale investment (new industry, jobs and private housing) in this area as the line planned knits together two banks of the river Thames.

The Jubilee line, Stage II, will provide an interchange with the BR North Kent line and, by linking the two banks of the river, encourage people living in Docklands to work and shop in Woolwich. After Croydon, Woolwich is probably one of the most important suburban centres in London which, at the present time, is largely isolated by the river from a potential catchment area to the north. Beyond Woolwich, the proposal is to extend the line to Thamesmead, and the GLC see the provision of a direct link from Thames-mead and Docklands to central London as being an important part of the whole concept.

The estimated cost of Stage III is put at £180 million, which together with Stage II, means an overall cost of £280 million over a lengthy construction period, expenditure which cannot be justified in purely transport terms.

So far, central government has been unconvinced by the arguments put forward by the GLC and the Docklands Joint Committee in favour of expansion, and no part of the project has received financial authority. Because of this the GLC is trying to find a way of improving railways in the area quickly and economically, while modernization and improvement of BR services is going ahead. The GLC is also proposing that the Woolwich Tunnel section of the Jubilee line should be built before Stage III and they await the reaction of the Department of Transport.

# CONCLUSIONS

The population of London is on the decline and problems with peak congestion of the public transport system has eased slightly, which means that the
case for new  underground railways across central and inner London has
become rather more difficult to justify. Unfortunately, London is unlike many
expanding cities such as Hong Kong, San Paulo or Mexico City where major
development in public transport is going ahead in response to pressure created
by that expansion, and whose overwhelming need for the provision of vastly
increased capacity on the public transport system has to be satisfied.

# Section Three
# Sea Transport

The initial chapters in this section provide a picture of the shipping industry some three decades ago. Gedge's chapter relates to an era when passenger cargo liners maintained regular schedules between the UK and the world's major ports. The second contribution, from Laws, serves as a reminder that today's dense network of roll-on/roll-off ferry services is of very recent vintage.

The changes in the maritime scene since that time owe much to containerization. This revolution in cargo-handling methods provides the theme for the next two selections. The chapter by Tilsley outlines container operations at an early stage in the changeover from more labour-intensive methods. Tatman, in contrast, looks at the consequences of containerization from the perspective of 1979, when traditional forms of freight movement by sea had largely been superceded.

Next, Asteris examines the reasons for the decline in the UK merchant fleet during the period 1975-1983 and concludes that it was a necessary response to adverse trading conditions.

The focus of the reprints then shifts to UK ports, which have had to adjust to both the container revolution and the shift in the pattern of maritime traffic from the west coast to the east coast. Evelyn discusses these developments with reference to the growth of the East Anglian terminals, while Francis, in Chapter 23, looks at the history of the Humber ports and their links with the rest of the world.

151

The final piece in Section Three focuses on the effect of the Fixed Link on the pattern of North West Europe's deep-sea cargo movements. The chapter argues that Britain's ports are likely to prove sufficiently competitive to prevent this country degenerating into a maritime appendage of the Continent following the opening of the Channel Tunnel.

# 17 Ships and the carriage of goods by sea

*Paper presented to the Preston Centre by*
*J.D. Gedge*
*January 1961 issue*

Generally speaking ocean going ships are of 3,000 tons gross upwards and are engaged in either regular trading or tramping from one port to another in any part of the world. The carriage of large quantities of specific cargo has caused the development of special types of vessels, such as oil-tankers, colliers, ore-carriers, banana ships, refrigerator ships.

The "tramp ship" trades from one port to another and may not return to its home country for two years or even more. It is usually of the simplest design and construction. The regular traders, cargo-liners, passenger-liners, fruit carriers, are more elaborate in design and construction. The reasons for this will no doubt prove themselves as this paper progresses.

The passenger cargo liners engaged on regular schedules between the United Kingdom and the main ports of the world carry a large number of passengers and cater for them extensively. They also have a large cargo carrying capacity, whilst the cargo-liners, engaged on regular services are principally cargo carriers. Specific cargoes are usually carried and the ships are suitably constructed for efficient handling and safe speedy carriage of their cargoes. Into this category come, what may be termed the dual purpose ships, as they carry general cargo outward from the United Kingdom, returning with a specific cargo such as fruit or meat. Their holds are insulated for this purpose.

The short sea traders are vessels of 1,500 tons to 3,000 tons gross and limit their trading to Scandinavia, Iceland, Spain and the Mediterranean ports.

These smaller vessels are divided into similar categories. Coasting vessels also fall into these same categories, but are restricted by law to trade between the ports of the United Kingdom and Eire and those of the Continent between the river Elbe in the North and Brest in the South. Tonnages range from 100 to 1,500 tons gross but colliers are usually a little larger and are specially designed for speedy loading, despatch and discharge of coal.

During its life a vessel has to stand various stresses and strains on its structure. Such strains as hogging and sagging are experienced when a vessel is in a seaway. When bow and stern are supported on two waves the centre is said to tend to sag. When the centre is supported on a wave, the stem and stern tend to droop and are said to be hogging. The vessel may receive heavy blows from breaking seas and she is then said to experience racking strains. In a seaway her bows may on occasion, in her progress through the sea, contact a breaking wave and she is then said to pound. All these strains and stresses have to be taken into account and the vessel suitably strengthened against them. In consequence frames are usually closer together at the bows and stern. Most ships have a sheet girder keel, the bottom of which has the ship's bottom plates joined to it, whilst the top some 2ft. 6in. or 3ft. high, forms the hold bottom. This gives the vessel a double bottom which is divided into sections by a horizontal girder, to give extra strength. The space thus provided is not wasted because it is so constructed as to make sealed compartments, which are used for water ballast or oil fuel bunkers.

Having touched very briefly on the strengthening of the vessel, let us now consider its interior structure and how it is arranged for the different types of cargo that it is designed to carry.

Most cargoes are by no means devoid of active characteristics and many of them are most susceptible to the action of the ship in the water. Many of them make bad travelling companions and may even be a source of danger to the ship. They may suffer from undue exposure to the elements, from climatic changes or merely from the passing of time. Every provision must, therefore, be made for their safe keeping during the voyage, different cargoes having different requirements.

In the simpler type of ship, the bulk cargo carrier, this fact is particularly noticeable. These ships, which carry grain and coal in bulk, have their interiors divided into a small number of separate compartments by bulkheads fore-and-aft of the engine room for strength and safety. Grain or coal is simply fed into these compartments until there is sufficient weight in the ship to bring her load-line to the level of water in which she is floating. To meet these simple requirements all we require is a single-deck vessel with transverse bulkheads and openings in the deck to give access to each compartment. The larger the opening, the easier it is to load or discharge. The compartments can be loaded to their utmost capacity without the necessity of employing trimmers to spread the cargo into the extreme corners of the upper hold under the deck. On the other hand, the larger the openings in the deck the more is the vessel weakened.

These bulk cargoes are liable to spontaneous combustion and adequate precautions must be taken to ensure that there is sufficient ventilation in every hold throughout the voyage. Cargoes of a loose nature, such as grain or small coal, have an alarming tendency to shift and in consequence upset the stability of the ship. Means must be provided to prevent this movement and the holds are subdivided longitudinally by shifting boards. These break up the bulk of the cargo into smaller units and prevent the transfer of weight from one side to the other in a seaway. Grains of a small cubic capacity do not require the whole cargo space provided. In this case, in a four hold vessel for instance, the two centre holds are filled to capacity and the forward and after holds are loaded as required to bring the ship to her load-line marks and suitable trim. The Board of Trade has laid down laws for the loading of ships in this manner. The usual practice is to bag a percentage of the cargo in these two holds. The filled bags are stepped up from the hold floor on the sloping surface of the loose grain to the upper deck, as an added precaution against shifting.

The nature of the traffic normally carried by a cargo liner demands a larger number of decks. By an arrangement of 'tween decks the deep holds are divided into shallower layers. A fantastic assortment of cargo is carried on every voyage of the cargo liner. It varies in weight and size from very small packages to 20 ton boilers and in quality from tea to vegetable oils or chemicals and even wild animals. The ports of loading and discharge often vary considerably in climate and custom. The large number of compartments provided are specially designed to meet the needs of the various cargoes carried on the route. Carcasses of meat cannot be left on deck for a voyage from Australia, nor can a cargo of grain be stored in an upper compartment. Refrigerated compartments must be provided for the former, whilst the latter must be carried in the deepest part of the ship. Cargoes of oil are carried from time to time; very often a deep tank is provided near the engine room which can be used for carrying this type of cargo or alternatively (in oil burning ships) for the carriage of extra bunkers. Awkward cargoes have to be catered for and rolling stock, for instance, which by virtue of its length is carried on deck. Decks must be strengthened and eyebolts securely fitted to the decks to take the necessary lashings this type of cargo requires.

The carriage of fruit, meat, dairy produce and other perishable commodities demand special care. Ships regularly engaged in this type of trade are provided with insulated holds and extensive insulating machinery. Many ships have part of their hold capacity insulated and the remainder of normal type for general cargo. Other vessels, such as the m.v. Hornby Grange, are fully refrigerated. This vessel is engaged in the meat trade between Argentine and Great Britain. She has 78 separable insulated compartments and can carry 7,300 tons of chilled meat.

Not all commodities can be carried at the same temperature; fruit especially require a wide range of temperatures. Apples should be kept just above freezing point whilst bananas, which are loaded green and ripen on the voyage in well ventilated holds, require up to 54° Fahrenheit. Their sea voyage must not take too long and, therefore, ships with a fair turn of speed are required. Citrus fruits are prone to breathe and would contaminate any other fruit or commodity with which they come in contact or proximity. They are often carried in gas-proof chambers, into which air can be pumped or extracted according to the readings of the instruments which record the gas content of each compartment.

Ventilation is of paramount importance in the carriage of goods by sea. It may not be generally realized that such cargoes as canned goods require careful ventilation. When a ship passes from warm to cooler water, considerable condensation occurs and large drops of moisture run down the side or drop from overhead beams. Means of preventing this humidity from affecting the cargo must be provided. Severe damage can be caused to such widely different cargoes as maize and tobacco. Precautions must be taken to prevent bags of sugar from coming into contact with the steelwork and thus becoming stained by rust or damp. In consequence, various systems of ventilation, dehumidifying and air-conditioning have evolved for the protection of cargo. Particulars of action taken during a voyage with regard to such systems are recorded in the ship's logbook.

Fire damage is a risk which is evident in most cargoes with particular reference to such commodities as case-oil, chemicals, whilst irreparable damage can be caused to the ship and other cargo by leaking containers. Inflammable cargoes must be kept well ventilated and completely separate from the remainder of the cargo and, in general, are best carried on deck. Liquid cargoes in bulk are always carried in "Tankers" specially designed for the purpose. The danger of fire in these vessels is by no means the greatest difficulty to be overcome, and their design is almost wholly governed by the characteristics of the cargo.

Liquid cargoes tend to shift, much more than does loose cargo such as grain. A free mass of liquid would play havoc with the stability and control of a ship in a seaway. Therefore, the principle of sub-division must be extended as far as possible to contain the movement of the liquid. The tanker's hull is thus divided into a large number of small tanks by means of frequent transverse bulkheads and at least one longitudinal bulkhead running throughout the length of the cargo compartments or tanks. This creates a honeycomb effect and limits the liquids movement fore and aft. A large number of hatches are thus required, but as oil is pumped in and out through pipelines this is not a disadvantage and may have little or no effect on the strength of the vessel. As oil tends to expand or contract with variations of temperature, room for expansion must be allowed. A partly filled tank means too much play for the free surface of the liquid; the tanks are, therefore, filled but vents are provided so that expanding oil can find its way into an expansion trunk which runs along the centre line of the ship under the hatches. Crude oil at low temperatures becomes semi-solid while other tanker cargoes such as bitumen are normally carried in a semi-liquid state. To enable them to be discharged steam heated coils are provided in the tanks. Another characteristic of oil cargoes, particularly in the refined state, is their corrosive effect, whilst lubricating oils are so penetrating that they may work their way through riveted joints. The life of a tanker may therefore be shorter than that of a dry cargo ship. As a precaution against the many eventualities in connection with oil cargoes, specially strengthened cotterdams are built at either end of the line of tanks to separate them from living quarters, engine room and spare spaces. Special precautions against fire must be taken throughout a voyage, but particularly during loading and discharging when tankers are kept well clear of other shipping. Loading and discharging points are usually isolated sections of a port.

The physical disposal of the cargo from the ship, whether it be liquid or dry, liner or tramp, requires careful attention and calculation. A badly distributed cargo will have a serious effect on trim and stability and may make the ship unseaworthy. Ballast tanks are provided in every ship, to compensate for lack of cargo, usually in the fore peak and stern, as well as the double bottom tanks. They are not designed to compensate for badly stowed cargo. In cargo liners the problem is often more complicated, for cargoes of varying weights or density may be stowed in different holds or in different parts of the same hold. A further complication in this case is the fact that the cargo may be due for discharge at several different ports so that cargo for the first port must be easily accessible and not buried under cargo for subsequent ports.

The ship builder and owner endeavour to produce a suitable vessel for its respective trade but the ship's officers and the stevedores are responsible for preparing the cargo plan which shows the kind of cargo, its destination, distinguishing marks and distribution throughout the ship.

The criterion of a successful port administration is the speed and dispatch with which incoming ships can be served. Ships must pay for such services as pilotage, towage, stevedoring, repairs, maintenance; any increase in the cost of these services is reflected in the cost of sea transport. The longer the ship is delayed in port through inefficient services or insufficient equipment the higher these charges mount and the less chance a ship has of earning her freight and making a profit.

Most of the important ports of the world are situated on rivers, considerable distances from the sea. The nearer the ship can penetrate to the centre of production and consumption the cheaper the cost of carriage, providing always that there is sufficient depth of water to admit the most economical type of vessel, and that the cost of maintaining that depth does not cancel out the other advantages. In certain cases it has proved economical to provide artificial waterways, such as the Manchester Ship Canal which is 35 miles long with a depth of 28 feet connecting the Mersey at Eastham to the Port of Manchester, situated in the heart of the industrial area of South-East Lancashire.

The natural resources of any country dictate to a considerable extent the nature of its overseas trade and influences the types of ports which are provided to handle it. Comparison of the characteristics of the various ports of the world will serve to illustrate this. In our own country we have the rivers Clyde, Mersey and Thames upon which are situated the ports of Glasgow, Liverpool and London. They are outstanding as commercial ports because they are navigable waterways which penetrate into the centres of industry and population. They have excellent road and rail communications radiating inland. The Thames and Mersey have the advantage of an inland waterway system connecting them with the industrial Midlands and in fact connecting one another. These ports are well situated for handling the various essential imports of food and raw materials and exports of manufactured goods.

Ports provide sheds, warehouses and storage facilities of all kinds, commensurate with the normal volume and character of its trade, quays for transit of road and rail vehicles and cranes and other handling equipment.

Our greatest natural asset is coal which is also an important export. The coal trade gave rise to ports in North-East England and South Wales as for example, Blyth, Newcastle, Sunderland, Seaham, Swansea, Barry and Cardiff. These ports have developed mainly for the handling of coal, not only for

158

export, but also for transport to other ports around the coast in competition with rail. A depression in coal has a worse effect upon the South Wales ports than upon those in the North-East as the latter also enjoys a constant flow of general trade with Northern Europe and the Baltic ports, due to being on the natural direct route.

Passenger traffic has its own requirements and passenger liners tend to use ports which afford the quickest means of communication with great centres of population and trade. Southampton with the phenomena of four tides has become a terminal point for the trans-Atlantic express passenger services in which speed of transit is a major consideration. Overall journey speed has resulted in Dover becoming the port for Ostend and Calais, Folkestone for Boulogne, Newhaven for Dieppe and Liverpool and Holyhead for Dublin.

Fishguard and the many other small ports must not be considered unimportant for they exist to serve and are supported by the coastal shipping industry which is vital to the nation. The coastal services cheapen the cost of transport of a great many commodities carried coastwise between many parts of the country and for imports and exports by trans-shipment to and from ocean-going vessels in the larger ports. A strong fleet of small ships is essential to the nation in time of war and the Transport Act (1947) indicated how much this fact was appreciated by laying down, as a statutory requirement, that the "Transport Commission" maintain an efficient coasting service.

Ports are usually managed by a Harbour Master who is in supreme command. Subordinate to him are the various Dock Masters and Pilots, all of them Master Mariners, who have usually been in command of a ship. The Harbour Master is responsible to the owning authorities.

All on board ship are subordinate to the Master or Captain. He is responsible, at all times, for the safety of the ship and all on board. His responsibilities are numerous and include navigation, loading and discharge of cargo, stability and trim of the ship at all times. He signs and accepts receipts for all cargoes at ports of loading and discharge. He also engages the crew, who sign "Articles" setting out the terms of their engagement in the presence of a Superintendent of the Mercantile Marine Office (Board of Trade). He is in fact the sole representative of ship and owner at all times.

The second in command, the first officer or "Mate", is responsible for the general running of the ship and deck department and he supervises the loading and discharge of the cargo. The upkeep of the ship and her equipment and stores are his responsibilities and he is assisted by the other officers except the 2nd officers. He is concerned with the navigation of the ship at sea and the

159

upkeep of instruments and charts in port. He is directly responsible to the master for plotting the ship's position and course.

The number of officers and men varies with the size of ship and the nature of her duties. Minimum scales are laid down under the Merchant Shipping Acts regarding the number and grades of officers and ratings that must be carried in a foreign going ship of British registry.

The crew is made up of Able Seamen and Ordinary Seamen, the rating depending on length of sea-service. At sea they normally work in watches. They may be employed as look-outs, at the wheel or on general duties maintaining the ship's paintwork and cargo gear. In port they are employed on general duties, preparing holds for cargo and in some cases working cargo.

The Chief Steward is responsible for victualling the ship, he supervises the tables, linen and the galley or kitchen staff.

In the Engine-room the Chief Engineer is in charge and is responsible to the Master for running the engines as efficiently and economically as possible. They must be ready to respond to any demand from the bridge, the nerve centre of any ship. His responsibility extends to all forms of machinery in the ship, auxiliary engines, electrical plant and equipment, cargo handling gear, refrigeration machinery, windlass and steering gear. Bunkers repairs, maintenance and stores are also under his control. In refrigerator ships and tankers he is closely concerned with the loading.

He is assisted in his duties by a number of engineers, his immediate subordinate being the Second Engineer who is the "Mate" of the engine-room. The Petty Officer of the engine-room is the Donkey Man, so named because he is responsible for the Donkey boiler which maintains the steam supply whilst the vessel is in port. The number of firemen carried is governed by the numbers and size of fires in the ship.

Great strides have been taken to train men under the Merchant Navy Training Board. This organization which consists of representatives of Ship-owners, Maritime Trade Unions, Government departments concerned and representatives of the Sea Training Establishments.

Before an entrant joins a ship he has a minimum of four months training at an approved training establishment. After two and a half years as Ordinary Seaman he may pass an examination which qualifies him for the rating of Able Seaman and so becomes eligible for promotion to Petty Officer. He then has an opportunity of becoming navigating officer.

Every British foreign-going ship, and many others, must sail with a properly certified Master, and at least one other fully certified officer, according to the provisions of the Merchant Shipping Acts. To obtain a 2nd Mate's certificate for example, the applicant must be at least 20 years old and have served a minimum of four years continuous service in a foreign-going ship or six years in a home-trade ship as seaman or apprentice. A candidate for 2nd Class Engineer's certificate must be 21 years old, have served four years in specified types of workshops from the age of 15 and at least 18 months as an engineer at sea on regular watch.

To become a Radio Officer it is necessary to pass the examinations held by the Postmaster-General for a certificate of proficiency in radio-telephony and radio-telegraphy, generally after a course at one of the approved colleges.

Within such a vast industry which, by virtue of its nature, is both national and international, a great amount of organization is necessary. In consequence, shipowners have found it to their mutual benefit to form associations local to the ports they use. Examples are the Bristol Shipowners' Association, London General Shipowners' Association and the North of England Shipowners' Association. These associations discuss ways and means of securing improvements for the mutual benefit of the members or of preventing developments which would adversely affect the local shipping industry. Stevedores, pilots, tugowners, ship-repairers also have their associations.

The local Shipowners' Association play an important part in the relations between the industry and the Port Authority. Shipowners partly comprise some Port Authorities.

The Chamber of Shipping represents the industry as a whole and it has an important function to perform in organizing, formulating and presenting the opinions of expert shipowners on a wide range of subjects. Decisions may have to be made on matters of policy, national and international, on innumerable technical subjects and matters affecting relations with Government departments, matters of general and universal applications concerning such things as port facilities or management, dock and harbour dues, pilotage or navigational aids, Panama or Suez Canal dues, shipbuilding costs, Government subsidies, import and export trades, coal and oil bunkering, road and rail competition, air transport and a host of other matters.

The fact that British ships and associated maritime industries, professions, and services which depend on them operate to such a large extent in an international sphere illustrates the need for some sort of international organization. Ships of all flags are engaged in the same trades and use the same ports and waterways, paying the same dues, observing the same regulations and conducting their business by similar methods of commercial practice. There are many exceptions to this broad generalization but the fact remains that all nations have similar interests in many spheres of the business of the carriage of goods by sea. Consequently there has grown up a network of international organizations which tend to multiply as the years go by.

Leading maritime nations drew up a Convention which formulated a set of international rules for sea transport. These rules known as the International Regulations for the Prevention of Collisions at Sea were brought into effect on 13th October 1910. Other international Conventions deal with such matters as the regulation of radio wavelengths for use of ships at sea to prevent "jamming", and among the more important are the International Conventions for the safety of Ships at Sea and the International Loadline Convention.

In conclusion I must mention Lloyds Register of Shipping which records the condition and other important data concerning the risks an Insurance Broker may be asked to underwrite. Lloyds is a voluntary Society maintained by the shipping industry and its committee of management is composed of shipowners, ship-builders, engineers and marine underwriters. Naval architects, master mariners and others with specialized qualifications and knowledge serve on the technical committee. Through a world-wide organization of surveyors, initial classifications are made when ships are built and maintenance surveys are carried out periodically or whenever the ship's structure suffers damage from any cause whatsoever. Lloyds Register surveyor's test and approve, during its manufacture, the material intended for use in the ship's structure, her engines or boilers, they survey refrigerating machinery, supervise the testing of chains and anchors, and are the competent authorities for the assignment of freeboard to all classes of ships in accordance with the provisions of the Merchant Shipping Act and Loadline Regulation.

A vessel when ready for her maiden voyage, duly passed by Lloyds surveyor as A1, may well be considered a fit vessel to brave the elements, for A1 at Lloyds is tip-top in any language.

# 18 Continental ferry services

*Paper presented to the Manchester Centre by*
*N.J.H. Laws*
*April 1959 issue*

If we draw a series of ever increasing circles, with Manchester as the centre, we find some rather interesting geographical facts. Paris, Brussels, Rotterdam are as near as Glasgow and Edinburgh. To most exporters Paris, Brussels and Rotterdam have constituted problems. They are "on the other side", thus selling, packing and shipping have required special treatment, but I don't suppose any of us would give a second thought as to how to send goods to Glasgow or Edinburgh. Two years ago we might have been forgiven for looking at European markets as problem children and excusing ourselves for lack of sales in those countries, accepting too easily that the Germans, Italians and the Swiss were in that much closer proximity to those countries and in fact one to the other, and could logically sell more easily.

During the last two years many of the difficulties and the traditional costs which we were previously up against have been smoothed out by the introduction of a vehicle drive on drive off system, using wartime L.S.T's for a commercial service which runs three times a week both ways between Tilbury and Antwerp.

There are other services and further new ones will be introduced. My paper is confined to experience as opposed to what we hope to have available within the coming months.

The principle of this drive-on-drive-off system is to treat all goods, no matter the type or class, as an ordinary road transport problem, by putting them on a truck or trailer at the point of origin and the same trucks or trailers going through to the European destination without load trans-shipment, thus making the European customer almost as accessible as the customer in Glasgow or Edinburgh. Quite naturally, there are certain complications. You cross international frontiers and that strip of water which has at times been a blessing but in times of peace has proved a stumbling block in giving those free trading conditions, about which there is so much talk at the present time.

The system provided by the Ferry Service has helped to break down these barriers and difficulties, whether real or creations in the exporter's mind. As a regular and reasonably big user of the service I can say without fear of contradiction that it is simplicity itself. Hitherto, exporters had to case goods for protection due to the many handlings undergone during the journey from factory to port, on board the vessel, stowage, unloading and redelivery. With our system we take a semi-trailer to the supplier's warehouse and goods are loaded on the bed on the trailer without packing or any form of protection whatsoever. The goods are lashed and tarpaulined.

Whilst this is going on, someone has to prepare documentation, certified invoices for compilation of the customs entry and ensure that import licences if necessary, letter of credit are arranged so that there will be not any delays en route. Assuming this has been done, the semi trailer will be hauled to Tilbury arriving an hour or two before the drive-on-drive-off vessel, the "Bardick Ferry" is due to sail.

That is of utmost interest to anybody who wants to ship quickly. There isn't that need to get goods to the dockside in cases hours or even days before the ship sails. Whilst the vehicles are journeying to Tilbury, the Shipping Agents look after the customs entry and documents. The customs officer has had a preview of the papers and decides whether he wishes to inspect the load. If he does it is comparatively simple as, due to the manner of loading, he can easily inspect the goods. Previously he would have broken open cases, made his inspection and then repacked.

If everything is in order, the tractor unit unhitches the semi-trailer and one of the Stevedoring Company's tractor units moves the trailer into the hold of the ship. Trestles are placed at the front end of the semi-trailer to ensure stability during the voyage, the sides and the rear sections are secured and it is impossible, no matter what sort of sailing conditions are met, for these semi-trailers to move during the voyage. The lower hold of these ships will take 30 vehicles of 24ft. x 7ft. 6in. floor area.

The voyage from Tilbury to Antwerp takes approximately 17 hours and puts your goods into one of the most convenient centres for ultimate distribution to most points on the Continent. The Belgian hauliers have really laid themselves out for this job and their organization is very good indeed.

At Antwerp, the Belgian haulage contractor brings his tractor unit into the hold of the ship, hitches on the semi trailer and draws it out on the quayside for customs inspection. And here is a rather interesting feature. Apart from one occasion when we were at fault with the documents, we have never experienced a delay of longer than an hour on the quay in Antwerp. This is due to the extreme co-operation which the Belgian Government generally and the customs officials particularly are offering to ensure that the time factor is reduced to the absolute minimum.

The customs clearance at Antwerp covers goods for all destinations in Europe and whilst in some cases it is necessary to raise a customs bond, clearance at Antwerp is adequate for most points this side of the Iron Curtain. Once these formalities have been completed and the documents handed to the driver, he can proceed on his way and when I say proceed I really do mean proceed.

These Continental hauliers really get down to the job in hand and whilst there are limitations within City precincts, speeds of 60-80 kilometres per hour are expected and attained on most journeys.

The regulations covering working hours are not nearly so severe as they are in this country and whilst I have doubts about the advisability of drivers working 12-14 hours at a time, the job is done speedily and economically.

If we calculate the total time it takes for such a trip from Manchester to Paris, say Manchester to Tilbury nine hours, two hours at Tilbury for customs formalities, 17 hours on board, say another two hours at Antwerp for procedures, and 10 hours maximum to Paris, a total of 40 hours for a journey of some 500 miles, of which the sea voyage represents 40 per cent in time and 30 per cent in distance.

Now if I may come down to details for technical, financial and documentary requirements. We have three factors predominating. Firstly, equipment to be used on a venture of this sort, secondly how do the costs for these drive-on-drive-off vessels compare with charges made by normal shipping lines and thirdly, how is the documentation simplified, how is the exporter's life made easier?

As regards the equipment, one can use a British trailer of any current specification, although I would recommend strengthening of the chassis and fitting slightly larger tyres. There must be air brakes, two line system, and flashing indicators at the rear of the trailer. The coupling is perhaps an all important requirement as most of the Continental hauliers use the American system, i.e., the S.A.E. kingpin.

A feature found to be of inestimable value, is a through tie bar around the outer edge of the trailer platform to enable continuous roping of the load. This pleases the customs authorities because they can place a seal at one end of the continuous rope knowing that it will not be possible for the load to be tampered with en route.

The costs of operating this method must be treated not as a straightforward comparison between road transport costs and orthodox shipping costs, but a combination of all the expenditure which would normally be incurred by an exporter sending goods abroad including packing.

The insurance of high valued commodities is considerably cheaper on trailers than would be the case for an ordinary shipment.

A 12-ton load occupying a trailer area of 24ft. x 7ft. 6in., would cost from Manchester to Tilbury the same whether going by the Transport Ferry Service or by ordinary shipment. Let's look at the charges from that stage onwards.

At Tilbury we have 15/- per ton for the dock authorities, calculated on the gross weight of the load and the trailer, in this case being some 15 tons costing £11 5s. 0d: The sea freight - at the rate of 5/- per square foot for laden trailers and 4/- per square foot for unladen trailers (allowing pick-a-backing). There is no limitation on the weight taken on the trailer. The shipment costs £45 to Antwerp which related to ton weight being carried is about £3 16s. 0d. per ton, which compares very favourably with current shipping rates. The charges at Antwerp are nominal - roughly 6/8d. per ton so there we have a further £5.

One of the most important people in the chain of communications in this operation is the Continental Agent. We count ourselves particularly fortunate in this regard as we have someone who really knows what to do and works with the utmost efficiency. They normally charge us a figure of £7 per trailer load irrespective of the weight or value.

The biggest item in our cost build-up is the Continental haulier's charges. You will appreciate that if your trailer is going a considerable distance this could amount to 50 per cent of your overall costs. Antwerp to Paris is some 350 kilometres. The Continental haulier charges considerably more than his English counterpart and for a journey to Paris, we are expected to pay a rate of approximately 2/6d. per mile on the overall there and back distance. In other words we pay a cost of £45. To this we must add our standing charges and a profit giving us a total all in charge for the journey of approximately £175, i.e., just over £14 per ton, which I think is fair and reasonable. I might state that previously it was costing a little over £14 per ton for packing and delivering to F.O.B. British port only. You cannot obviously make a straight comparison of a point-to-point charge. The exporter has had innumerable advantages in terms of financial saving, time saving which must be taken into the overall appraisal of the situation, giving his customer the goods in factory fresh condition ready for immediate use; so the customer will also save money because he avoids using labour to unpack and perhaps making good discrepancies on his supplies.

# 19 World containerization: A progress report

*Paper presented to the Annual Conference by N. Tilsley*
*Containerization International*
*July 1968 issue*

The single most important development in international freight transportation has been the advent of the container as we know it today, which serves as both a therapeutic and, at the same time, a disabling factor in industry. It is therapeutic in the sense that ocean shipping companies may now be in a position to eliminate peaks and valleys in their operating charts and grow in a more orderly fashion, while simultaneously operating on a more profitable basis. It could be disabling, on the other hand, because the container will undoubtedly bring with it the failure of many shipping lines and the drying up of cargo handling in many areas.

But it is not only at sea where the container is having a disabling effect - as some long-distance public hauliers have already discovered. Adopting the door-to-door concept of physical distribution, the giant shiplines currently switching over to full containerization, wisely according to some, prudently according to others, are fighting for control over the whole distribution chain from factory door to customer reception dock. Thus, conventional shipping and forwarding agents, and even road carriers, could find their very existences at stake in the future world of containerization for, make no mistake about it, whether we like it or not; whether there will be the great savings the pundits have forecast or not; containerization is here, and here to stay.

Anyone now participating in the transport industry, or employed by a manufacturing plant in connection with distribution, who refuses to accept this fact and does not take steps to see how his particular organization can participate, maybe not immediately but in the "near immediate" future, is not only doing himself a disservice but, more important still, is doing a disservice to his shareholders and customers. Already, too much capital has been committed and, in most areas of the world with the exception perhaps, of the developing countries, containerization is well past the point of no return.

Having set the scene as bluntly and as strongly as I can and no doubt having laid myself open to considerable contradiction, especially from some conventional diehards, may I say how honoured I am to be invited by the Institute to be your first speaker at your Conference for 1968, a year which I regard as "D minus one" year as far as containerization in the United Kingdom is concerned. May I say, too, how much I welcome this opportunity of speaking to men whose main interest is in road transport, a field of activity and a mode of transport with which I have been associated for many years as a journalist; an area of activity in which, moreover, I have family connections, though I ask you not to hold that against me!

The angle that I have been asked to take in this paper is particularly suited to me, having for over a year sat in the editorial "hot seat" for a truly international journal dealing specifically with this new method of handling freight. Acting, if you like, as a kind of international monitoring service, sorting, annotating and eventually "delivering" news and comment to and from all parts of the world. In such a position one has the advantage of being able to travel, in my particular case throughout Europe and the United States, to talk to operators and users alike, and to form impressions and make comparisons of what is happening in this exciting new world of freight transportation.

At this moment in time it would be impertinent of me to insult your intelligence and bore you with long utterances about what is containerization; what are the advantages of using containers, and so on and so forth. This has been dealt with so many times in the last few years, and still is being propounded, I note with some disappointment, at symposiums, seminars and conferences in this country. I say this with great respect to the eminent people who take part in them, but with a great deal of feeling for the people who attend them, who pay quite sizeable sums in delegate fees in the hope of learning more about this fascinating subject. We are now, I hope, out of the kindergarten stage in containerization. We must now exchange generalities for technicalities.

Containerization was born of inefficiency, and labour intensive material handling methods. The function of the cargo transportation industry is to place a product in its intended market by the most efficient and economic means.

Properly used, containers will do just that. The container concept was designed to serve as an integral link between the manufacturer and the ultimate customer. By eliminating as many as 12 separate handlings, containers should minimize a cargo's exposure to loss or damage; they should speed delivery and reduce overall expenditures. Thus they should satisfy the three principal considerations of distribution: safe, prompt and inexpensive delivery.

If I follow my brief properly, I must now ask (and then try to answer) the following questions. "Is containerization fulfilling these functions? Or are we all really being hoodwinked by the shipping lines and railways who, in most cases, stand to gain traffic by the adoption of containerization?"

Before answering this, let us cast our minds back over the last few years. Four or five years ago international, intermodal containerization, as we understand the term was only known in this country to the few who had travelled to the United States and seen developments between the east and west coasts to Puerto Rico and Hawaii respectively; or who had travelled on the railroads and seen the giant demountable boxvans travelling on the Southern Railway or New York Central System (now merged with the Pennsylvania Railroad Company). Like our own Northern Ireland-UK unit-load services, these systems were purely domestic in nature, with none of the problems attaching to documentation, banking, Customs and insurance. Of course, our own and other Continental railway companies had been exchanging containers for years, but these were heavy wooden boxes which, in many instances, weighed as much as, and often more than, the goods they carried.

Here, between the UK and the Continent, goods were travelling "quite nicely thank you" on road vehicles, using roll-on-roll-off ferries and operating under cover of TIR carnets. Both here, and on the Continent, the tilt-topped semi-trailer which could be loaded virtually from all angles -the top, sides and rear, was becoming more and more popular.

Then followed the Yankee "invasion" of Europe with containers making the ocean passage on conventional cargo ships run by Moore McCormack, States Marine Line, US Lines, Lykes Line and Sea-land. At this time there was considerable user resistance in Europe - especially regarding some of the "through-transport" methods adopted ashore. There were technical difficulties, too. The 40ft. unit was too large and unacceptable in many countries. Even the Sea-Land 35-footer was "out of gauge" on British roads. In any case, delivery points were often physically unable to accommodate such monsters. I well recall a well-known Southampton haulier who was at that time experimenting with States Marine Line container deliveries, having to park a 40ft. container and unload it in the street, so restricted was access. At this time

171

the haulier was breaking the law as regards the then prevailing Construction and Use Regulations as far as length was concerned, but he allowed us on the journal that I was working for, to photograph his vehicle and the container in an effort to have a test case brought against him by the Ministry of Transport.

Apart from this question of access, Customs, documentation, and particularly the traditional Bill of Lading, insurance and even tariffs imposed on many ship lines by the Conferences, were just not geared to containerization, to say nothing of the capacity of the ports to handle them.

There was considerable prejudice, moreover, in the fact that the Americans were said to be pushing themselves almost a little too far and were taking traffic from European ocean freight carriers who were facing considerable declines in trading.

The proof of the pudding was in the eating, however, and the salesmen and agents were doing their jobs well. Soon whisky, books, toys and electrical goods to mention but a few commodities of which I have personal knowledge, were containerized internationally, while Dr Beeching's now proved and much publicized freight liner system was making inroads into long-distance road haulier traffic in Britain, despite teething troubles and labour difficulties and the almost hereditary prejudice against rail on the part of some shippers and distribution men. This, then, was the big breakthrough.

Europe's counter-attack against the American invasion was meanwhile being planned, in the form of a trans-Atlantic service of "combo" ships, deigned to carry both vehicular traffic in the roll-on/roll-off fashion, and also containers carried above deck. Atlantic Containers Line came into being, formed by leading shipping companies (who were competitors on the North Atlantic) in Sweden, Holland, France and in Britain with Cunard.

Services started last year from Sweden and Holland linking Gothenburg, Bremen, Rotterdam, Antwerp, New York, Baltimore, Virginia, and four ships are providing a weekly service. The intention was to "Beat the Americans at their own game", as Mr Van Houten, the Dutch chairman of the consortium, put it to me during an interview last autumn.

Nearer home, some of our largest groups of shipping companies had similarly joined forces and formed consortia to containerize traffic between Europe and Australia on a door-to-door basis. Names that we are all familiar with now - Overseas Containers Ltd. and Associated Container Transportation (or OCL and ACT as they are known) came into being and both started planning inland container stations here and in Australia, studying and experimenting with various types of goods and containers, using, for the time being, their existing services.

During this period - back in Europe again - we have had the battle of the

172

ports with, on an international scale, verbal clashes by port authority officials on whether Tilbury, Rotterdam or Dunkirk should be Europe's one and only trans-Atlantic terminal, and on a domestic basis competition between Liverpool, Southampton and Tilbury for the distinction of being the UK's main container terminal (with Grangemouth and Felixstowe, Britain's only true container ports at the time, quietly knocking up their totals of trans-Atlantic and European containers handled). Rotterdam, nearby Amsterdam and Antwerp have been similarly vying with each other in the Low Countries; Bremem and Hamburg in Germany, and a three-cornered fight has been going on - still unresolved, between Dunkirk, Le Havre and Marseilles.

Meantime, crane, mechanical handling and vehicle manufacturers have been designing new and strange-looking devices for the handling of the containers between ship and shore, between rail wagon and road vehicle and to lift containers from ground level to skeletal trailer and vice versa.

Last year container fever appeared to be at its pitch, but there seems to be no abatement in the middle of 1968. In the spring of 1967, only a few months after the results of a successful North Atlantic container experiment had shown that containerized loads had crossed the Atlantic door-to-door quicker and more safely than if they had travelled break-bulk, we had the McKinsey Report. Commissioned by the British Transport Docks Board at a cost of £50,000-plus, McKinsey, a firm of American consultants, forecast freight savings of 50 per cent. Also forecast was a 70 per cent reduction in cargo ships on the North Atlantic run, and a 90 per cent reduction in the number of dockers and stevedores handling general cargo. Recommendations were made to reduce drastically our ports for ocean-going ships; development of short sea trade routes in ports that take full advantage of low inland transport costs; subsidies for low-cost unit trains to container berths; rationalization of our shipping industry to ensure a high-volume market, and the promotion of integrated transport systems by importers and exporters. Container enthusiasts throughout Europe immediately adopted McKinsey as their bible while trade union men, shipping and forwarding agents and hauliers, in the main, preferred to ignore its existence.    Last year, too, saw the laying of the keels of the OCL and ACT consortia vessels, and some measure of the type of money being expended by these organizations can be gleaned from figures given out by OCL at the time. Total cost of the venture will exceed £42 million, representing £30 million for the six, 1,130 container capacity vessels, and the balance being the cost of 11,000 containers and inland facilities.

Other important happenings in containerization last year were the formulation of external dimensions for containers -the ISO recommendations of 8ft. x 8ft., by modules of 10ft., 20ft., 30ft. and 40ft. being adopted, despite understandable pleas by the pioneers Sea-land and Matson who had, and still have, vast fleets of 35ft. and 24ft. containers respectively. Standards were also formulated last year by Lloyds for the construction and testing of containers and also, after an initial strike and other labour difficulties, LIFT (which stands for London International Freight Terminal) became operational at Stratford, bringing British Railways, diverse shipping and forwarding agents and road hauliers together to handle road, rail and container traffic under one roof (several roofs, actually, but within one compound).

Apart from the fact that 1967 also saw the real getting together of shippers, bankers and insurance underwriters, there were important happenings in Europe. For instance, the railways of Europe got together and formed Intercontainer, an independent company under the chairmanship of a British Railways Board member, to handle all through movements of containers on rail on the Continent. There was also the Leber Plan in Germany - a scheme by the German Transport Minister which makes Barbara Castle's transport bill seem very "small time" by comparison. Apart from completely barring certain bulk commodities of goods from the road altogether, Leber aims to tax other goods so heavily that they will be forced on to rail; and this includes containers. Another important happening last year was the arrival of the first containers in Japan from London using Europe and Asia as a landbridge. MAT Transport forwarded ten containers of household goods and office equipment via Russia and the Trans-Siberian railway. Apart from possible savings in time of up to 2½ weeks, the overland route cuts the sea journey mileage almost in half.

This year - bringing us up-to-date - containerization has continued to progress by leaps and bounds. At home British Railways has continued to expand their Freightliner services -last month they inaugurated an overnight service to Paris. their fully-cellular Harwich - Zeebrugge container service also commenced operations just over a month ago, although they have so far not allowed any journalists near Harwich to see for themselves, preferring, no doubt, to keep their teething troubles to themselves! As far as the ports are concerned, Tilbury's container terminal became operational at the beginning of the year, with the inauguration of European Unit Route's first containership (EUR is a subsidiary of the General Steam Navigation Company) and this year sees the opening of US Lines Tilbury terminal.

Deep-sea services are expanding, too. The original American west coast container pioneer, Matson, has extended its successful Hawaii pineapple service to Japan and Australia, while American Export Isbrandtsen Lines, parent company of Container Marine Lines which operates the North Atlantic to Europe, has inaugurated a much-needed container service to the Mediterranean area. Here there are some serious lifting problems in the Italian ports caused through a lack of adequate cranage. There is also considerable activity on the other side of the world where the Japanese are busy building containership and terminals, in Japan and on the US west coast, while plans have been laid for the commencement of a container service to New Zealand.

Such, then, is the progress of containerization throughout the world. You will realize that most of my paper has dealt with the progress of the providers of containers and container services. With this gigantic swing towards full containerization - a state of affairs that could well be arrived at in this country in the early 1970s - can it be said that the shipper who generates the cargo is going to benefit at all?

The two consortia who plan to operate containerships to Australia early in 1969 - D-year - have issued "indicative tariffs" for the guidance of prospective shippers. They give detailed examples of shipping different kinds of goods as full container loads and less-than-container-loads. For shipping 8 tons weight of machinery from Wolverhampton to Melbourne they show a saving over conventional shipping of £40. For moving 6 tons of refrigerators between Cardiff and Sydney they give a saving of £44. Another shipment, this time of confectionery between Edinburgh and Sydney, showed savings of £41 on a 7-ton load. In these days of continual rising costs, such examples are encouraging, although they are considered by some to be extremely conservative and cautious.

As stated earlier, these are merely indicative tariffs. We carried an example of the costings of an actual container movement recently in Containerization International. One ton of machinery travelling between Sheffield and New York showed a saving in cost of £8 7s. 5d., and a saving in time of 17 days. The facts, in this case, speak for themselves. Containerization can afford savings not only to the carrier but also to the shipper; and journey time is considerably cut. As regards safety there have been some serious incidents of damage, damage mainly to the containers themselves through bad handling, careless fork-lift truck driving and mistakes on the part of crane or straddle-carrier operators. There have also been instances of damage caused by the elements. For this reason, insurance is presenting some operators with difficulties, and this even applies to the consortia. Deciding who is responsible for the damage (when it is eventually discovered) is one of the problems; another is the question of packing. Contrary to what has been said in the past, containers must be packed carefully to avoid damage due to movement during rough seas. The reluctance on the part of ocean carriers to accept responsibility for damage to goods they have not themselves packed is understandable.

175

Insurance should be cheaper, because the goods are less exposed to damage or pilferage; yet more often than not this is not the case. These difficulties remain to be resolved.

One thing that should be mentioned is the position of the shipping and forwarding agent. Current feeling in the industry is that generally speaking the forwarder has failed to fill the gap created by modern advances in technique and thought regarding through-shipping methods. The situation is rapidly approaching when the small man, because of apathy and stubbornness to recognize the advent of the container, will lose his clients to the larger forwarder who can offer through container services. A new breed of transport man has appeared in the States, and there are one or two of them here in the UK. They are called "Intermodalists" - which in lay language can be interpreted as "container operator". Organizations selling space in containers - either their own containers or leased ones. These are "middle men" with a difference. Without them the consolidation of less-than-container-loads could not be effected.

I have been asked to give my views on how containerization has affected the haulier. Progress of containerization in the field of road haulage has been considerable. Generally speaking, because the railways are less labour intensive, containerization favours rail. The dividing line between road and rail operations varies according to circumstances (in America one large consultant organization puts this figure as 500 miles; in Europe 300 miles is reckoned to be break-even point). Essentially, therefore, where large land masses are involved, road haulage may be confined to the role of collection and delivery. Hauliers, with few exceptions, do not want to own containers.

Obviously this criteria does not apply to the United Kingdom mainland (England, Wales and Scotland) because of the small area involved compared with the American or European mainlands. However, because of the density of traffic between certain populated areas, for instance, between London and Glasgow or Manchester, unit trains can offer a better tariff proposition. On these rail trunk routes containers will obviously travel by rail. The haulier, provided the Government allows him to participate, will probably make his money hauling other people's skeletal semi-trailers and containers. His only capital outlay in the future, as far as equipment is concerned, will be his tractive unit.

There seems to be an uneasy lull on both sides of the Atlantic on the question of dockside labour. In the States the mighty ILA (International Longshoremen's Association) previously collected a "royal" fee for each container handled, which was subsequently shared out among the members of a particular gang. But the ILA has recently made it clear that it does not want compensation for redundancy in containerization. As it's President, Tim Gleasson, told me in an interview recently "The men don't want money - they want their jobs." They are to insist on their men supervising the loading of containers at inland containerizations. We are likely to see similar demands being made here as more containers come in.

To return to my main theme - world progress in containerization - I would like to stress that although we, in Britain, entered the container race several years behind the Americans, the general feeling is that containerization here is more sophisticated than it is in the States. One instance is the through Bill of Lading. We have it here, but the Americans are still waiting for a bill to go through Congress.

It is to be hoped that we do not arrive at the situation such as exists now between New York and Puerto Rico. While in New York recently, I was told of a protest meeting that had been convened by forwarders there to draw attention to the serious delays afforded to general, break-bulk cargo destined for Puerto Rico. Apparently there are now so many cellular containerships on this run that "out-of-gauge" traffic like long steel bars and bulk powders are being delayed sometimes as much as 10 weeks. With such large operators as US Lines switching over completely to cellular containerships in the near future, such a state of affairs could well happen on the North Atlantic. There will always be room for the conventional shipper but, as I stated in opening, transport men all over the world owe it to themselves and their companies to consider containerization and their places in it in the future.

# 20 Containerization: Some facts and figures

*Article by H.E. Tatman*
*September 1979 issue*

During the past two decades the main ports throughout the world have undergone many radical changes in order to cater for the coming and going of huge fleets of container vessels which have largely replaced the long existing cargo steamers whose numbers have since rapidly diminished.

The main ingredient of this technological revolution is the container - a strong, rectangular box, most commonly built of steel or aluminium. The basic type has doors at one end and has been specially devised to meet the needs of shippers. It is today the most widely used method of transporting large volumes of general cargo from supplier to consumer.

From the original 'box' concept containers have been adapted and developed to cater for a wide range of specialized goods and from the basic general cargo box there have evolved a number of other types for special purposes.

Numbered among them are insulated and integral refrigerated, half-height, open top, flat rack, open sided, dry bulk and bulk tank containers. All these types are approved by Lloyd's Register of Shipping and conform to the recommendations of the International Standards Organization.

## TYPES AND SIZES

The most widely used type is the 20ft general cargo container which can carry a payload of up to 20 tonnes and has a capacity of about 28 cubic metres. Also available in the range are 30ft. 35ft. and 40ft. boxes.

Moving meat or fresh fruit presents no problem when housed in the ideally suitable 20ft. refrigerated container with its integral refrigeration unit and such perishable goods invariably arrive at their destination in mint condition. Likewise such goods can be forwarded in insulated containers which are connected to the ship's refrigeration system during the sea voyage.

Large or awkward items (e.g. machines, wheels and oddly shaped products) have the facility of the 20/40ft. open top container into which, by removal of the header bar above the door, the cargo can easily be lowered from above.

The 20ft. dry bulk container is ideal for moving granular substances and powders and as for cars, trucks, heavy machinery or bulky items of that nature, the flat rack will accommodate them adequately. The basic 'flat' has removable slatted boards on each end to make for easier loading. There are numerous lashing points and also provision for removable stanchions.

For the carriage of dense cargoes such as steel, pipes and tubes the 20/40ft. half-height container is the type for the job and is a boon to the shipper whose premises have a restricted height for loading. There is a choice of two types - either with a tarpaulin top or solid removable top. Both have fixed sides but with end door opening facilities.

The understandable risks in moving hazardous cargo such as timber, plywood and similar products have now been greatly reduced by the introduction of the open sided container which has either wire mesh, non-load-bearing gates or full height gates which may be completely removed and stowed inside the container if not required.

When moving bulk liquid cargoes the 20ft. tank container is the answer. Standard ISO steel frames support the tanks, which are equipped with hatches to allow access for cleaning purposes.

This brief summary indicates the variety of containers in use but many permutations can be provided by the shipping lines for particular needs beyond the normal scope.

# ECONOMIES

The economies achieved by a shipper who containerizes his goods immediately become apparent when the otherwise high cost of wooden cases, crates or heavy duty cartoning is eliminated. Again, labour costs become minimal and these two factors together - the one giving an important weight reduction and thus reduced freight charges, the other giving a reduction in loading time - must prove beneficial to the shipper.

As a practical example, let us consider a product widely used in most offices throughout the world: the ordinary filling folder, of which 100,000 units (boxed in 50s) are to go to Singapore. As a conventional shipment such folders would pack into, say, 250 master cartons of 400 to give a workable handling weight of 50kgs per carton.

It would be reasonable to assume that the cost of 250 seaworthy cartons plus around 80 hours' packing labour (approx 3 per hour) would far exceed the cost of containerizing the folders - a matter of less than three hours' work. Further, to carton pack could mean up to two days' work for the packing room - and a possible missed sailing.

Assuming that this quantity of folders would nicely fill a 20ft. general cargo container, they could be stowed, sealed and on the way in three hours.


# STUFFING

To 'stuff a box' is another way of saying 'to load a container'; so let us now examine the aspects of this very important stage.

First and foremost, cargo that is to occupy the same box should be selected on the basis of compatibility, as damage could be caused by incompatible goods or packing. Ideally, of course, the shape and dimensions of the package should be an optimum module of the container and in the case of the aforementioned example this would be so. But this is not always possible.

Certainly the container must be stowed as tightly as possible so that lateral and longitudinal movement is impossible during transit. Shoring, lashing, wedging and locking are the commonest methods of securing the cargo.

There is no simple formula for securing cargo. The built-in securing points should always be used and dunnage (e.g. old tyres polyurethane slabs, rolled cardboard, paper pads etc.) can be utilized as required to ensure a tight stow.

Palletized cargo presents less of a problem provided the load is effectively strapped to the pallet. Fork lifting palletized goods into the container reduces the time element and securing is not normally necessary if the distance between pallets and container wall is 4 inches or less. Wedging, by the use of wood block or lengths of timber, is recommended where space exceeds this. It is also beneficial to insert sheets of board between pallet loads to protect against chafing.

Whatever means are adopted to secure the cargo, it is vital that distribution of the load must cover the full width and length of the container. Each ton weight of cargo should be spread over at least two of the floor members, which run transversely under the container floor at 1ft. centres. In no circumstances should the closed-end half of the container carry more than 65 per cent, or the door-end half more than 60 per cent of the total load. It should, of course, be unnecessary to say that heavy items should always be stowed at the bottom with light packages on top.

## STRESSES

Containers are subjected to all stresses experienced by road, rail and sea. A container which is being loaded on a trailer will be subjected to vertical forces of 1.8 times gravity aboard ship and it is therefore not sufficient to load as one would load a lorry.

Containers are designed to accept maximum payloads which must not, on any account, be exceeded. Negligence in this respect must be viewed seriously in the light of safety regulations and the container line should always be consulted when in doubt.

It is also worth mentioning that certain countries (such as Australia) have strict quarantine laws and any product of a vegetable or animal nature (including wooden pallets or dunnage which has not been treated before stowing must be fumigated before arrival. A certificate showing that this has been done must be produced to the authorities at importation. If this procedure is not carried out a shipper could be liable to a heavy fine or even confiscation of the goods.

One important factor that the shipper must keep in mind is the time element for loading a container (FCL) at his premises. The shipping line will normally allow 3 hours to load a 20ft. box and 4 hours for a 40ft.

Should these times be exceeded the line could then charge demurrage, on average about £8 per hour. If the shipper has prepared his goods for containerization well in advance of the arrival of the box he should, generally speaking, have ample time to load within the above limits.

The shipper's final job after completing the stow is to close up and seal the doors. Containerline seals are provided for this purpose if required or the shipper's own seal may be used if preferred. In any event, once sealed, there can be no tampering with the cargo by an unauthorized person and the shipper can be confident that his goods will arrive at his customer's door in mint condition.

The cost of a container is not easy to calculate because so many factors must be considered. The freight charges imposed by the shipping line are normally applied according to the type of product being shipped. With this in mind, let us examine the advantages of the Liner Conference System, which has been in operation for many years.

By definition, a Liner Conference is a group of two or more vessel-operating carriers which provides international liner services for the carriage of cargo on a particular route or routes within specified geographical limits and which has an agreement or arrangement, whatever its nature, within the framework of which they operate under uniform or common freight rates and any other agreed conditions with respect to the provision of liner services.

Consequently, if a shipper signs a contract with, for example, the UK/Far East Freight Conference (assuming he has regular shipments to that area) he has the opportunity of using any suitable vessel of a Conference line member and obtaining the same freight rate from whichever line he chooses, coupled with the fact that the Conference provides regular, dependable sailings to the ports within the area.

Taking the aforementioned example of the shipper with folders for Singapore, who, assuming he has signed a contract with the Conference, will have an agreed freight rate for the product and can thus compute the total charge for the box. The rate, incidentally, is applied on one metric tonne or cubic metre, whichever yields the greater profit.

## COSTING

Thus, if 100,000 folders have, say a weight of 10 tonnes and a cubic measurement of 26m$^3$ at a freight rate of £50, the total cost would amount to £50 x 26 = £1,300. Add haulage from the shipper's premises to the terminal, plus terminal charges and the total sum will be the cost of shipment to the port of arrival or destination.

A shipper who does not feel justified in signing with the Conference may of course use the Conference vessels but would be required to pay a higher freight charge. On the other hand, he can use a non-Conference vessel and negotiate with the shipping line a rate which often might be lower than Conference but he would, in all probability, have less choice of vessel and the likelihood of a lengthier sea voyage.

A good deal therefore depends on the regularity of orders being exported by a shipper to a particular destination and it might be well worth his while to compare the freight rate from both Conference and non-Conference and check out the frequency of shipping services each provides.

## LCL CONSIGNMENTS

Full container loads, generally referred to as FCLs, are usually completed at the shipper's own premises but what happens in the case of the shipper who has a LCL (less than container load) consignment? Special inland clearance depots have sprung into being for just such a situation and ICDs are now in operation all over the country to receive LCL shipments and containerize them.

At these depots, containers are filled with compatible goods which are shipped out to the equivalent ICD in the country of destination, where the boxes are de-stuffed. Individual consignments are then onforwarded to the intended customers. This consolidation service is of course a boon for shippers having LCL consignments. Sophisticated and expensive packaging is dispensed with because of the containerization by experts at the ICDs.

The next stage in the transit chain (whether the FCL goes from the shipper's premises or the ICD), is to move the containers to the main deep-sea terminal.

There are two basic types of skeletal trailers capable of carrying 20ft. and 40ft. containers. Dimensions vary slightly according to the source of manufacture but as a general guide the approximate maximum length (20ft. box) is 22ft. 6 ins with prime mover between 31ft and 35ft (9.4m and 10.6m). Maximum width is 8ft. 2½ins (2.5m) and the loading height is approximately 5ft. 1in above ground level.

## DIMENSIONS

The skeletal trailer carrying a 40ft. box may have dimensions which vary slightly but are generally 40ft.3¼ in. (12,278mm) in length and with prime mover between 48ft. and 52ft. (14,625mm and 15,850mm). The maximum width is 8ft. 2½ in. (2,500mm).

Such statistical data is useful to keep in mind, especially for shippers who may have fairly tight loading facilities. Incidentally, the boxes are still referred to as 20 or 40 footers and not in metric lengths. It is a fact that old habits die hard and UK shippers still tend to call a 40 footer just that and not a 12.2 metre box.

## LONDON DOCKS

It is clear that giant containerships and the berthing facilities required for them could never come within the scope of the traditional London docks. These are now a mere shadow of what they once were and the absorption of the large dock labour force into the ICDs has occurred as a consequence. The docks still cater for vessels carrying conventional cargo but the trade is visibly declining as more and more containerships are built.

The two main terminals in southern England are at Tilbury and Southampton. Others at Liverpool, Manchester and Glasgow serve the north.

A deep-sea terminal takes on a truly Wellsian aspect to the uninitiated. Acres of land, adjacent to the berth, are thickly littered with countless rows of containers waiting to be loaded into the vessel. Giant straddle carriers like mechanical dinosaurs rumble among the boxes, stacking them in piles, often up to five containers high, or pulling them out to move them over to the massive gantry which spans the area between the vessel's deck and the quay.

## MANOEUVRING

The mind boggles at the ease with which these huge juggernauts can manoeuvre 20 ton boxes as though they were mere bricks. Plucked from the ground, the container glides over the quayside and stays hovering over the vessel's deck for manoeuvring into an allocated slot. The OCL container fleet, one of the largest in the world, has in service vessels capable of carrying around 2,400 TEUs (Twenty Foot Equivalent Units). A number of these vessels are up to 950ft. long and are able to travel at some 26 knots. The captain and his small crew occupy quarters at the stern end, whilst the rest of the vessel houses the containers.

The construction is such that the boxes are lowered into individual slots below deck and when all slots are occupied the top deck is utilized for additional layers of boxes. Although a fully loaded vessel is a fantastic sight the captain sees only a continuous line of container tops extending almost up to the bows.

The role provided by a reputable forwarding agent can play an important part in relieving a shipper of most of the tedious work relevant to the shipment of his goods. Briefly the agent will act for him throughout the transaction by booking the box with the shipping line, arranging forwarding, completing all Customs formalities and offering expert advice on all aspects of the movement. He can be of invaluable assistance to the 'green' shipper and for a moderate fee (on average around 5 per cent of the freight charge) he will do most of the spade work.

Many such agents will, as part of their service, collect the goods from the shipper's premises in their own transport and stow the cargo into the box, thus relieving the shipper of this function should he be without the necessary handling equipment.

Forwarding agents are well informed in respect of sailing and arrival dates of vessels and will be able to determine the earliest suitable vessel for the shipper. Most UK agents have their own clearing agents in the overseas ports who, on arrival of the goods, will see the clearance through Customs and deliver to the customer's warehouse.

## DOCUMENTS

Many countries (in the Middle East for example) demand certain documents to be submitted before clearance can be effected. A Certificate of Origin and invoices certified by a Chamber of Commerce and duly legalized by the appropriate Embassy are essential. The agent, when asked, will carry out these requirements for the shipper, thus ensuring that the cargo is forwarded without hitches or delays due to lack of, or incorrect, documentation.

When in port, with the aid of the modern mechanical methods of loading and unloading, vessels can berth - and sail - at a fast pace. Often, 60-hour turnrounds are achieved and fast voyage times (e.g. Southampton to Hong Kong via Port Keland and Singapore) average a mere 24 days. After arrival at the port of destination, the containers are discharged in the same way as at the home port, ensuring that the ship's time on berth is kept to a minimum and a fast, overall service is maintained.

## SAFEGUARD

The container system provides the means to expedite and simplify the transport of cargo in large, easily handled units, from the shipper's premises to the customer's warehouse thousands of miles away. It minimizes possible damage to the cargo in transit, provides a safeguard against pilferage and forges a bond of confidence between the shipper and his customer, who both know that orders are passing from one to the other in the fastest and most economical manner available.

It is well to mention here that some countries make it a condition that goods are inspected for quality and quantity before shipment. At the moment this only applies to cargo destined for Ivory Coast, Zambia, Tanzania, Ghana and Kenya but the list is likely to extend to other countries in the near future. A shipper with cargo for a customer in any of the aforementioned countries must call in the authorized cargo inspector prior to arranging shipment. After inspection, he will issue his certificate and the shipper may proceed. The only exception to this rule is that inspection is not required if the cargo is of a value below the amount stipulated by the country.

# 21  British shipping in decline

*Article by M. Asteris*
*Portsmouth Polytechnic*
*December 1983 issue*

Britain once dominated international shipping but sadly, during the past eight years, the UK merchant fleet has shrunk by more than half. This article looks at the causes and consequences of this contraction and asks what, if anything, can be done about it.

First, however, it is necessary to consider what has been happening. Table 1 sets out details. Figures there show that the UK fleet expanded by more than a third during the first half of the seventies, to reach a peak of almost 50 million deadweight tons (dwt) in 1975. This represented about nine per cent of the world total. Since then, UK tonnage has declined to less than 25m dwt. The world fleet, in contrast, has continued to grow - albeit very slowly of late. Consequently, the UK fleet now constitutes around four per cent of total world tonnage.

Contraction of the fleet is the result of a number of influences. To begin with, technical innovation has raised the efficiency of vessels so reducing the tonnage required to carry a given volume of cargo.[1] The switch to container shipping illustrates the savings in tonnage arising from technical change. A single container ship can transport as much cargo as half a dozen, or more, conventional vessels.

Another factor which needs to be taken into account is the changing pattern of British trade. In 1970, distant former Empire countries, such as South Africa and Australia, still featured prominently in the pattern of UK exports and imports. Today they no longer do so because UK trade has shifted

189

towards Western Europe. There has, therefore, been a swift growth in short-haul shipping and a relative move away from traditional routes, such as those to Australia.

Nor has the shift towards short-haul traffic been confined to dry cargo. In the past few years, the size of the British tanker fleet has been adversely influenced by the changing pattern of world trade in oil. This results partly from an increase in the output of crude from sources, such as the North Sea, close to major areas of consumption.

Nationalism and protectionism have also adversely influenced British shipping. For both political and economic reasons, developing countries wish to raise their share of ocean transport. Measures aimed at reserving a proportion of cargoes for national carriers, at the cost of cross traders, are therefore increasingly common. Indeed, in many parts of the world, the efficiency of shipping services takes second place to considerations such as "cargo generators' rights".

TABLE 1

UK MERCHANT FLEET

UK Registered Vessels Directly Owned By UK Companies

Tonnage at end of year　　　　　　　　　　　thousand deadweight tons (dwt)

| Date | Passenger vessels | Cargo liners | Container vessels | Tramps | Bulk carriers | Tankers | Total |
|------|------|------|------|------|------|------|------|
| 1970 | 518 | 6,371 | 433 | 1,972 | 5,519 | 18,812 | 33,625 |
| 1972 | 371 | 4,724 | 1,130 | 1,664 | 9,643 | 22,670 | 40,202 |
| 1974 | 280 | 4,536 | 1,288 | 1,454 | 12,215 | 27,975 | 47,749 |
| 1976 | 193 | 3,928 | 1,259 | 1,353 | 12,874 | 28,065 | 47,672 |
| 1978 | 184 | 3,197 | 1,665 | 1,049 | 10,246 | 26,289 | 42,630 |
| 1980 | 177 | 2,477 | 1,478 | 815 | 7,324 | 23,448 | 35,720 |
| 1982 | 162 | 1,597 | 1,465 | 614 | 5,831 | 15,079 | 24,746 |

Source: Business Monitor, MR15, July 1982, table 1.3 (iii) and
Department of Industry.

Since its initiation in 1964, the United Nations Conference on Trade and Development (UNCTAD) has been in the forefront of attempts to replace relative competitiveness in shipping by a more discriminatory approach. The UNCTAD Code of Conduct for Liner Conferences reflects this desire most clearly in its cargo-sharing provisions.[2] These incorporate the so-called 40:40:20 principle which allocates 40 per cent of conference trade to countries at either end of a particular route and 20 per cent to cross traders. When the Code is brought into force shortly (some nine years after it was first mooted) it is clear that efforts will be made by many countries in the Third World to apply its principles to other sectors of international shipping.

New technology, changing trade patterns and discriminatory practices have all played a part in the contraction of British shipping. But these factors were in evidence before the present period of decline. The main causes of the shrinkage must therefore be sought in two recent developments, the prolonged world recession and a deterioration in the competitiveness of British shipping.

During the 1950s and 1960s, shipping reflected the optimism of the period. Owners ordered tonnage, confident that the demand for maritime transport would continue to increase rapidly. As is evident from Table 2, which shows the growth in seaborne trade from 1965 to 1981, until the oil price rises of 1973/74 this was very much the case. But in the mid-seventies, the world entered a long slump with the result that (as is shown by the lower portion of Table 2) there has been little rise in the demand for sea transport since that time.

Nevertheless, new tonnage has continued to swell the supply of shipping, encouraged by favourable loan conditions to owners and subsidies to shipyards. These stimulants are reflected in excess shipbuilding capacity. Rather than face the task of drastically reducing this surplus, governments compete for orders by artificially lowering the costs of buying new vessels. This, in turn, helps to perpetuate the disequilibrium in maritime transport. Over-capacity is a feature of all the major sections of the shipping industry. Recently the tanker market has suffered not just from the change in the pattern of the oil trade, which was noted earlier, but also from the absolute decline in seaborne oil indicated by Table 2. Dry bulk shipping has fared little better. Optimism in the earlier part of the decade, with respect to growth of cargoes such as coal, has proved premature. Nonetheless several million tonnes of extra bulk carrier capacity is now competing for business. Even the more specialized sectors of the industry, such as the container trades, have suffered from the recession.

The excess supply of shipping has resulted in very low freight rates even though operating costs have risen steeply. Fuel and labour costs, in particular, are much more significant than a decade ago. Between the early seventies and the early eighties, bunker costs rose some seven-fold though operators faced similar increases irrespective of nationality. It has therefore been changes in crew costs which have played a crucial role in determining competitiveness. This has proved detrimental to the European shipping industry because the gap between its manning costs and those of low-wage Asian fleets has widened. The differing crew costs of a 'handy-sized' bulk carrier of some 25,000 dwt illustrates how fierce competition from the new-industrialising countries has become. On average, in 1981, manning costs in Europe for this type of vessel, at around $2,600 a day, were $1,000 higher than those of Eastern operators.[3]

TABLE 2

THE GROWTH IN SEABORNE TRADE 1965-1981

| | | | | Per cent variation per annnum | | |
| Period | Tonnage Shipments | | | Ton-Mile Transport Performance | | |
| | Oil | Dry Cargo | Total | Oil | Dry Cargo | Total |
| --- | --- | --- | --- | --- | --- | --- |
| 1965-66 | +10 | + 6 | + 8 | + 7 | + 7 | + 7 |
| 1967-68 | +13 | + 7 | +10 | +20 | +10 | +16 |
| 1969-70 | +15 | + 7 | +11 | +15 | +11 | +14 |
| 1971-72 | +10 | + 5 | + 7 | +16 | + 4 | +11 |
| 1973-74 | - 1 | +10 | + 4 | + 4 | +11 | + 6 |
| 1974-75 | - 8 | - 4 | - 6 | - 8 | - 3 | - 6 |
| Average 1965-75 | + 7 | + 5 | + 6 | +12 | + 8 | +10 |
| 1975-76 | +12 | + 6 | + 9 | +15 | + 4 | +11 |
| 1977-78 | - 2 | + 5 | + 2 | - 7 | + 5 | - 3 |
| 1979-80 | - 9 | + 4 | - 3 | - 12 | + 5 | - 5 |
| 1980-81 | - 12 | 0 | - 5 | - 12 | + 1 | - 6 |
| Average 1975 - 81 | - 1 | + 4 | + 2 | - 3 | + 5 | + 1 |

British trends in manning costs have been particularly disturbing in that they have risen more rapidly than those of many other European countries. This situation is partly the result of high wage settlements and improvements in fringe benefits (such as increased leave entitlement). These characterized the period of high inflation following the first oil crisis. At the same time, UK flag companies were slow in achieving manning reductions. To some extent, this reflects Britain's comparatively low manning costs at the start of the recession. They made the need for crew reductions appear less than urgent. Whatever the reasons, a representative sample has shown that in too many cases British vessels are often 25 per cent or more overmanned compared with their best European competitors.[4] The outcome has been that the UK has lost its position as a relatively low-cost supplier of seafarers compared with other major Northern European shipping nations. This fact is emphasized by the data in Table 3.

TABLE 3
RELATIVE MANNING COST INDICES 1981
(Bulk Carrier $\pm$ 25,000 dwt)

| Flag | Index |
| --- | --- |
| Dutch | 100 |
| British | 82 |
| (Br/Indian crew) | |
| Norwegian | 76 |
| Italian | 76 |
| Finnish | 76 |
| Singapore | 56 |
| (Ge/Sing crew) | |
| Liberian | 54 |
| (Nor/sp crew) | |
| Hong Kong | 50 |
| (Eur/Chinese crew) | |
| Greek | 40 |
| Indian | 29 |

Source: the Impact of Inflationary Cost Tendencies on Dry Cargo Shipping Operations. H. P. Drewry (Shipping Consultants) July 1982.

Caught between low revenue and high operating costs, UK companies have been forced to sell, or scrap, labour-intensive vessels which are unlikely ever again to find profitable work under the national flag. In short, the UK fleet is contracting because assets are being switched to more lucrative activities. While regrettable in many ways, this diversification does have the merit of improving the resilience of UK shipping in the face of adverse trading conditions.

## WHY DECLINE MATTERS

The shrinkage of the fleet is a matter of concern for both economic and security reasons. Anxiety on economic grounds has focused on balance of payments and employment implications.

Shipping is a much less important source of foreign exchange than it was three decades ago but ships owned by UK operators have made a valuable net contribution of around £1,000 million per annum to the balance of payments in recent years. Unfortunately, in real terms, net earnings have fallen as the fleet has shrunk. This adverse trend is obviously of considerable importance to a nation which, for more than a century has sought to compensate for a tendency towards deficit in its merchandise transactions with the rest of the world by earning a healthy surplus on invisible trade.

The manpower implications of the fleet's shrinkage are no less disturbing than the loss in foreign exchange earnings. Since 1976, the number of seafarers has fallen from almost 82,000 to less than 50,000. In addition there have been substantial losses in shore-based jobs. Contraction on such a scale is obviously worrying in the context of recent heavy unemployment in the UK. What makes the situation even more unpalatable is that the continued loss of skilled mariners could have adverse implications for the security of the nation.

The Falklands conflict demonstrated the military importance of British shipping. More than 50 merchant vessels, manned by some 2,000 sailors, were needed to support the relatively small military force which took part in the campaign. Thus, as in previous emergencies, the Merchant Navy met the military demands made on it. However, the shrinkage of the fleet has emphasized the need to maintain a hard core capacity, not just to support the Royal Navy but also to ensure the continued supply of the UK home base.

The present official stance is that the Merchant Navy is adequate for defence purposes and that the problems of defence planning arise not so much from the size of the fleet as from its configuration.[5] Even so, if recent trends continue, then the fleet, considered economically viable by the shipping industry, could well fall below the level considered adequate for defence purposes. In such an event, the Government of the day would probably feel compelled to intervene in some way, for example, by creating a reserve fleet of specific types of merchant vessel.

To date, the decline of the Merchant Navy has not had critical consequences but the economic and military benefits from a large shipping sector are being steadily eroded. What then can be done to arrest and even reverse present trends?

While discriminatory policies have become increasingly important in shipping, it is apparent that, apart from the recession - which British shipowners are powerless to do anything about - the prime cause of the shrinkage in the UK fleet has been a loss of competitiveness. Broadly therefore, two approaches are possible: (a) for the state to intervene so as to insulate the industry from the effects of its competitive deficiencies; or (b) to encourage British shipping to respond to the pressures of the market place.

At first sight protectionist measures would seem to offer a quick solution to the problems of the shipping sector. Flag discriminatory devices, such as cargo reservation, could be introduced so as to raise the proportion of Britain's trade carried by the national fleet.[6] At the same time, the cost of operating UK vessels could be lowered by means of generous subsidies.

However, experience elsewhere suggests that protection and unconditional subsidies discourage innovation and technical change. The attempt to avoid adjustment would therefore further weaken the UK's competitive position. Moreover, protectionist measures would reduce, rather than increase, the volume of cargo available to British shipping. Unlike the fleets of many developing countries, UK vessels earn more from cross-trading than from national trade. They are therefore vulnerable to retaliation.

Apart from its adverse impact on the shipping industry, resort to protection would constitute a burden for the British economy as a whole. In effect, seaborne goods would be subject to a freight tax, an undesirable situation for a country which uses maritime transport to convey 95 per cent of its foreign trade.

Britain's approach to the problems of the shipping industry has been to reject protectionism in favour of adjustment through market forces. Measures such as cargo reservation or special subsidies have been repudiated. Instead, strenuous efforts have been made to stem the tide of protectionism, so as to leave as large a portion of maritime trade as possible free from state regulation. The European attempt to avoid government-imposed cargo reservation in trade between developed countries has therefore received the enthusiastic backing of the UK. In line with this stance, Britain has sought to dissuade the United States Government from signing bilateral shipping agreements with Third World countries.

However, where a free exchange of shipping services has not been attainable then diplomatic pressure has been used to secure a reasonable deal for national carriers. The understanding reached with the Soviet Union in 1982 provides an instance of such an initiative. The Russians have used the monopoly power of their state trading organizations to secure about 90 per cent of the United Kingdom - Soviet Union liner trade. Under the new arrangement, British vessels will be certain of a greater share of the trade.

Despite inherent problems, the approach of encouraging the industry to reshape itself is yielding results. UK companies have drastically reduced their ownership of labour-intensive vessels which, in many cases, are not in accord with the level of British crew costs. Of course, much remains to be done. Faced with a prolonged recession and an absence of additional government assistance, owners are naturally anxious to achieve greater efficiency. It is therefore imperative that items such as vessel utilization, port charges, taxation and the level of general and administrative expenses should be closely monitored. In short, good management is essential if the industry is to prosper.

In the search for lower operating costs, Merchant Navy unions are being asked to agree to reductions in manning and changes in shipboard organization. Interchangeability of ratings was introduced by UK shipowners in the 1960s; the next step is to initiate similar flexibility in the technical and supervisory grades. In addition, as the entire ships crew becomes more highly skilled it should also be possible to introduce integrated social facilities, and thus effect further savings.

Contraction of the UK fleet is a necessary response to adverse conditions.[7] Fundamental changes are taking place in shipping and the Merchant Navy must adapt to the new situation. To this end, outdated and inefficient units have been removed from the fleet. The remaining vessels are those which are likely to be in greatest demand when the market improves. British shipping will thus emerge from the present process of restructuring much reduced in size but well-placed to participate profitably in an expansion of world trade. Ultimately, continued competitiveness offers the best prospect for preserving the economic and defence benefits which the UK enjoys as the result of processing a merchant fleet.

# NOTES AND REFERENCES

1.           Though the speed reductions and over-capacity of the past decade have tended to dissipate some of the productivity gains.

2.           Liner conferences are essentially shipping cartels concerned with scheduled cargo services.

3.           H.P. Drewry (Shipping Consultants) The Impact of Inflationary Cost Tendencies on Dry Cargo Shipping Operations, July 1982, p.21.

4.           I. Sprout, House of Commons Debates (Hansard) 18 March 1983, Col. 292.

5.           Ibid, Cols. 291-292.

6.           In 1980, UK vessels carried 31 per cent of UK imports by weight and 37 per cent of exports. See Business Monitor, MR 15, July 1982, Tables 3.2(ii)and 3.2(iv).

7.           In 1982 total tonnage ordered by UK owners for UK registration amounted to only 318,000 dwt. The flow of orders could be increased by raising the tax offset level to 140 per cent, as suggested by the GeneralCouncil of British Shipping. Such a move could be justified on the premise that the present reluctance to invest in the industry denies it the means of adjust. On the other hand, the additional stimulus would not be in the long-term interest of the industry if it encouraged overexpansion.

# 22 The role of East Anglian ports

*Paper presented to the Annual Conference by*
*J. Evelyn*
*Port of Ipswich*
*December 1976 issue*

## TRADE

Recent years have displayed dramatic changes in the fortunes of Britain's ports. In particular, the apparent decline of London, Liverpool and the traditional major ports of the country has brought with it major industrial relations and financial problems as the industry has attempted to readjust to modern requirements and conditions.

The scale of change can be indicated by a simple comparison between 1965 and 1974. In 1965 the fifteen largest ports handled 86 per cent of the general cargo tonnage for the country; by 1974, those ports' share was 59 per cent. With such a marked change in market share taken with a reduction of registered dock workers in the industry from 45,728 in 1965 to 2,911 in 1974, it is no small wonder that the industry is having problems with changing its shape and size. It is, of course, easy to draw the wrong conclusions from isolated statistics and it must be recognized that the impact of the change I have illustrated varies considerably from one port to another. To some extent, some of the major ports handle large tonnages of 'non-general cargo' besides the vast tonnages of petroleum which is a category of cargo I don't intend to discuss. In those ports, the bulk cargoes have helped to cushion the rapid changes of general cargo tonnage. The fact remains that although total foreign trade excluding petroleum has grown by 19.48 per cent, for Britain as a whole, the major ports growth has been less than 4 per cent whilst the smaller ports have more than doubled their tonnage - to be precise a growth of 109 per cent.

Let us consider the changes which have taken place in those nine years. By far the most spectacular has been the unit load revolution. So much has been written and said about containerization. The technique has certainly changed the English language with its associated jargon. Words and phrases like intermodal, land/water interface and TEU have proved to be expensive words to port operators. Expensive in terms of capital investment with a reasonable container terminal costing in excess of £4 million, expensive also in the effect on mobility of the trade, since once a deep sea service becomes containerized the economics which held the conventional service in a port no longer apply and the trade is quite likely to change its terminal port. A good example is the Far East trade, traditionally handled on Merseyside but which containerized at Southampton. Since every port worth its salt makes provision for handling containers, this sort of mobility has the two-fold effect of depressing the market price for the service and allowing some terminals to remain badly under-utilized. One can with all the accuracy of hindsight look back and criticise those ports who have this excess capacity for over-investment, but in most cases this sort of criticism is facile and in any case unconstructive.

My point on mobility of deep sea trade is linked with two factors concerning Europe: firstly, the faster economic growth of Continental countries which makes them emerge as a vastly bigger market than the UK, coupled with our own drift in trade away from the traditional partners - mainly commonwealth and ex-colonial countries towards Europe and the short sea trade partners.

This means that for many deep sea trades there is a tendency for ships to make a UK call linked with a Continental call or else a Continental call with the UK being fed by trans-shipment. The growth of Southampton as the only major UK port on the deep sea route to Europe bears this out. In fact, Southampton has made the greatest gains of any UK major port -from 1,193,000 tonnes in 1965 to 3,690,000 in 1974. The growth of unit load traffic (containers and roll on/roll off) has more or less run parallel with trade growth, excluding fuels, over the past few years. For example, in 1970 total British trade (excluding fuel) was 111,266,000 tonnes of which 22,768,000 tonnes were ores and scrap. Unitized cargo accounted for 16,880,000 tonnes leaving 71,618,000 as other break bulk. By 1974 the total figure had reached 123,056,000 tonnes but ores and scrap had grown to 23,226,000 tonnes and unitized cargo to 30,640,000 tonnes leaving 69,190,000 tonnes as other cargo.

This comparison suggests that our category of other cargo had in fact dropped back by about 2.5 million tonnes during those four years (Table 1).

## TABLE 1
## BRITISH TRADE (EXCLUDING FUEL) 1970-4
### x 1,000 tonnes

|      | Total Trade | Ores and Scrap | Unitized Cargo | Remainder |
|------|------------|----------------|----------------|-----------|
| 1970 | 111,266    | 22,768         | 16,880         | 71,618    |
| 1971 | 109,300    | 20,223         | 19,307         | 69,770    |
| 1972 | 113,710    | 20,250         | 22,460         | 71,000    |
| 1973 | 126,833    | 25,729         | 28,456         | 72,648    |
| 1974 | 123,056    | 23,226         | 30,640         | 69,190    |

I mentioned earlier the change of emphasis in Britain's trade patterns. This can best be illustrated by trends in near sea and deep sea tonnages between 1965 and 1975.

Near sea is taken to be trade with the Irish Republic, EEC countries, Scandinavia, the Baltic, Iberia and the Mediterranean. Deep sea is, of course, the rest of the world: Africa, India, Arabian Gulf, Australasia, the Far East and the Americas.

Short sea trade has grown by 65 per cent against deep sea 3 per cent and perhaps more significant to the fortunes of the UK's various ports the share of total trade has grown from 47 per cent to 59 per cent. It is particularly significant to note that the fastest growing segment has been trade with the EEC - now the largest trade area.

I apologise for having used so many statistics in my paper but the growing and now dominating part played by EEC trade does account for the success of East Anglia's ports. Taken as a group, the Haven ports alone have now outstripped all other UK ports with the exception of London in non-fuel tonnage. Funnily enough, the only port in the area which was set up to give this type of service - connecting Europe to the industrial centres of Britain - was Harwich Parkeston Quay. The other ports evolved mainly to serve their own local primarily agricultural hinterlands. The Railway Company did, however, build with a view to a through transport link at Harwich.

Only in the last twenty years has Felixstowe grown to reflect the emergence of the new market and in that port its name has been made in United

States container traffic as well as the now faster growing European business. Yarmouth and Lowestoft have each more than doubled their foreign tonnage since 1965 but altogether the East Anglian ports have increased throughput almost four-fold. There has, of course, been considerable capital investment in each of the ports and most of all at Felixstowe. Capital employed quickly mounts up when land reclamation is involved and in an increasingly capital intensive industry where a single item of plant such as a straddle carrier costs around £100,000 and cranes are at half a million pounds or thereabouts. The main danger faced in this kind of market is of over-reaching the ports ability to service the loans whilst the new facility builds up to optimum working level, a very real risk since the individual ports are relatively small commercial entities.

Although road links still leave much to be desired, inland connections particularly to the Haven Ports have been steadily improved. The A12 is a dual carriageway practically all the way to London and the A45 to the Midlands has been up-graded with a number of by-passes either open, in the course of building or else at an advanced planning stage.

As well as liner services to the USA and West Africa, between them the ports offer at peak times an average of nineteen daily sailings and serve no less than 71 European destinations. Since the Haven Ports are on the direct line between Britain's industrial Midlands and Europe's most concentrated market area - the Ruhr, they can be quite reasonably called the gateway to Europe.

The future looks equally promising with EEC trade forecast to grow faster than any other sector through to the mid-1980s. By 1985 it is anticipated that the EEC will account for 39 per cent of all Britain's trade. East Anglian ports are in a prime position to serve this trade. My colleagues and I look forward to serving many of you as customers.

# 23 World-wide from the Humber

*Article by J. Francis*
*March 1975 issue*

From time immemorial the Humber has provided a series of havens for vessels trading with places overseas. Although patterns have changed time and again, the ancient ports have kept pace with the various developments. In the year 1205 it is recorded that Hull was paying large sums in import duties and before the end of the century was England's third port in respect of customs dues, at that time London being the leader and Saint Botolph (Boston) second. Hull still claims third place today. Richard II, in 1382, granted what is now the River Hull as a haven to the burgesses of Hulme, the beginning of the name of Kingston-upon-Hull.

## DEVELOPMENT AT HULL

Over the past two centuries an extensive docks system has grown up at Kingston-upon-Hull. What was known as the Queen's Dock was opened in 1778, serving until 1930 when the site was filled in, later being converted into pleasure gardens. In 1809 came the Humber Dock, to be followed 20 years later by Prince's Dock. Between 1791 and 1824 the traffic rose from 181,500 tons to 365,867 tons. Regular services from Hull to Hamburg commenced in 1819. The coming of the railway to Hull in 1840 was followed by the construction of the Railway Dock. Humber, Princes and Railway Docks have been closed and later were sold to Hull Corporation.

Victoria Dock came in 1850 and by the time the next new dock was opened in 1869 (Albert Dock) the annual traffic had reached two-million tons. The early 1880s saw the opening of the William Wright and the St. Andrew's Docks. The latter, dedicated to the patron saint of fishermen, was quickly given over to the sole use of the fishing industry. Albert and William Wright were closed to commercial shipping in 1972 and it was proposed to move the fishing activities there from their present location. Alexandra Dock opened in 1885 and in 1907 the demand for quick turnround for provision vessels brought into being 2,500 ft Riverside Quay. This was completely destroyed by enemy action in 1941, to be replaced in 1959 by a shorter concrete construction. Just before the start of World War I the King George Dock commenced operations. Here the £27½ million Princess Margaret Terminal was opened on October 30 1974. The first of the Salt End Jetties, location of the petrol and chemical industries, started in 1914. The £6¾ million Queen Elizabeth Dock was inaugurated by H.M. the Queen in 1969.

## GRIMSBY, IMMINGHAM AND GOOLE

On the south side of the Humber is Grimsby, the oldest chartered borough in the country, dating back to 1202. Its twin community of Immingham is a twentieth century creation although that was the point from which the Pilgrim Fathers sailed to the Netherlands in 1608 before setting off across the Atlantic a few years later. Some 50 miles inland from the North Sea is Goole, a tribute to 19th century enterprise which developed the district from 1820 onwards as an outlet to the sea for the Aire and Calder Canal and its connections with the growing industrial areas of South Yorkshire and the East Midlands.

## TRADE

Many members of the Institute will already be shipping via the Humber to many destinations; for the benefit of others we give a summary later in this review of the freight liners working out of the different ports. Figures for 1973 show total traffic, inward and outward, through the Humber ports of around 33 million tonnes, 14 million of this being petroleum passing through Immingham. Passengers numbered close on 320,000. Apart from 1¼ million tonnes of petroleum, principal cargoes through Hull were: outward, chemicals and fertilisers, iron and steel, machinery, cereals and other foodstuffs;

inward, timber cereals, molasses, sugar and other foodstuffs, oilseeds and nuts, building materials, iron and steel.

From Grimsby the chief outward cargoes are iron, steel, machinery and other manufactured goods, and chemicals. Inward the emphasis is upon timber, woodpulp, iron and steel, foodstuffs, dairy produce and fish.

Outward from Immingham go petroleum, coal, coke and patent fuels, iron and steel goods, chemicals and fertilisers, vehicles, machinery and other manufactured goods. Leading inward cargoes in 1973 - after petroleum - were iron ore and roasted iron pyrites (3.2 million tonnes), followed by chemicals and fertilisers, iron and steel, non-ferrous ores, woodpulp and timber.

Goole's main outward cargoes were coal, coke and fuels, iron and steel, chemicals and fertilisers, and building materials. Inward the leaders were iron and steel, timber, wood and paper manufacturers, chemicals and fertilisers, machinery and vehicles. The last-mentioned include many Renaults which are imported by means of a roll-off service.


## PASSENGERS

For the visitor to Kingston-upon-Hull the principal passenger services that offer the possibility of a quick trip to the continent at reasonable cost are of obvious interest. Passenger services from the Humber have long made a strong appeal to travellers from the North of England but the development of the vehicle ferries over the past decade has brought the great upsurge in this traffic.

From the King George Dock, at Hull, North Sea Ferries operate a passenger roll on/off service seven times a week to Rotterdam and three times to Zeebrugge. Similar services are run by Tor Line from Immingham Dock, three times weekly to Gothenburg and once weekly to Amsterdam

North Sea Ferries drive on/off ferry between Hull and Rotterdam (Europort) commenced in 1965. This organization is a consortium of British, Dutch and German shipping interests, the largest holding being that of the P&O with 45 per cent. They have built up the trade with the 4,000 ton "Norwave" and "Norwind" on the Rotterdam run. These two ships have recently been replaced by the 12,500 ton "Norland" and "Norstar", which are stated to be the largest of their kind in Europe and carry some 1,240 passengers with berths for 1,072. The smaller ships, each carrying 249 passengers, have been transferred to the Hull-Zeebrugge route.

The run between Hull, King George dock and Rotterdam Europort Beneluxhaven operates daily including Sundays, leaving the terminals at

18.00 hr and arriving at the destination at 08.00 hr the following morning. The Hull, King George Dock - Zeebrugge Prins Filipsdok service departs at 18.00 hr, reaching the destination at 09.00 hr. In each case these are supplemented by a freight ro/ro ferry having passenger accommodation for a dozen; these vessels can carry hazardous cargo not accepted by the line's passenger ships.

Tor Line has been operating the Immingham-Gothenburg route since 1966. This summer they are due to bring into service the 15,500 ton "Tor Britannia" and a sister ship of similar size.

At the time of writing this feature, the "Tor Anglia" and "Tor Hollandia" work the Immingham Dock to Gothenburg service and the Immingham-Amsterdam. Currently there are three sailings weekly to the former destination and one to the latter. For passengers there are coach connections from Gothenburg to Stockholm; from Stockholm there are frequent ferry links to Turku (Finland).

"We have more than doubled our passenger traffic on the Immingham-Gothenburg route during the past five years," said Mr. Andrew Olszowski, "and are confident about the future." Tor plan to carry over 320,000 passengers on their North Sea routes during 1975. The new ships will accommodate 1,234 passengers with berthing for 722. Vehicle decks can accommodate (say) 400 cars and 13 trailers or 50 cars and 65 trailers. Car ferries sail from the Humber to Gothenburg on Mondays, Thursdays and Sundays, the passage taking 25 hours. Amsterdam sailings are on Friday at 20.30 hr. the destination being reached in 13 hours.

Altogether Tor have 12 freight-only services a week out of Immingham, all of the roll-on/off class. They serve Gothenburg, Halmstad, Helsingborg, Copenhagen and Rotterdam. In co-operation with Fred Olsen Lines and Norwegian Transport Services there are weekly facilities to Oslo and Western Norway respectively.

Starting at the beginning of 1975 a new roll-on/off merger was concluded with Nike line of Sweden joining Tor. Behind this development are the Salen shipping group, now with a two-thirds share-holding in Tor Line AB of Gothenburg, and Transatlantic of Sweden who hold the remaining third. KNSM of Holland who previously had a quarter share in Tor sold their holding to Transatlantic as at the end of 1974.

From Grimsby's Royal Dock, Esbjerg has two or three roll on/off services weekly by DFDS A/S. A weekly lift on/off service is provided by Norwegian Transport Services to Stavanger, Sandnes, Haugesund, Skudesneshavn and Bergen. There are thrice-weekly life/-on/off sailings from Hull's King George Dock jointly by Ellerman Wilson and Svea Line to

Gothenburg. Similar frequencies apply to the departures from the Alexandra Dock by the Royal Netherlands Line to Amsterdam and the Argo Line to Hamburg/Bremen. From Hull's Queen Elizabeth Dock a lift-on and roll-on service is provided to Leningrad every 10-12 days by the Baltic Shipping Co. From the Queen Elizabeth Dock there are weekly sailings, all lift-on/off, to Helsingborg and Copenhagen by Svea Line, to Oslo, Fredrikstad and Larvik by Ellermans, to Nantyluoto/Turku and to Helsinki/Kotka by Finhumber Ferries. Twice-weekly there are departures by Deutsche Seerederei to Rostock and Hamburg, also by Ellermans-DFDS (UK) Joint to Esbjerg. Nantyluto is served every ten days by the Meri Shipping Line.

## CARGO SERVICES

Connections to all parts of the world are offered by the Humber cargo liner services. Cunard Brocklebank jointly with P&O serve Ethiopia, the territory of Afars and Issas, Jordan, the Maldive Islands, Saudi Arabia, the Seychelles, Somali Democratic Republic, the Sudan, Yemen Arab Republic and the People's Democratic Republic of Yemen, all from Hull. Ethiopia is also covered by Ethopian Shipping Lines. The Termaris Line provides for Algeria and Tunisia, from Goole. Gracechurch Line ships go from Goole to Greece, Italy and Libya. Ben Line carry from Hull to destinations in Indonesia, Japan, Thailand, Hong Kong, Korea, Malaysia, the Phillippines, Sabah, Sarawak, Singapore and Taiwan. Bennett Line vessels leave Goole for Belgium and France, Kirsten Line from Hull for West Germany and the Rhine. Brussels-Goole Line also sail for Belgium.

Pacific ports of Canada are reached from Hull by the Euro-Pacific Line, also the Panama Canal zone, and the US Pacific ports. Ellerman City Lines cover Cyprus, from Hull, also Greece, Israel, Malta and Portugal. From Hull Jugolinija operate to Yugoslavia, also the Italian ports of the Adriatic. The Caribbean and Pacific ports of Central America and the West Indies are the concern of Hapag-Lloyd, Hull. Holland is served by SSM lines from Goole and Grimsby. Consortium Line from Goole goes to Morocco and Spain.

Among other services are those to Brazil (Lloyd Brasilerio, Empresa de Navegacao Alanca SA, and L. Gigueiredo Navegacao, all from Hull), China (Toho Line, Hull), Denmark (Bork Line form Goole), France - Rouen (Sequana Maritime from Goole), East Germany (Deutsche Seerederei from Goole), Iceland (Samband Line from Hull), India (British India Steam Navigation from Immingham), Indonesia (Indonesian National Line from Hull), Iran (Caspian - Volga - Balt Line from Hull), Norway (EWL - Transport division of Ellerman Lines, Goole, also from Grimsby by EWL, and by Fred Olsen Line, also Nordenfjeldske Line), Pakistan (British India Steam Navigation, also National Shipping Corporation of Karachi, from Immingham), Poland (Polish Ocean Lines and United Baltic Corporation-joint, from Hull), Sri Lanka (Ceylon Shipping Corporation, from Hull), Sweden (Berg Line, also Mathies Reederei Swedendienst GmbH, from Goole), Sweden (EWL from Grimsby), USSR (Soviet Line from Hull).

## BACAT SYSTEM

Of particular interest was the arrival of the Bacat system in the Humber last year.

This is designed to give a regular through service from the inland waterway system of the North Midlands and East Yorkshire to the waterways of Germany and the North European area. "Bacat 1" is of semi-catamaran design with a closed bow, twin hulls and an open stern, the carrying capacity being ten Bacat barges of about 145 tons each and three Lash barges of about 370 tons. The object of the system is to keep handling costs to a minimum and to avoid trans-shipment troubles. The Lash barges can work on the Humber and its connections as far as Gainsborough and Selby. With the Bacat barges that are designed specially for the narrower English waterways it is possible to reach destinations much further inland such as Leeds, Wakefield, Rotherham and Nottingham. Scope of the Bacat operations on the Continent includes Belgium, the Netherlands, Luxemburg, France along the Rhine, Germany and Switzerland; in Britain the Tees is served in addition to the Humber.

The Port of Goole is linked to the inland waterway system, the busy Trent and the Yorkshire Ouse. It was set up as the terminal point of the Aire and Calder Canal in 1826, giving connections to Knottingley, Leeds, Sheffield and South Yorkshire. Britain's most inland port, Goole actually stands on the Ouse, eight miles west of the confluence of the Trent and Ouse at the head of the Humber estuary.

Even to many experienced transport men commercial inland waterway traffic is a thing of the past. In this region, however, water-borne transport can be seen in full swing, with hundreds of thousands of tons carried regularly by this means.

# SHIPBUILDING

Before leaving Humberside one should touch briefly on shipbuilding, not an industry for which the area is well-known to the world at large. As in any centre of shipping there is a substantial quantity of repair and reconditioning work. In addition, no fewer than 2,000 are employed in new construction, for Humberside is a great producer of ships up to 350 ft. length including advanced types of fishing vessels, naval craft, off-shore oil rig supply ships and tugs.

Building facilities extend from Hull to Beverley, to Barrow-on-Humber, Goole and Selby, and to Thorne and Knottingley on the Yorkshire canals. When I was in the neighbourhood a few months ago the Hessle yard of the Richard Dunston group was constructing two 3,500 ton d.w. chemical carriers, the largest to be built there. With the coming of the Becat service over 50 dumb barges for this system were constructed by the Yorkshire Dry Dock Co. Ltd.

# 24 Deep-sea freight trans-shipment and the Channel Tunnel

*Article by M. Asteris*
*Portsmouth Polytechnic*
*August/September 1990 issue*

## INTRODUCTION

As June 1993, the scheduled date for the opening of the £7.6 billion Channel Tunnel draws closer, the debate concerning its impact on freight movement in Europe grows more intense. The effect of the Fixed Link on the pattern of North-West Europe's deep-sea cargo movements is an important aspect of this debate. Since the mid-1960s, trans-shipment - the movement of UK deep-sea trade via mainland European ports, rather than on direct services to and from this country - has increased. This is the antithesis of reverse-trans-shipment, whereby, until a few decades ago, Great Britain handled part of the Continent's commerce with the rest of the world. Some commentators regard the advent of the Tunnel as an opportunity for Britain to regain an element of this former 'European Gateway' role. Others argue that the Tunnel will greatly facilitate trans-shipment of UK freight, thereby threatening to turn this country into little more than a maritime appendage of Continental Europe.

These conflicting forecasts reflect the uniqueness of the permanent link. In the absence of suitable data from which to extrapolate, a wide range of assumptions are possible, leading to a spectrum of outcomes.Nevertheless, while the threads of experience are thinly spread, it may be possible to pull sufficient of them together to shed instructive insights on future developments. Indeed, the Marquis of Halifax, once remarked that the best qualification for a prophet is a good memory. With this observation in mind, the purpose of the present paper is to examine the historical record on trans-shipment and then, in the light of its lessons, to try and assess the Tunnel's likely impact on the pattern of deep-sea freight movements.

To summarize briefly, this article argues that, in terms of the trans-shipment of deep-sea freight, the post-war era can be divided into two phases. The first witnessed the demise of Britain's historic role as a gateway for Europe freight. The second, triggered by containerization, was characterized by a growing tendency to transport UK long-distance cargoes via mainland European terminals such as Rotterdam. During both of these phases, labour problems seriously blunted the competitive edge of Britain's ports. The opening of the Channel Tunnel will herald a third phase by increasing the attractiveness of using shuttle-service feeder transport systems for container freight. Britain's ports will, therefore, have to provide at least as credible a service as that offered by Continental rivals if they are to retain existing deep-sea freight and win new trade. In this context, the abolition of the National Dock Labour Scheme is a very important development because it paves the way for a more efficient use of resources.

## BRITAIN'S RE-EXPORT TRADE

For some 200 years, from the mid-18th century onwards Britain enjoyed a substantial re-export trade. Cargo from overseas would enter UK ports, particularly London and Liverpool, and then be trans-shipped immediately, or after some degree of grading or processing. In essence, therefore, Britain constituted a freight interchange, mainly linking North American and European ports. This intermediary trade was facilitated by low handling charges because dock labour was extremely cheap.

However, as other nations acquired merchant fleets and improved their port facilities, it was inevitable that transiting through the UK should decline. From around 20 per cent of total British exports in the late 19th century, re-exports dwindled to less than 5 per cent during the 1950s. By the close of the 1960s, the entreport trade had almost ceased.

# CONTAINERIZATION AND THE GROWTH OF TRANS-SHIPMENT

The virtual end of the re-export trade coincided with the introduction of containerization, whereby capital intensive methods of handling general cargo rapidly replaced labour intensive systems from the mid-1960s onwards. The mobility available to freight in unitized form was such that substantial trans-shipment via the UK or near-Continental ports could once again be contemplated. Moreover, the situation with respect to feeder routes was, in many ways, similar to the present. Then as now, cross-Channel services were about to be revolutionized. Today the Tunnel is the instrument of change: two decades ago it was the roll-on/roll-off freight system which, apart from a few train ferries, did not exist prior to 1966.

In principle at least, the mid-1960s thus appeared to hold out the tantalizing possibility of reviving Britain's former role as a landbridge between North America and the mainland of Europe. In fact, no such revival has occurred.

The growth of trans-shipment via near-Continental terminals - particularly Rotterdam and Antwerp - has, on the other hand, deprived British ports of deep-sea freight which they would otherwise have handled. As early as 1968 almost 3 per cent (by weight) of UK long-distance imports were being transported via Dutch ports. By 1984 these ports, together with Antwerp, had raised their share to 15 per cent. In that year trans-shipment also accounted for some 8 per cent of exports to deep-sea countries. Averages, however, tend to disguise the fact that on certain important routes the degree of market penetration has been far higher. This point is emphasised by Table 1, which shows UK trade trans-shipped through the Netherlands and Antwerp by deep-sea region. For example, it is clear from the table that in 1984 no less than 42 per cent of UK imports from the USA were handled at Dutch and Belgian ports, compared with 25 per cent in 1976. Ironically, therefore, trans-shipment of UK trade is most pronounced in imports from a region for which this country once provided a landbridge to the Continent.

TABLE 1
PERCENTAGE OF UK DEEP-SEA TRANS-SHIPMENT VIA THE
NETHERLANDS AND ANTWERP, BY REGION, 1976 AND 1984

|  | 1976 | | 1984 | |
|  | Imports | Exports | Imports | Exports |
| --- | --- | --- | --- | --- |
| USA | 25 | 8 | 42 | 3 |
| Canada | 3 | 5 | 9 | 9 |
| Australasia | 31 | 2 | 27 | 4 |
| Central & South American | 2 | 6 | 8 | 6 |
| Far East | 17 | 6 | 22 | 17 |
| Gulf | - | 5 | - | 27 |
| Africa | 1 | 3 | 7 | 15 |
| India & Pakistan | 3 | 7 | 26 | 16 |

Source: Derived from Trans-shipment of UK Deep-Sea Trade 1976-84, British Ports Association and Department of Transport, 1986, Table 8.

It is clear that containerization acted as a catalyst for the rapid growth of trans-shipment while failing to reactivate reverse-trans-shipment. What accounts for this unbalanced outcome? In essence, the explanation is to be found in the contrasting experience of the British and near-Continental ports in recent decades.

The volume of cargo handled by ports such as Rotterdam has risen dramatically since the 1950s. This has produced a vast and highly competitive shipping market, yielding attractive freight rates. For example, on the North Atlantic route, container rates are often 10 or 20 per cent below British levels. The Continental ports also offer low port charges as a consequence of high levels of operating efficiency and generous subsidies. While Britain adopts a narrowly commercial approach to the ports sector, most Continental nations tend towards a 'socially orientated' philosophy. This encourages substantial assistance for items such as breakwaters, land reclamation and navigational aids. As a result of lower costs, port charges for container traffic on the North European seaboard are often around two-thirds of those prevailing in the UK. The final advantage of ports such as Rotterdam is that they have earned an enviable reputation for reliability and quality of service.

214

In contrast to their Continental counterparts, Britain's traditional major ports were, until very recently, caught in a vicious circle of stagnant trade, high freight rates, high port charges, low efficiency and poor reliability. The implications of this state of affairs in terms of shipowners' costs and port competitiveness were very significant. Consequently, when, in order to derive adequate economies of scale, container lines were compelled to make extensive use of hub-and-spoke systems, they tended to select mainland terminals for their deep-sea vessels. 'Peripheral' areas such as the United Kingdom were catered for by means of feeder services.

The result of this pattern of operations was a decline in direct liner services to many UK ports. Where calls continued to be made, the desire to serve both Britain and the Continent with one vessel implied a preference for ports on the South East coast because of their geographical juxtaposition to mainland European terminals. The West coast ports, whose initial expectations of containerization had been high, thus found themselves in a very weak position with respect to major traffic flows.

## LABOUR PROBLEMS

After due allowance is made for geographical factors and historical trends, it is evident from the discussion thus far that the post-war demise of Britain's re-export trade and the growth of trans-shipment can be attributed to relatively high costs, low efficiency and poor reliability. Lamentable industrial relations made a major contribution to this trio of ills.

An excess supply of manual labour, resulting in low wages and poor working conditions, had long been a prominent feature of the ports industry. The National Dock Labour Scheme, introduced in 1947, was an attempt to redress the long standing imbalance between workers and employers. Utilizing a registration arrangement introduced in 1940, the Scheme covered all the significant UK ports of the early post-war years. It allowed only registered employers to employ Registered Dock Workers and provided for joint management and trade union control of the register. Moreover, 'dock work' was reserved for Registered Dockers, who were guaranteed a minimum wage even if there was no work to offer them.

Far from heralding an era of industrial peace in the docks, the introduction of the Scheme was the prelude to a long period of unrest. Sadly, labour difficulties in the ports epitomised what became known as the 'British Disease'. The 1965 Devlin report considered that the main cause of unrest was the continuance of elements of the casual labour system. Decasualization was therefore implemented nationally in 1967.

Unfortunately, this action coincided with the start of containerization which required a huge reduction in the dock labour force. Understandably, the dockers resisted the loss of work, especially when it took the form of a transfer of some dock functions to inland depots. Between 1965 and 1969, during the early stages of containerization, more working days were lost per thousand employees than in any other industry, including motor vehicles. These were hardly the conditions in which Continental shippers could entertain trans-shipment via UK ports!

## THE IMPACT OF THE TUNNEL

From the outline of events presented in this article, it emerges that, in terms of the trans-shipment of deep-sea freight, the post-war era can be divided into two phases. First, that to the mid-sixties, which witnessed the demise of Britain's residual European gateway role; and second, the period since then, characterized by the growing tendency to transport long-distance cargo via Continental terminals. The opening of the Tunnel in 1993 will herald a third phase, by increasing the attractiveness to shipping lines and their clients of using a shuttle-service/feeder transport system for container freight.

The Tunnel will enhance the attractiveness of trans-shipment in two ways. Firstly, via a price effect - it will be cheaper, in real terms, to move freight across the Channel. How much cheaper will be determined by market forces. Tariff reductions will reflect both the efficiency of the Eurotunnel system and the impact of its opening on existing modes of transport. In particular, the greatly increased competition will force ferry operators to become more efficient or risk being left without an adequate market. In recognition of this fact, operators are introducing much larger vessels than hitherto on major routes so as to take advantage of economies of scale. Moreover, P&O European Ferries, the company with the largest ferry fleet, has cut crew costs (the largest single item of ship operating costs) by introducing less expensive manning arrangements. Once the Tunnel is open, the major companies are also likely to be permitted to co-operate closely so as to rationalize their sailing schedules.

In the second place, trans-shipment will be encouraged as a result of the Tunnel's non-price effects. These will consist of three related benefits: time savings, increased reliability and convenience. The impact of these non-price effects will be determined to a considerable degree by the extent to which transport routes on either side of the Channel are upgraded in the near future. In this connection, much will depend on the response of British Rail. Its freight activities have been in retreat for several decades, so it will require time to adjust to the radical improvement in its market position following the opening of the Tunnel.

Between them, the price and non-price effects of the Fixed Link will create the potential for greater indirect movement of deep-sea freight. This potential will be enhanced by the completion of the Single European Market by the end of 1992. This will eliminate the frontier and regulatory impediments which governments have traditionally placed in the way of freight movement in Europe. In essence, therefore, the removal of barriers, both physical and governmental, will create a unitary freight market in North West Europe for the first time in history. In such circumstances, it is inevitable that interport competition for deep-sea cargo will intensify. In particular, the Tunnel will extend the number of ports in direct competition on major trade routes. For instance, it is already evident that French ports, such as Le Havre and Dunkirk view a fixed link as effectively enabling them to add the UK to their international hinterland.

How then will the Tunnel effect the pattern of trans-shipment? Are we about to witness a renaissance in reverse-trans-shipment, together with a winning back of some of the UK freight which currently uses Continental terminals, or will an even larger portion of Britain's deep-sea trade migrate across the Channel?

## GATEWAY STUDIES

Unfortunately, recent research findings strongly indicate that the cost and time savings likely to be derived from reverse trans-shipment following the opening of the Fixed Link will be insufficient to justify its introduction on any scale. For example, in its 1987 report 'The European Gateway', Transmodal Industries Research tested the hypothesis that carriage of deep-sea freight via the Fixed Link could replace direct calls on the Continent. The analysis was based on a container vessel with a capacity of 2,000 TEUs (Twenty-foot equivalent units) achieving a load factor of 90 per cent. Stevedoring costs were excluded, thereby making the implicit assumption that handling costs are the same at UK and Continental ports. The results of the work are set out in Table 2.

217

## TABLE 2
### COST PER TEU BETWEEN USA AND EUROPEAN INLAND
### DESTINATIONS ($)

| Port | Netherlands | Belgium | Germany | France | Austria | Switzerland |
|------|-------------|---------|---------|--------|---------|-------------|
| Rotterdam | 217 | 233 | 260 | 284 | 440 | 400 |
| Clyde | 394 | 374 | 414 | 386 | 532 | 492 |
| Liverpool | 337 | 317 | 357 | 329 | 475 | 435 |

Source: Transmodal Industries Research, The European Gateway, 1987, p.4.

The figures in this tabulation indicate that savings in sea costs to all major European destinations were insufficient to make either the Clyde or Liverpool competitive with Rotterdam on the basis of price. Moreover, reduced inventory costs were unlikely to compensate shippers for the additional expense of using a west coast port unless one assumed high interest rates and/or cargoes of very high value, which tend to be the preserve of air freight services. The overall conclusion of the study was that there could be some scope for a premium service calling at Liverpool or the Clyde. Even so, on the basis of prevailing prices, the potential market is very restricted, mainly because of the high costs of land transport. The negative results of the Transmodal research with respect to establishing a landbridge to Europe were supported by the 'Eurowestport: Prefeasibility Study' carried out in 1987 for the Clyde Port Authority. This investigated whether it would be economically feasible to use the Clyde as a forward terminal for European trade with North America. It concluded that....'from a practical and economic point of view all shipping lines and most freight forwarders saw the prospect of a Eurowestport on the Clyde as unattractive'.

## ABOLITION OF THE DOCK LABOUR SCHEME

Aside from any possible European Gateway implications, the advent of the Tunnel will constitute a major challenge to the ports in terms of retaining existing deep-sea trade and regaining some of that which has been lost. Post-war history teaches that success in this respect will be determined by the ability to offer at least as credible a service, in terms of price, quality and

218

reliability, as that offered by Continental competitors. What are the prospects of this happening?

The UK ports have enjoyed rapid increases in efficiency during the past two decades, but in the absence of satisfactory data on productivity differences between ports the extent of the relative improvement in their position is far from clear. European terminals have certainly not been standing still since the late 60s, so average performance in the UK remains significantly below that of leading competitors.

The debilitating effect of the National Dock Labour Scheme has been a major factor in producing this regrettable state of affairs. The rigidities of the system resulted in highly inefficient practices. The most common was one in which, as a result of over-manning, up to a third of a gang employed to load or unload a ship could be absent at any one time. Another custom was to pair a registered docker with any worker brought on to the docks. Port employers claimed that, in aggregate, arrangements of this sort added perhaps 12 per cent to costs.

So as to escape the inflexible arrangements of the Scheme, shippers made increasing use of non-scheme ports - their share of cargo rose from 10 per cent to nearly 30 per cent in the 20 years to the late 80s - and trans-shipment via the Continent. Recent trends in the ports industry are therefore not simply a response to changes in the geographical and commodity composition of UK trade.

Faced with the threat of losing much of their throughput, major ports such as Liverpool and Southampton produced commendable performance improvements within existing arrangements. Even so, port employers had long sought the removal of the artificial constraints imposed by the Scheme. Its abolition was therefore welcomed as an important step in meeting the increased competition arising from the completion of the Single European Market and the opening of the Channel Tunnel. Ending the arrangement has given port managers the flexibility to shed excess labour and alter working practices so as to achieve rapid improvements in productivity.

In due course, these changes will be reflected in more competitive port charges, which will encourage those ports which were never part of the scheme to trim their tariffs. Termination of the Scheme thus implies that British ports will be at less of a cost disadvantage than hitherto in competing with foreign rivals. Nonetheless, there will continue to be a discrepancy in port costs as a result of differences in financial regimes. Unfortunately, the European Commission does not regard port subsidies as a matter demanding urgent attention. From the perspective of the British ports industry, however, it is important that, where possible competitive distortions should be removed.

## CONCLUSION

In examining trans-shipment trends this article has not attempted to make detailed predictions. Rather the intention has been to provide the background against which qualified judgements can be made.

Looking back over the period since 1945, it is clear that improvements in transport facilitated the transfer of an important segment of Britain's port activity to the Continent. Fortunately, there are grounds for believing that by 1993 the ports industry will be more competitive than hitherto. Relative retardation offers the opportunity to achieve spectacular productivity improvements following the abolition of the National Dock Labour Scheme. Hence, though the development of even a limited European gateway role is open to question, Britain's ocean terminals are likely to prove sufficiently competitive to prevent this country degenerating into a maritime appendage of the Continent following the opening of the Fixed Link.

# Section Four
# Air Transport

The final group of reprints commences with an overview by Evans of Britain's internal air services during the 1950s. The significance of this chapter is that it underlines the vast changes that have taken place in British civil aviation during the intervening period. The two following chapters, by Childs and Tilsley, respectively, explore the advantages of air freight, which has expanded dramatically since the end of the Second World War. Next, Lawson's 1974 paper explains why the UK needs an aircraft industry and sketches the background to the Concorde airliner.

The extremely rapid growth in air travel has been accompanied by the evolution of complex fare structures. Hanlon (chapter 29) explains why this has happened and examines the link between pricing policy and the economic difficulties faced by international airlines. Chapter 30 focuses on the likely benefits and possible risks of liberalizing Europe's passenger airline industry. It contends that extensive reform of the regulatory framework is highly desirable.

The two concluding works are concerned with airports. In his second contribution to this section, Hanlon identifies the growing importance of HUB airports as one of the clearest trends to emerge from airline deregulation. Recently, congestion at Britain's major terminals has become a fairly frequent occurence at certain times of the year. In the light of this fact, Spurling in the final chapter considers the role that the price mechanism might play in alleviating capacity constraints by altering demand patterns.

# 25 Britain's domestic air services

*Paper presented to the Southampton Centre by*
*L.J. Evans*
*April 1960 issue*

First, a little about the history of domestic flights - that is those on which passengers, mail or freight are carried from one or more points to other points within Great Britain. The first such flight recorded was made in August 1910, when mail was carried from Blackpool to Southport and then in 1911 a cargo of Osram lamps was flown from Shoreham to Hove - but these seem to have been once only efforts.

For a fortnight or so in the autumn of 1911 the Coronation Mail or Aerial Post was flown between Hendon and Windsor. Attempts to fly domestic services with any regularity then ceased until after the First World War when throughout the summer of 1919 a service was maintained for passengers between Manchester, Southport and Blackpool. This is generally accepted as the first domestic air service. Thereafter in October 1922, a service was started from London to Manchester which lasted until March 1924. This is listed as the first sustained domestic air service. From 1925 until the outbreak of World War II in 1939 many more services were started, a large number of which failed for lack of support and from competition with the railways and road transport, both of which were then practically as fast as many of the aircraft of the period.

The aircraft used have been vastly improved during the fifty years since the first service was flown. The small biplanes with open cockpits seating a maximum of four persons were replaced by slightly larger aircraft after the First World War. These flew at only a few hundred feet.

Today fully pressurized aircraft seating up to 58 passengers and cruising at heights in excess of 20,000 feet at over 300 mph are in use. The main burden is borne by the American Douglas DC3 twin piston-engined aircraft which has now been in service for some 24 years and is used by the majority of British airlines operating domestic flights. It is capable of flying into and out of airfields with only grass runways. Larger planes require hard runways of concrete or asphalt. Other aircraft in use vary from the twin-engined De Havilland Dove, seating only 8 passengers up to the four-engined Lockheed Constellation and Vickers Viscount seating in the region of 60 persons.

In common with all forms of transport the problem is to operate vehicles - which after all include aeroplanes - capable of lifting the largest possible loads but the limiting factors insofar as air transport is concerned are the sizes of the available airfields and the strength of the runways, whether of grass or hard construction.

British European Airways provide all the year round passenger services within the United Kingdom between London, Scotland, Northern and Southern Ireland. Additionally, flights are made between Scotland and Ireland and various provincial towns and cities.

Those who benefit particularly from the regular air services are, however, the inhabitants of the many islands served by BEA, for instance, the Isle of Man, the Western Isles, Channel Isles, Orkney and Shetland.

Generally speaking, services to the various islands are well patronized. Even in the far North of Scotland it is necessary to employ two aircraft as far as Orkney due to the amount of passenger traffic, only the last leg of the journey to Shetland being flown by one aircraft.

In the islands the limiting effect of the airfields is a problem - only the Isle of Man and Jersey can be reached by Viscount airliners but the runway at Guernsey is being extended for that purpose. In Orkney and Shetland use is made of former wartime airfields with concrete runways but at Barra in the Hebrides, landings are governed by the tides, the aerodrome being a convenient stretch of sandy beach.

To serve Barra and a number of other Scottish Islands, BEA maintain two DH Heron 15-seater airliners and, similarly, the service from Penzance to the Scilly Isles is flown by three 7-seater de Havilland biplanes kept especially for that particular job.

Helicopters, the only form of aircraft currently in service which can take off and land vertically, are from time to time hailed as the ideal vehicles to operate inter city routes or between the centres of cities and the major airports which serve them. So far, however, helicopters have not established themselves on any particular service for a prolonged period. They have been used

224

to carry passengers between London and London airport, between London and Birmingham and for a short period flew into Southampton each weekday from London. British European Airways, which operated these flights, looked upon them as experimental. The aircraft only carried 4 passengers and the timing of the flights was such that a person arriving in Southampton by helicopter from London Airport had only a quarter of an hour or so to transact any business before boarding the aircraft again for the return flight.

The GPO, in co-operation with the BEA Helicopter Unit, have also carried out experiments in East Anglia where mails were flown from outlying districts. However, the saving in time did not warrant the heavy cost of trans-shipping the mail from vans into the aircraft and back again into vans to finish its journey.

The question of whether it is worthwhile to travel by air between two places on the mainland which are less than 200 miles apart, other than as a means of gaining flying experience, is debatable - especially if the sector flown is part of, or an extension of an international service. In order to see for myself how well patronized was the Cardiff-Paris service of Cambrian Airways I flew from Bristol to Southampton. I chose to go to the airport by public transport to arrive by the specified time but here the fun began as, although my flight was to end at Southampton, the aircraft with the majority of its passengers was to travel to Paris. Also due to the intensive operation of the aircraft, when it arrived to take on passengers at Bristol for Paris it had flown from Jersey and still had passengers aboard for Cardiff. As a result all passengers had to pass through Customs before boarding the plane.

After a score or so passengers had been processed we boarded the plane which landed at Cardiff Airport within a quarter of an hour. Here everyone was asked to leave the aircraft and walk to the reception building where all passengers, whether travelling only to Southampton or abroad to Paris, were introduced to an immigration officer. This occupied about twenty minutes which followed by a flight of only forty minutes gave a total of approximately 2¾ hours to cover the 80 miles or so between the centre of Bristol and Southampton Airport.

On the flight just described and a similar one made a year or so ago from Southampton to Bristol my relations with the Customs and Immigration Officials were most friendly but before the flight to Bristol it was a little disconcerting to be asked to declare how much money I was carrying. Experiences such as the foregoing tend to discourage potential air travellers no less than the other hazards, for example, air sickness, either experienced by themselves or possibly more disturbingly by their fellow passengers. To encourage the passengers to enjoy their flights attractive hostesses are in attendance and take a genuine interest in the welfare of their charges.

Charter flying is carried on by all operations from BEA down to the smaller one/two aircraft firms in Britain. It forms only a very small portion of the business of the nationally managed corporation but in the case of the smallest operators covers 100 per cent of their work.

The aircraft used may vary from Viscounts to 2/3 seater types and this side of the business is not limited to any particular period of the year. Some of the uses for which aircraft are chartered are to fly parties to and from football matches, race meetings and the like or when the saving of time is a first consideration for instance for newspapermen. Parties may be flown by oil companies to visit their refineries, or by shipping concerns to witness the launching of their ships. Automobile accessory manufacturers sometimes fly their dealers and distributors to conferences or exhibitions. These forms of charter are generally limited to say one or at the most, two flights but other charters are provided on a long term basis. During the construction of the London-Birmingham motorway aircraft, both fixed wing and helicopter types, were chartered by the various construction firms engaged on the project to fly their executives to and from the scene of operations. In addition the aircraft were employed to fly above the motorway to enable the engineers to obtain a birds eye view of the work in hand.

From charter flying it is but a short step to company owned and operated aircraft, although it is unlikely in Great Britain that the expansion of aircraft purchase by commercial undertakings for their own use will ever approach that in the USA There is, nevertheless, a steady increase each year of such aircraft registered in and to, a large extent operated within, the United Kingdom.

Now a look at British European Airways' current operations. The Corporation was formed in August 1946 and, included in its terms of reference, is the requirement to maintain passenger, mail and freight services within the Untied Kingdom; and of such it is the largest single operator serving 26 airports from Jersey in the south to Shetland in the north, Dublin in the west to Gatwick in the east. Thirteen of these airports are located on islands, thus involving over water flights from the mainland. The longest of the flights takes an hour or so to complete, a journey which by sea can be in the region of eight hours. A limited amount of freight can be carried, in addition to mail on any advertised passenger flight, the rates comparing favourably, particularly in view of the speed of transit, with other forms of transport.

Passengers are carried in two classes, First and Tourist. The aircraft used are basically similar but the seating is more spacious when the aircraft is adapted for first-class use.

In addition to the basic first class and tourist fares, in which return tickets are available, for 12 monthly periods, slightly cheaper rates are in force for monthly and fortnightly periods. All the fares vary between seasons so that winter travel is cheaper than high summer.

Generally speaking, the mainstay of the inter city traffic in Britain is business travel on the five working days of the week. Summer weekend traffic is kept at a reasonable level by holiday travellers but winter weekends were poor until last winter when fares, barely in excess of rail/sea rates were introduced as 8-day excursions between London and Manchester, Belfast, Glasgow and Edinburgh. As a result the aircraft were 80 per cent to 90 per cent loaded as against the previous year when they flew with only 60 per cent to 70 per cent of the seats occupied.

Freight traffic has reached such proportions that a nightly "Freight only" service is operated between London, Manchester and Glasgow and more freight is being handled each year.

Mail carried on behalf of the GPO has been reduced slightly during the past year or so. The saving in time does not warrant the higher cost of air over surface transport. Hardly any mail is now sent by air on Saturdays as there is little point in reaching its destination on that day when the delivery will not be made until Monday. This has reduced BEA revenue by at least £10,000 per year.

BEA make no secret of the fact that their domestic routes give them quite a number of headaches. From the financial angle, in the year to March 1959, their international services produced a profit of about £2 million but against that sum had to be set a loss of some £1¾ million on domestic services leaving a net profit of only £¼. Of the £1¾ million loss it is estimated that the routes to the Scottish Islands and in the Irish Sea area cost £½ million each.

Inevitably there are fluctuations in traffic carried, due largely to the overall economic position of the country; but even a period of foggy or stormy weather can have a marked effect on the number of passengers carried. However, during the past 5 years there has been an increase of over 50 per cent in the numbers travelling, and over the past 10 years an increase in excess of 200 per cent.

BEA operate flights on a charter basis at rates far cheaper than basic fares, in a similar manner to the rates charged for comparable services by Motor Coach line or party travel by rail. Their helicopters are chartered for a variety of uses which include crop spraying.

Other air lines with which BEA is associated and which operate domestic routes are Aer Lingus (or Irish Air Lines), Cambrian Airways and Jersey Airlines.

Now what of the future for BEA domestic services? Traffic tends to build up into peaks and fall away in troughs for various reasons throughout each day, week or year, such as the needs of business men who wish to travel from London to Glasgow at 8 am and return at 8 pm, or holidaymakers who fly to the Channel Islands or the Isle of Man on Saturday afternoons throughout the summer. A determined effort is to be made to even out the traffic flow by the introduction of cheap fares on mid-week flights and even cheaper fares for particularly early or late flights. Some of the piston engined aircraft have been flying with BEA for more than 13 years and a large number are due for retirement. These will be replaced by Viscount aircraft, (themselves displaced by bigger new aircraft) on routes serving airports with suitable runways -but there remains the problem of serving certain islands. It is accordingly proposed to commence helicopter services between Penzance and the Scillys next year using 6-seaters, these to be followed in due course by the Rotodyne type of aircraft when they become available. For services to the Islands of North and West Scotland the Government are to supply three Handley Page "Herald" Turbo-Prop aircraft to replace the existing twins piston engined types. Apart from the network of services operated by BEA roughly a dozen smaller independent private enterprise airlines provide services to and from many airports throughout the country.

In the British Isles many airfields are used for both international and domestic flights - but a considerable number are only used for internal traffic. Let us therefore examine the facilities provided at a few of our airports. First, London Airport where nothing is lacking from either the passengers' or operators' standpoints. The former can await the departure of his or her service in comfort with access to a restaurant or snack bar and drinks can be obtained. Moreover, various shops are housed under the same roof. The only possible drawback could be overcrowding on summer holiday weekends.

To assist the operator there are first class radio and radar aids and when the aircraft have landed refuelling and oiling is promptly attended to by one or other of the oil companies who provide the refuelling services at the airport. In addition, there are depot repair shops for electronic equipment and a tyre service.

Secondly, Southampton Airport, which I will describe for want of a better word as an intermediate airport. Here are handled both international and internal flights, but the former of an essentially short haul nature, the most distant destination being Paris. The accommodation provided is reasonably in keeping with the nature of the traffic - adequate except during the five summer months when hopeless overcrowding can occur at weekends. From the operators' point of view however, Southampton's main draw-back is its lack

228

of a hard runway plus the comparatively short length of the longest grass runway, which is less than one mile.

Lastly, St Mary's Airport in the Scilly Isles, which replaced the original landing strip on the Island's golf course in 1940. Here the passenger accommodation is not lavish but comfortable; outside, however, the main grass runway is a mere 1,800 feet long and is hump-backed.

Having reviewed past, present and future operations in the domestic field, I will try and outline the advantages and disadvantages of the use of such air services for the transport of both passengers and cargo. The prime advantage of getting from one airport to another at speeds of up to 300 miles per hour can easily be outweighed by the time taken for the passengers to reach the airport from the town or city in which their journey originates and also to reach their destination after landing at the airport which serves it. Thus, the overall time taken from London to Birmingham by air is 2hours 20minutes; a little longer than the time taken by express train between the two cities. However, on longer journeys the flying time becomes an advantage. London-Manchester being reached in 2½ hours against 3½ hours by rail. A particular problem for the passenger is how to reach the airport before the flight and leave it after landing. If no friend is available with a car, a taxi can of course be used; alternatively there is a coach service provided between most town centres and the local airport. The coaches are scheduled to leave in ample time so that they arrive at the airport up to half an hour before the aircraft departure time. Another drawback is the requirement that passengers shall check in 20 minutes before the flight which they are to use is due to depart. It is, strictly speaking, not essential to book prior to the check in time but it is advisable to do so on account of the limited accommodation afforded by an aircraft in comparison with, say, a train. Should a passenger miss the 'plane after booking in advance he must forfeit 25 per cent of the fare, minimum £2. At present the system of ticket issue for domestic flights is a little cumbersome, the name of the ticket holder, for example, has to be written into the ticket along with details of the flight number and route.

The amount of luggage which can carried free is only one third of the amount which can be taken by rail.

The meals and refreshments served on certain flights are said to be free, but some part of the fare must, of course, be assumed to cover their cost. Aircrew members are forbidden to accept tips, which is directly the opposite to one's experiences when travelling by surface transport either on road, rail or by sea. One rule which I heartily endorse is that which excludes animals from the passenger accommodation. I am fond of animals in appropriate places but find them very annoying in the confined space of a railway compartment or bus.

There may be a disadvantage to the air traveller in that sometimes the flight is rough or bumpy due to atmospheric disturbances which would not be felt with land travel. In the view of many passengers who formerly had to undertake equivalent journeys by sea the shorter duration of a flight is an advantage in spite of the bumps and higher cost.

So far as cargo is concerned the advantage is in the speed of transit between airports. Illustrations of items which are particularly suitable for despatch by air are fresh flowers and early strawberries, where the value to weight ratio is comparatively high. It is essential to know the timetables as the flights are not as frequent as the number of journeys made daily by British Railways.

Traffic control problems exist today no less in the air than they do on the roads. Fortunately, there have been no collisions between civil aircraft over Britain in recent years but several near misses have been reported, one incident involving an aircraft flying on a domestic service and an RAF plane being the subject of a question in the House of Commons. Thus it will be appreciated that a part of the cost of operating domestic flights is attributable to payments which must be made towards the maintenance of an efficient ground control system for all aircraft airborne at any given moment. The aircraft must be flown at specific heights, and on specified routes and in some cases this has the effect of adding a considerable mileage to a particular flight.

A use of aeroplanes developed during the past decade has been of both fixed wing and helicopter types as giant agricultural spraying machines. It is claimed that crops sprayed from the air are more effectively dealt with in a matter of minutes than similar crops on which farmers have spent days spraying from the ground.

Another much used service is that provided by firms who operate their own aircraft and specialize in aerial map making. British Railways for instance have had many miles of their track and the surrounding areas, photographed from the air in connection with their modernization pro-gramme. In common with similar concerns about to undertake major engi-neering projects they found that only their surveyors were capable of visual-izing, when looking at a conventional map, how the area depicted would look to a person actually standing on the site, whereas aerial photographic prints can be easily interpreted by both expert and layman.

Regarding the future, it is my opinion that the services provided will have to be co-ordinated to a far greater extent than at present so as to achieve a regularity of service over as great a route mileage as possible if the maximum number of passengers and tonnage of goods are to be carried. Travel by air between points within the British Isles will undoubtedly increase, larger aircraft will be used to carry the traffic and fares will reduce until they are competitive - at least at first class level - with those charged by British Railways.

Helicopters although making a slow start compared with fixed wing aircraft will I am certain come into their own during the next five to ten years as bigger machines of this type are built.

I suggest that a system of air routes centred on, say, Birmingham or Derby would prove to be extremely useful to the businessman or tourist. On the assumption that certain airfields at present not having hard runways and first class navigational aids are brought completely up to date, routes such as the following might be flown: Portsmouth-Southampton-Derby-Newcastle: or Exeter-Cardiff-Derby-Edinburgh. Thus Derby would be the exchange point and aircraft would be timed to arrive there from the various airports of origin within a space of a few minutes so that through passengers would not be held up unnecessarily. The inception of such a system would involve hard work on the part of planning staffs and quite an amount of give and take on the part of the operators but there is no reason why such an idea should not be made to work.

It can fairly be said that the use of aircraft as a means of transport by the general public is still only a fraction of what it will become in the future.

# 26 Air freight

*Paper presented to the Manchester Centre by*
*E.H. Childs*
*Manchester Airport*
*January 1966 issue*

Probably the earliest use of air freight was for the carriage of mails for which it was obviously suited. Other than this air freight between the wars tended to be confined to items for which expense was no object, e.g. emergency medical supplies, and items of a very high value/weight ratio which could accept the necessarily high transport charges. The Second World War showed the potential of air transport in such operations as the supply of vital war materials to the Chinese across the Himalayas. The early post-war years showed a more remarkable example in the Berlin air-lift, when for many months the western sectors of that city were entirely supplied from the air with all the necessities of life.

The rapid expansion of air passenger travel after the war stimulated the development of larger and faster aircraft. These larger aircraft often had reasonable space available for freight, and its carriage on passenger services provided a useful addition to revenues. The ever-increasing pace of passenger aircraft development culminated in the jet buying spree of the late fifties and early sixties. The new jet aircraft had very superior passenger appeal and with the limitations imposed by the IATA fare structure all operators had to join in or go under. One of the effects of this re-equipment with jets was to make available a considerable surplus capacity in the form of fleets of large piston engine aircraft with many years of useful life left. Many of these were adapted for freight work and although they were not ideal for the purpose, they increased considerably the freight capacity on offer and gave impetus to the drive to sell air freight. Graphs began to rise sharply and although it is doubtful whether much profit was made out of pure freighter operations the possibilities of air freight became more apparent. This led finally to the development of aircraft designed specifically for air freight of which a notable early example was the Argosy. The CL44, although owing a lot in its ancestry to the Britannia was yet another example. The latest developments of freighter versions of the newest jet aircraft, notably the Boeing 707-320 and Douglas DC 8F which have been ordered in numbers will add enormously to the capacity available on the long haul routes.

Figures for the last ten years show a four-fold increase in the use of air freight and it is obvious that more and more shippers are beginning to find it an attractive method of moving their goods. In the wide commercial world attraction boils down in the end to cash. For all practical purposes one can say that air freight will never compete with surface freight in simple terms of pence per ton mile. A proper assessment of the relevant economics of air and surface transport requires a consideration of all the costs involved and this is now expressed familiarly in the air transport world as the "total cost concept". An examination of all the direct costs usually narrows considerably the differentials in pure freight costs between air and alternative methods. Goods sent by air often require considerably less packaging or crating which is an economy in itself and also reduces the total weight of the consignment. Insurance premiums are invariably lower for air freight. Air freight rates are inclusive Airport to Airport and many of the costs associated with other methods such as transport warehousing do not appear. Documentation costs are also usually lower.

However, it is in the field of indirect costs that some of the greatest savings of air transport are revealed. The guarantee of speedy delivery by air often means that stock holdings can be considerably reduced or even eliminated. This can result in large economies in warehouse rentals and in the administration costs associated with stocks and inventory checks. Losses due to deterioration and obsolescence may also be avoided. There is also, of course, a considerable saving in not having large amounts of capital tied up in stocks.

Some of the other benefits of air freight are perhaps not amenable to accurate evaluation but their importance may be the determining factor. Quicker delivery times associated with punctuality and reliability lead to greater customer satisfaction and hence increased sales. With air freight there is a smaller risk of pilfering or damage which help to produce the lower insurance premiums already mentioned but also have great customer appeal. In modern parlance there is also the value of the image of a firm which is modern and progressive and uses the most up-to-date means of transport.

The airlines of the world are endeavouring to reduce even further the differentials between air and surface freight charges. The direct operating costs of the new large jet freighters should help to bring a reduction in general rates. In addition air freight is being made more competitive in many areas for many items by the adoption of specific commodity rates which are permitted under the IATA rate structure. The situation has now been reached in which a great variety of goods is being carried by air and the old idea of air freight consisting of perishable luxury goods is no longer valid.

Much emphasis is being laid on reducing still further delivery times by air particularly by a reduction in the time spent by aircraft on the ground in turn-round. Improvements in this respect increase the productivity of expensive aircraft by permitting greater utilization and thus directly lowering operating costs. At the same time it underlines the major asset of air freight which is speed. Turn-rounds are being speeded up by the ever increasing use of palletization and the use of special containers. Various incentives are offered to shippers to spread the use of these systems which are fundamental to operations with a new freighter aircraft. Associated equipment includes scissors platform and purpose-built trailers. Extensive use of rollers is made within the aircraft and on the loading platforms and trailers to facilitate the speedy and easy movements of pallets from warehouse to aircraft fuselage. Similar methods can be used within the warehouse and, in its final development, air freighting should be a completely integrated system from the factory to the sales point.

One irksome form of delay in the movement of air freight arises from documentation requirements in respect of Import and Export Regulations and Customs Clearance. Airlines are more conscious of these than other carriers because time spent in these formalities is likely to be disproportionate to the time taken to carry the cargo from point to point. Airlines have reduced their own paper requirements to the minimum and much has been achieved through the work of the International Civil Aviation Organization and the International Air Transport Association in simplifying Government requirements. It is to be hoped that the logic of adapting Government controls to the speed of transport will eventually prevail.

I should like to turn now to the air freight picture as it is seen at Manchester in particular. In terms of tonnage handled the rate of increase has kept well up with London. The current annual total, including mail, is running at 25,000 tons a year. Annual increases have been particularly marked in the last few years averaging 25 per cent. This represents a doubling every three years. The North Atlantic route has been particularly active and very large

235

increases can be expected as the big jet freighters come into operation.

A very useful network of pure freighter services operates from Manchester. BOAC operate at present a three times weekly west bound service with CL 44's to North American destinations but these will shortly be replaced by 707 jets and the frequency increased to six west bound and three east bound services. A wider variety of points in North America will also be covered. KLM operate five DC7 services a week to Amsterdam and Sabena four DC3 and one DC6 services a week to Brussels. BEA offer three Viscounts a week to Paris, six Argosy services to London and six Viscounts and one Vanguard to Belfast. Aer Lingus operate six mail flights a week with Friendship aircraft and five cargo flights with Carvairs to Dublin. In addition to this freighter network, air cargo facilities are available on the extensive passenger aircraft network operating in the summer and the less extensive but still very useful network in the winter.

As an act of policy Manchester Airport carried out exclusively the actual loading and unloading of freight and baggage, although each airline is responsible for providing supervision directly or indirectly. Although not universally popular this system has considerable merits. Overall it must be more economical in the use of manpower and equipment and helps to reduce congestion in the Apron areas.

It has been the fashion to talk for some years now of the breakthrough in air freight. There are perhaps more solid reasons now for believing that it has arrived. The very sharp increases recorded in recent years, the large capacity now becoming available and the intensive sales drives presently being conducted could result in dramatic developments in the next few years. In the offing are further aircraft developments, including the enormous C-5A which could have a tremendous impact on the air freight scene. As the largest provincial Airport in the country favourably situated with respect to the industrial heart of the nation, Manchester Airport is watching developments closely.

There are good reasons for believing that it may become a most important centre for air freight and plans are being made to ensure that its development will be equal to the demand.

# 27 How airfreight can cut distribution costs

*Article by N. Tilsley*
*April 1988 issue*

The role played by airfreight in the modern world economy is assuming increasing importance. With greater emphasis being placed on more efficient methods of procurement, production and distribution, more and more exporters and importers are turning to the use of airfreight - and understandably so. Indeed, such is its status that airfreight can rightly be said to have added a third dimension to transportation.

Why, one may well ask, with surface overtonnaging on both the North Atlantic and to and from the Far East, has there been an almost doubling of the amount of world cargo moved by air in the last decade? When operating costs have spiralled, pushing up all ancillary charges across the board, why is airfreight becoming the 'norm' for exporters moving cargoes overseas whereas, not so long ago, airfreight was only considered when emergency situations arose involving, for example, heavy cost penalties through a production plant having to be shut down for the want of an engine component -the so-called 'fire brigade' syndrome?

Today, more companies are turning to planned airfreighting for the same reasons that were given a score or more years ago by the pundits of the business, supported by the much-publicized Stamford Report which was prepared by the Stamford Research Institute in 1963 for the Emery Airfreight Corporation. This dramatically made the point that the high speed and skilful handling inherent in air transport brought in its wake several cost reducing factors, the most important of which can be summarized under the headings of packing, insurance, stockholding, warehousing, capital utilization and lost production opportunity. It was pointed out then - and this still applies today - that savings made by the so-called 'spin-offs' of using airfreight, frequently more than outweighed the higher air cargo rates.

## PACKING

Packing for airfreight can be, and should be, minimal. Bearing in mind that air transport systems provide ultra short transit times (rarely more than two or three hours within Europe, ranging up to a maximum of ten hours on the long haul) as well as skilled handling and careful stowage and therefore little damage and full protection, it is no wonder that certain industries such as electronics and hitech, are 'traditional' airfreight users to the exclusion of surface containerization.

Expensive softwood or plywood packing is totally unnecessary for pure air cargo, and this was the reason why in the early days of the computer one well-known manufacturer switched to air in the first place. Such were his savings in packing when sending a computer from London to Paris that two computers could be sent by air for the price of one sent by surface transportation. (In this case the cost of the packing for surface containerization was £1,700 whereas the cost of the packing by air was £600. This represented a saving of £1,100 per computer, while the cost of sending it by air was well below this figure.)

Similarly, a study made into the movement of household goods showed that the weight of the consignment for transport by sea was almost three times the airfreight weight.

High quality and high value goods such as oscilloscopes, television sets, radios, record players and washing machines, traditionally travel by airfreight, and these are examples of goods which move in large quantities with only the minimal of packaging necessary to protect their services.

Fabrics and other clothing materials, cut flowers frozen foodstuffs, ice cream, fresh carcases and seafoods, are also regularly shipped with the minimum of packaging material. In the case of the carcases, for example, they are palletized and covered only in gauze; while the frozen foods (i.e. those that remain frozen for some hours) travel well and without the necessity for expensive temperature controlled units, even to the tropics.

## INSURANCE

Brokers have long recognized that damage and pilferage by air cargo are negligible, when compared with the transit of goods by other transport modes, and their quoted rates reflect this fact. Freedom from pilferage obviates the need to ship out an expensive replacement, or the loss of valuable customers, production schedules help up or capacity diverted to meet replacement needs.

## STOCKHOLDING AND WAREHOUSING

With the emphasis on the need to carry less stock but to give a customer high speed service to in turn service their purchases, airfreight has really come into its own. Stocking and warehousing are closely related of course; the industry urges companies to reduce their stocks in order to reduce their warehousing requirements. Often, companies build up stocks when sales or production requirements are difficult to predict on a day-to-day basis. Customers cannot, or seemingly will not, wait for the goods to be transported. When air cargo makes available the commodities at the time and place required, then stocks can be reduced or eliminated.

Levels of stocks are determined by two main factors: frequency of demand, and the lead time for re-orders. The use of air cargo has no direct effect on demand frequency but, conversely the use of airfreight has considerable effect on lead time. This means lower stockholding to meet the same level of consumer service. If goods can be replaced within two or three days, then it is necessary only to hold stocks sufficient for this period rather than the one, two or three weeks required by surface transport.

The despatch of small, regular shipments by air means that supply can be accurately matched to demand and equally important - when demand drops, the supply can be cut off without expensive obsolescent stock in the pipeline.

Traditionally, there are three main areas of costs in holding stocks against demand:

(a)   unproductive capital (the major area);
(b)   the cost of keeping goods in the best condition; and
(c)   if the goods are subject to physical deterioration, changes in style or commercial obsolescence their sale  may be forced at a loss.

## INVENTORY CONTROL

As supply closely follows demand when using airfreight, so there is a steady flow through the warehouse, and rarely any expensive or costly storing. Warehouses can thus often be reduced in size if not entirely eliminated. There is little point in utilizing the speed offered by air transport if consignments are then to wait in storage. (The Bermuda Public Works Department at one time flew out tons of anchor chain from the UK which were held in stock until required by the Ports and Harbours Department. A distribution cost study revealed that these types of goods would better be sent by surface containerization and suggested that consideration be given to using airfreight for goods required urgently.)

## NEW MARKETING TECHNIQUES

With air transport new products or markets can be consumer tested without the necessity of setting up advance stocks. It also allows a company to take advantage rapidly of increasing sales; equally, to get out of a test market with the minimum expense in terms of warehousing and stock control should the venture prove wrong. (One of the side-benefits of close stock control is an accurate movement graph of sales which are rapidly available, as against an ill-defined figure which incorporates all or part of the supply line stock either awaiting dispatch, or actually en route.)

## LOST PRODUCTION OPPORTUNITY

Profits missed through lost production can never be regained. The difference in lead time throughout Europe, air versus surface, is anything between three days and three weeks. Most capital consignments should have earned more than their air charges during the extra production time gained through the use of air cargo. (Examples have been quoted concerning a European airline, which involved the carriage of some capital machinery which cost, in rates and ancillary charges, six times more to move by air than by surface. On examination it was found that the extra costs were more than outweighed by the profits from three weeks' extra production time. Similarly, the increasing practice of leasing equipment means that airfreight is a must. A few days lost rental, and any advantage surface rates has is lost).

# 28 Our purpose civil aviation: A manufacturer's viewpoint

*Paper presented to the Annual Conference by*
*I.D.N. Lawson*
*British Aircraft Corporation*
*December 1974 issue*

I am glad to have this opportunity of speaking to you on the subject of Civil Aviation. It is a large subject, and in this short talk, I would like to narrow the range by looking at civil aviation mainly from the viewpoint of the aircraft manufacturer. This will enable me to speak from first-hand experience, always an advantage when addressing a professional body such as yours. It will also allow us to consider one or two basic questions such as "Does Britain need an aircraft manufacturing industry?" and "Does Britain, and the world, need Concorde?".

First of all, let me sketch in the general background to our subject. The growth of civil aviation has been rapid - "explosive" is not too dramatic a word to apply to it. In a few decades it has developed from pioneering beginnings into a major world-wide industry and a dominant factor in the shaping of modern society. Journeys that were measured in weeks forty years ago are now measured in hours.

And that, quite simply, is the reason the sole reason, for the phenomenal growth of air travel. It is the airliner's ability to get from A to B fast that attracts the traveller. It is speed that has drawn the great bulk of medium to long-haul traffic away from the comfortable, leisurely ocean liner to the aeroplane. (And if some of you think I am preparing the ground for a Concorde sales pitch later on, you are quite right).

Thanks to the pulling power of speed, then, civil aviation is now an established fact of world transport life. The first air routes were developed for, and sustained by, the business traveller. As airliners became more economic, as route networks expanded and operational techniques improved, leisure travel by air grew to the point where it now accounts for the major proportion of the passenger traffic. As we have all seen, there are profitability hazards inherent in this situation.

Let us now try to tackle our first basic question: "Does Britain need an aircraft manufacturing industry?". In doing so, let's get right back to basics.

Transport is the circulation system of society. Without an efficient and dependable transport system, society will sooner or later collapse, and the more complex the social structure, the more rapid and complex that collapse will be. Britain forms part of an extremely complex world society, but in this country we are even more dependant than most nations on our transport "circulation systems", national and international.

As a trading nation, Britain has long recognized the economic and strategic importance of owning, and thus controlling a substantial part of the transport system by which its trade and commerce are carried on. In this company, I think there will be general agreement that Britain should at least operate its own air transport fleet, and in British Airways we have an airline that ranks with the best in the world.

We move on to more controversial ground when we ask whether Britain really needs the ability to produce its own air transport vehicles. Why not let somebody else take all the development risks? Why not sit back and buy our airliners off the shelf with all the teething troubles sorted out? This superficially attractive policy has its advocates in Britain, some of them in high places.

But I firmly believe that this policy is totally misconceived. To carry it through to its logical conclusion would lead to a complete transformation in Britian's position in the world. We are, I repeat, a trading nation, and to make both ends meet, we need to sell a substantial volume of goods and services to other countries. Nowadays, all the emergent nations are seeking to make themselves industrially self-sufficient, and it is only by being able to provide a range of products and services beyond the capabilities of the majority of other nations that we in this densely-populated island can survive and maintain a reasonable standard of living.

It is therefore a matter of economic life and death for Britain to keep up with the technological leaders. Aerospace acts as a spur to research and development in many other advanced-technology industries. The task of meeting the stringent safety, reliability and endurance requirements of modern civil aviation has hastened progress in such important areas as electronics, computers, machine tools, radar, plastics and rubber and glass technology. To fulfil the demands of aviation design - precision engineering standards on a heavy-engineering scale - new manufacturing techniques have been evolved. At Filton, we are using electron-beam and laser-beam welding on titanium and other exotic metals, and we have what is probably Europe's largest battery of tape-controlled machine tools. All this expertise will rub off in due course on other industries. There is "spin-off" from aerospace into almost every aspect of modern life: for example, the latest and safest in laminated car windscreens owes much to the development work its makers did in producing flight deck transparencies for Concorde.

Admittedly, it is a lengthy process to bring a large modern aviation project to fruition and on the way large sums of research and development money are absorbed. But, for the reasons I have just outlined, these sums should be regarded not merely as an investment in the specific project, but also in this country's technological future.

However, it is sometimes argued that two of the most successful industrial exporting nations in the world, Germany and Japan, have kept well in the technological forefront without the support of an indigenous aerospace industry. Both of these nations are in the specially advantageous situation of having had their major industries completely re-equipped from scratch after the Second World War, and they have both made very heavy direct investment in advanced technology. Nevertheless, in recent years, and as a matter of long-term policy, both Germany and Japan have been working assiduously to build up their own native aerospace capability.

They are doing this, I suggest for two main reasons. First, they have realized the value of aerospace as a technological pace-maker. This is the point I have already been trying to make in relation to Britain. Second - and this is a point we have not yet touched on in a British context -Germany and Japan are seeking to safeguard their future procurement situation. We need to take this second factor seriously into account in drawing up the aerospace balance sheet for Britain.

It is as well to emphasize that at the moment Britain is the only nation in the world outside the US and the USSR which has an all-across-the-board capability in aerospace. That is, we are able to produce airframes, aero-engines and all the associated avionics and the aircraft system. To put it at its very lowest, this is an invaluable bargaining counter in the international negotiations that lie ahead of us.

To adopt a "buy foreign" policy and to allow our own industry to wither away would not only prejudice our technological position and dissipate hardwon and irreplaceable skills, it would almost certainly put us, sooner or later, into the hands of the suppliers' cartel or quasimonopoly. In crude terms, we should have to buy from the US suppliers' ring at whatever price they decided the market could bear. The Middle East oil situation illustrates the power that can be exerted by a small group of producers who control the supply of an indispensable commodity.

There is one other point to be made in favour of retaining an independent British aerospace capability - and it is an important one. We have rich coal reserves, and we have - in prospect - rich oil resources, but undoubtedly, the most valuable asset this country possesses is the skill and the know-how of its people. Aerospace products make relatively little demand on imported raw materials but very heavy calls on our native stores of expertize; the labour costs in a modern airliner represent about ninety per cent of the total. The Swiss make a good thing of taking small amounts of metal and converting them into precision-built watches, and the British do the same with aeroplanes.

Unfortunately, the public image of our industry is somewhat tarnished. We have our failures and our cancellations, and the press remind us frequently of the "soaring" costs of such-and such an aerospace programme. (You will have noticed that in Fleet Street, costs never simply rise or escalate, they invariably soar). Being human, we make mistakes and errors of judgment, but most of our financial forecasting problems arise from the fact that we are working on the frontiers of knowledge. And I hope I have persuaded you that if Britain is to keep its place in the world, that is just where we ought to be working.

And, in fact, our successes far outweigh the failures and the near misses. If every major industry in this country achieved the proportion of exports to total sales that the aerospace industry does, we should have no serious balance of payments problem. At the end of August BAC's total order book stood at a record figure of £818 million, and of this sixty-eight per cent (£546 million) was for export. The latest published figures for this year show that up to July the British aerospace exports totalled £353 million, probably £600 million for the full year of 1974. Looking at the industry as a whole, we ought also to reckon the many hundreds of millions saved by way of "frustrated imports", that is, the value of the home-produced civil aircraft and defence equipment which we would otherwise have had to buy from abroad. All this should be borne in mind and set against the picture - the caricature, rather, - of an Oliver Twist industry eternally asking for more research and development funds.

So far, I have been considering the British aerospace industry in isolation, but the logic of events must compel one to take a wider view. The scale and complexity - and hence the costs - of major aerospace projects grow greater every year, and we have now reached a point where it would be impolitic for Britain or any other European nation to "go it alone" on a major project. Even the US giants, operating in their tough competitive "hire and fire" environment, are finding it difficult. Europe has recognized that it must work in co-operation if a viable European industry is to be maintained in the face of US competition.

My company has taken a leading part in the development of European collaboration in aerospace. On the civil side, the outstanding project is, of course, Concorde, on which we have been engaged with our French partners, Aerospatiale, (formally Sud-Aviation) for twelve years. You may think this is a pretty long gestation period, and you would be right, but I would like to come back to that point in a few moments. On the military side, BAC is involved in two major collaborative projects: with Breguet of France on the Jaguar strike/trainer and with MBB of Germany and Fiat of Italy on MRCA, the multi-role combat aricraft. Jaguar has recently attracted its first export orders - very substantial orders, totalling £80 million - and there will be more to come. In scale and significance, MRCA ranks with Concorde itself, and the flight test programme is now off to a very successful start.

How are these multi-national partnerships working out? I can only speak first-hand about Concorde, but I believe our experience there is paralleled to the other two projects I have mentioned. Nobody pretends it has all been smooth going working with the French on Concorde; no meaningful partnership ever is all smooth going. But when one considers that two large independent design and manufacturing teams were put together to work from scratch on the biggest technological project that Europe has ever taken on, the frictions and the personality clashes have been surprisingly few.

Over the years, we have come to know, understand and respect each other as engineers and as people. I have just referred to the long gestation period for Concorde, and there are two main reasons for that. The main reason is simply the inherent difficulties in designing and building a passenger aircraft for safe, comfortable and economic operation at a cruise speed of 1,350 mph. Those difficulties were formidable; we have overcome them, but it took time. Another element is the additional time involved in an international collaboration where decisions cannot be imposed by one party or the other, but have to be mutually agreed and accepted. This does take time, but both partners are now convinced that Concorde is a better aircraft than it would have been had it been produced as either an all-British or an all-French project. We are happy to acknowledge that the French are excellent engineers, more than that, they are - like us - fully-paid-up members of the human race. Many people at Filton - and I am one - have made firm personal friendships with French colleagues.

So far, European collaboration in aerospace has been somewhat piece-meal, but the first serious step towards concerted long-range planning in this area was the recently announced agreement between six of the leading aircraft manufacturers in Britain, France and West Germany. The companies, BAC, Hawker-Siddeley, Aerospatiale, Dornier, VFW-Fokker and Messerschmitt-Belkow-Blohm, have set up a working group to decide how best they can meet the long and short-haul requirements for Europe's three leading airlines, British Airways, Air France and Lufthansa, up to the year 2,000. To wrest even a part of this European market from the present US stranglehold will mean thousands of millions of pounds and tens of thousands of jobs. The stakes are high, and when the stakes are high enough, these European manufactures have already shown that they can sink national interests in a common multi-national enterprise.

At this point, perhaps, I ought to try to answer the second basic question I posed at the beginning of this talk: "Does Britain - and the world - need Concorde?".

All through history there have been people who wanted to arrest the march of progress at the stage it had reached in their youth. It is an understandable reaction; few of us really welcome change. In their turn, the spinning jenny, the railway train, the steamship, the aeroplane, radio and television were violently opposed by a strident minority. But the march of progress was not halted then, and it will not be halted now.

If civil aviation has grown and flourished through the sales appeal of speed, then there is assuredly a place for Concorde,. Concorde's cruise speed of 1,350 mph represents, in comparison with the fastest current subsonic speeds of about 600 mph, the biggest single speed advance in the history of passenger transport. Cruising at twice the speed of sound, Concorde can halve the present flight times on most of the world's long-distance route sectors.

This was the primary design aim, and the Concorde development aircraft already flying have conclusively demonstrated their ability to achieve this target. To quote one among many examples, in June this year, the second pre-production Concorde flew with a representative payload from Boston to Paris, spent an hour on the ground at Paris and then returned to Boston in a total elapsed time that was less than the time taken by an Air France 747 to fly the single journey Paris-Boston on the same day.

Concorde's sustained supersonic capability makes possible dramatic time-savings on inter-continental journeys. A day return business trip from London or Paris to New York becomes a practical possibility, and London and Sydney will be little more than thirteen hours apart. On the long trans-Pacific sectors, journey times will for the first time be cut to less than twelve hours and transport history shows that when this happens there is an upsurge in traffic. There was such an upsurge on the Atlantic in the early sixties when the first-generation subsonic jets broke the "twelve-hour" barrier. Concorde will do the same for the Pacific basin, an area of immense traffic potential.

Initially, Concorde's appeal will be to the business traveller, and to others for whom time means money. Operated as a single-class vehicle at premium fares (first class or first class plus 10 per cent or 20 per cent), Concorde will attract virtually all the present first-class passengers from the subsonics together with a significant proportion of the business travellers who now fly economy-class. This forecast is attested by market surveys already carried out in the US, Japan and elsewhere.

It is this attraction by Concorde of the high-revenue business traffic which gives rise to misgivings on the part of many operators and it is this that underlies the suggestion that it will be "uneconomic" to operate Concorde.

There will be no difficulty in achieving profitability in operation with Concorde, if this operation is considered in isolation. Our Chairman, Sir George Edwards, pointed out earlier this year that on British Airways' own estimates of Concorde operating costs, and at their estimated Concorde fare levels of between first class and first class plus 20 per cent, varying according to the route, an average load of 56 passengers is needed to break even after remuneration of capital. Before remuneration of capital the break even load falls to 50 passengers. In other words, the Concorde starts to make an operating profit as soon as it is half full.

However, an airline has to consider its fleet operations as a whole, and one solution which is being actively investigated is a new type of fleet diversification. In this, Concorde would be used for the priority traffic and the high-capacity subsonic jets, used as single-class "economy" vehicles, would cater for the mass travel market. This would improve the economics of the wide-bodies jets and give better hopes of at least stabilising fares for the mass market.

One cannot speak of Concorde without touching on the environmental factors. Many of the early fears about the impact of supersonic transport operation on the environment have been shown to be groundless. The effect produced by even 1,000 Concordes flying in the stratosphere would be puny compared with nuclear explosions or volcanic eruptions - and the stratosphere's cleansing mechanism has shown itself well able to cope with these. Supersonic operations on any scale that can be visualized will not have any adverse effect on world health or world climate, and monitoring will be an absolute safeguard.

The Concorde prototype aircraft had smoky exhausts, but this problem has been overcome in later developments of the Olympus engine with the result that Concordes now produce virtually no smoke and are among the cleanest aircraft in operation.

Aerospatiale and ourselves have stated that the airfield noise levels of Concorde at entry-into-service will be comparable with those of the 707 and the DC 8, and noise measurements made in Europe and in the U.S. bear out these claims. A programme of long-term research is in hand, to effect improvements on the entry-into-service levels.

Sonic boom is a phenomenon inseparable from supersonic flight. Concorde route planning will be designed to achieve the minimum disturbance, and this objective will not be too difficult to attain since about three-quarters of the total seat-miles on inter-continental services are produced over the oceans where sonic boom creates no problem.

The decision by the British and French Governments to authorize continuance of the manufacturing programme for the first sixteen Concordes means that the aircraft will be given the opportunity to prove itself in airline service - and that is all we ask. British Airways has five Concordes on order, Air France has four, and negotiations for sales to Iran and China are proceeding satisfactorily. Around the end of next year, Concorde will enter service with British Airways and Air France, and other operators will soon notice the effect on their business traffic. They will need to order Concordes to remain competitive.

Concorde has been a long time reaching the service stage, but its life as a front-line operational aircraft will be far longer - if only because the costs of developing an airliner offering any substantial increase in speed will be astronomical. Concorde and its direct developments will be in service into the nineties at least, producing continuing balance-of-payments benefits for Britain and France, and fast, better, international communications for the world at large.

# 29 The jungle of international air fares

*Article by J.P. Hanlon*
*University of Birmingham*
*December 1975 issue*

Recently, a further thickening in the jungle of international airline passenger fares could be observed. With the addition of such fare categories as APEX (advance-purchase excursion), IPEX (instant-purchase excursion) and ABC (advanced booking charter), the development of fare structures has come a long way since the early 1950s, when all (adult) passengers boarding an aircraft for a schedules flight over an international route were charged the same price. Now, the only uniform price is that charged for first-class travel; and, for economy-class, there are differentials between peak and off-peak periods, a range of excursion fares related to the length of the stay at the destination, reductions for groups of passengers, and discounts for those willing to book and pay in advance. Also there are special fares available to passengers within certain age groups (e.g., youths), in certain occupations (e.g. seamen) or with certain reasons for travelling (e.g., migrants). As a result of these developments, airline fare structures have rapidly become quite complex. This paper examines the motivations which led to the adoption of so many different fare categories, and analyzes the relation between pricing policies and the economic difficulties currently faced by the international airline industry. Particular reference is made to North Atlantic routes, a key market in which many fare innovations have been made.

## MAIN FARE CATEGORIES

Present fare structures have evolved from differentiation by three basic factors: class of travel, time of travel and market segment. Differentials between first and economy class reflect differentiation in the product supplied and, to some extent, the relative costs incurred; but the ratio of first to (normal) economy fares is often higher than the corresponding ratio of costs. The main objective of differences between peak and off-peak fares is to make it easier for airlines to match capacity with demand over time. In this regard, it is desirable to have a gradation of fares from peak through to off-peak, in order to minimize the risk of inducing local peaks and troughs in demand at the beginning and end of each period of validity.

The spread of promotional and special fares represents differentiation, some would say discrimination, by market segment. Excursion and inclusive tour fares can be purchased by any member of the travelling public, but the conditions attaching to these promotional rates are such that they afford little advantage to, for example, passengers travelling on business. Indeed, the availability of the fares has been designed with just this in mind: the airlines have been seeking to attract additional traffic by reducing the price to passengers whose demand is expected to be elastic with respect to changes in fares, without at the same time diluting the revenue received from passengers whose demand is inelastic. In the relation between price-elasticity of demand and revenue, a dilution of revenue will result if the proportionate reduction in the fare paid is greater than the proportionate increase in passengers, i.e. if demand is elastic. For good reasons, airline managements believe the demand of business travellers and of passengers travelling for urgent personal reasons (e.g., to attend a funeral) to be inelastic, and that of holiday-makers and of those visiting friends and relatives to be elastic.

These motivations are evident in the structure of N. Atlantic fares in Table 1. With two classes, three seasons and nine categories of economy-class fares, six of which are subject to surcharges for weekend travel, scheduled airlines now offer return flights at 42 different prices. A first-class ticket costs between 50 and 100 per cent more than a normal economy-class ticket which, in turn, costs almost twice as much as APEX ticket. In addition, there are lower ABC fares for charter services which, for London-New York return flights, range from £99 in the off-peak season to £139 in the peak season. But there are to be no IPEX fares on this route, at least for the time being: Laker Airways' "Skytrain" proposal for a London-New York "no frills" service at a single fare of £59 for passengers prepared to queue for a seat might well have attracted traffic paying normal economy fares to scheduled air-lines, and has not been given government approval. The next ramification is expected with the introduction of Concorde services: the fares for supersonic service have not yet been set by the International Air Transport Association (IATA), but most expectations are that, for a single class service, the price will be based on the first-class subsonic fare to which a premium of 10 to 20 per cent will be attached. It is anticipated that, even with this premium, supersonic services will appeal to many business passengers, especially those who are already travelling first-class.

## CURRENT PROBLEMS

We now consider the effects of these developments in fare structures on some of the major economic and managerial problems facing international airlines. As in other industries, the oil crisis, price inflation and recession have all led to severe difficulties, but the international airline industry has also to deal with underlying problems that have been building up for some time.

### 1. Excess capacity

Like that of any common carrier, the output for a scheduled airline cannot be stored. Unsold seats on a scheduled flight represent production that is wasted. For this reason, airlines strive for high load factors, something which is evidently becoming more difficult to achieve. On many routes, the growth in capacity has outstripped the growth in demand, and the underlying trend in the average passenger load factor on scheduled services of IATA carriers has been downward, from 66.4 per cent in 1951 to a low of 50.9 per cent in 1971. The introduction of large and more productive jet aircraft (the B-707 and DC-8 in 1958 and the B-747 in 1970) brought sharp increases in the number of seats available; and, at the same time, the successive "relegation" of piston, turbo-prop, and jet aircraft to non-scheduled operations opened up a new low-cost source of supply to price-elastic segments of the market. So, with almost a half of their seats empty, scheduled airlines have been strongly motivated to generate more traffic by extending their range of promotional fares. But, as a result of this policy, the proportion of passengers travelling at promotional rates has increased markedly - on the N. Atlantic, from 18 per cent in 1963 to 65 per cent in 1973 - and, despite increases in basic rates, the average revenue from passenger fares has declined. At a time when costs are inflating fast, reduced yields have meant losses for many airlines. In their last financial year, almost all of the major international carriers reported losses, perhaps the most

251

notable being that incurred by Pan American (of US $81.8 million in 1974 and US $256 million over the past six years). During the 1960s the N. Atlantic market was highly profitable but, in 1974, it was a market in which scheduled airlines were estimated to have lost about US $300 million.

With losses on this scale, there is broad agreement on the need to reduce capacity, the question is how. For their part, airlines have approached the problem by pooling services, exchanging routes and exploring the possibilities of mergers. Mutual agreements between airlines have resulted in some cuts in capacity, but only to an extent which is small relative to the magnitude of the problem. In the last week of June, 79 city-pair routes across the N. Atlantic were served by no less than 1,466 scheduled flights; these flights were operated by 27 airlines, and there were just about as many carriers operating charter flights. The scope for rationalization here is still great.

## 2. Currency fluctuations

Recent movements in foreign-exchange markets are causing further erosion of airline revenues. Since the 1940s, IATA has used sterling and the US dollar as base currencies for the setting of fares worldwide. Once agreed in terms of the base currencies, fares were converted into local selling currencies in accordance with a schedule of official IATA exchange rates that are drawn up annually. Following two devaluations of the dollar exchange markets became very unstable; and the relative values of currencies have changed so markedly that, in terms of the purchasing power of the currency with which it is bought, an airline ticket now costs significantly more in "hard" than in "soft" currency. Because of the impracticability of changing fare values swiftly enough, IATA has attempted to reduce the effects of currency fluctuations by instituting a system of surcharges and discounts on fares paid in hard and soft currencies, respectively. Under this system, fares are agreed in terms of the 1972 US dollar, and converted into local currencies at fixed parties (e.g., £ UK 1 = $ US 2.6057) plus or minus a percentage surcharge/discount periodically set to adjust for subsequent fluctuations in exchange rates.

The adjustments vary with the routes to which the fares apply and, for payment in sterling, N. Atlantic fares are surcharged by 11 per cent, UK - Europe fares by 16 per cent and UK - Japan/Australia fares by 14 per cent. With the continuing instability of exchange markets, it has proved difficult for IATA to update the adjustments so as to keep in line with the changing relationships between currencies. There has been disagreement within IATA on this question: members from countries with soft currencies have fought against increases in surcharges, for fear of the result which the effective

252

increase in price would have on traffic originating within their countries; and members from countries with hard currencies have been concerned about a diversion of sales and a dilution of their foreign-sales revenue. On this account, Lufthansa claims to have lost about DM 400 million between 1969 and 1972 and, with the 15-20 per cent appreciation in the external value of the Swiss franc between November 1974 and February 1975, Swissair expects to lose the equivalent of Sw. Fr. 132 million in the current financial year. To avoid all carriers being paid in relatively weak currencies, IATA has restricted fare payments to the currency of the country in which travel commences. But passengers can still avail themselves of unintended "currency discounts" by preferring single to return tickets, taking appropriate routes.    In some instances, "ticket running" can be highly profitable. For example, on long-haul flights from Zurich, it has been possible to save up to about £270 on an economy-class return to Sydney, by booking for travel from London via Zurich, paying in sterling, arranging for transmission of the ticket and discarding its London-Zurich portion. Strictly, this practice could be viewed as contravening - at least the spirit of-IATA regulations; but it is very difficult to check, or even to detect.

To overcome these difficulties, IATA has decided to adopt the International Monetary Fund's Special Drawing Right (SDR) as the basic reference for international fares. The SDR is an international unit of account, originally defined in terms of gold, but now based upon the relative market values of 16 currencies of countries which had at least a 1 per cent share of world exports, 1968-1972. Basically, the conversion from currencies to SDR's reflects exchange between each of the 16 currencies and the value in terms of SDR's of any other currency is determined through its market value in terms of any one of these 16. IATA intends to agree fare levels in SDR's, and local currencies. In essence, this will bring into being a regime of floating fares, the modus operandi of which has not yet been made public by IATA. SDR conversion rates are calculated daily by the International Monetary Fund but, presumably, certain tolerances will be allowed before movements in conversion rates are translated into changes in selling fares. It is anticipated that IATA fares will be negotiated in SDR's from late 1976.

## 3.  Constructed fares

At IATA meetings, agreement is sought on fares only for direct travel between two points. That is, specific fares are agreed for journeys between A and B, C and D, but not for travel over a route from A to D via B, B to D via C. It is considered impracticable for agreements to be reached on specific fares for all

253

routes in use, estimated at something of the order of 400,000 in number. So, for itineraries for which no fare has been agreed and published, a through fare must be constructed. Unlike the principle generally followed for other modes, a through fare is not simply the sum of sector fares along the route, but is calculated in relation to the point on the route with the highest fare for direct travel from the origin. This point is usually, but not always, the most distant from the origin and, providing that the route to be flown is no more than 20 per cent longer than the direct route, it is the fare to this point that is charged. Where the route flown is between 20 and 50 per cent longer, the fare is subject to a surcharge: for routes up to 25, 30, 35 and 40 per cent longer, the surcharges are levied at 5, 10, 15 and 20 per cent of the fare to the most distant point; and where the route flown is more than 50 per cent longer, the fare charged is the lowest combination of sector fares along the route.

Without entering into the technical complexities of fare construction, it is possible to indicate some of the difficulties to which this procedure leads. Firstly, travel over multi-sector itineraries more often than not require the use of services of different carriers, especially on International routes. Consequently, the revenue from a through fare must be shared between the airlines involved. Basically, airlines receive a proportion of the fare for each sector operated, this proportion being equal to the ratio of the through fare to the sum of the individual sector fares. So, whenever a through fare is less than the sum of sector fares, as is almost always the case, each airline receives less for the carriage of through passengers than for the carriage of local passengers. For example, if the through fare for a journey from A via B and C to D is constructed at £450 and the sum of individual fares for the sectors AB, BC and CD comes to £500, each airline would carry through passengers at an effective discount of 10 per cent on its local sector fare. This could result in serious revenue dilution to airlines operating sectors on which load factors are high, in which case there is a risk that local traffic may be turned away from flights fully booked with through passengers.

The London-Paris sector is one example where, for this reason, local airlines could be reluctant to accept through traffic: passengers from trans-Atlantic flights can, in most cases, fly over this sector at no extra cost, but local airlines earn 20 per cent less in revenue from carrying such passengers relative to full-fare local passengers; and load factors can be extremely high, particularly at certain peak periods. A related problem is that short sectors are inherently more expensive to operate than longer sectors. All the evidence and, economic theory, indicates that unit operating costs from an L-shaped relationship with distance should be reflected in the relationship between sector length and airline fares. Fares do tend to taper with distance, but not to the same degree as costs, and the taper is related, not to sector lengths, but to the total distance of the passenger's journey. Indeed, under the mileage system, passengers can complete their journey in any number of short hops at little, if any, financial penalty.

It is true that, recently, a number of excursion fares have been made subject to restrictions on the number of stopovers made en route but, for travellers paying normal fares, the incentive to follow circuitous routings can be great. And this can lead to directional imbalances in traffic flows, a problem that has been a particular feature of air travel between S. America and Europe: it has been observed that the flow of northbound traffic over this route has been consistently greater than that in the opposite direction, and it is strongly suspected that this is because passengers originating in S. America are flying direct to Europe and, taking advantage of the mileage allowances, return home via N. America. For example, the "triangular" journey Buenos Aires -London - New York Buenos Aires can be flown for only 10 per cent more than a direct return journey between Buenos Aires and London.

The airlines themselves are conscious of the effects of present methods of fare construction on traffic patterns, and have been considering various reforms. Some suggest that the mileage allowances should be reduced, and others that stopover surcharges should be extended to normal fares. More generally, there has been a proposal to replace the current system by charging through fares as the sum of sector fares minus a given percentage and plus a specific charge per stopover. This would have additional merit, if the coefficient by which sector fares are to be reduced is made a declining function of sector length.

## 4. Marketing and administration

The widening range of fares means that airlines must spend more on marketing and administration. The introduction of new categories such as APEX and ABC will have relatively little effect in stimulating demand, if a large part of the potential market is unaware of their existence. Also, the large number of promotional fares and the complex nature of the conditions applying to them poses problems in arriving at the most appropriate form of advertising. But it is not only the passengers who find present fare structures confusing. To reduce the tendency for the staffs of travel agencies to misquote fares, British Airways and the Association of British Travel Agents found it necessary to institute a training course involving 120 hours of study. And the work of airlines ticketing and revenue accounting departments becomes more complicated with every new fare introduced. On all these counts, simplification of fare structures would bring benefits in the form of reduced costs.

## CONCLUSION

International air fares have often been subject to criticism. Much of this has derived from suspicions of IATA's role as a price-fixing body, which some critics see as the reason why normal fares are at levels considered relatively high. International air travel can still be very expensive but, in real terms, the price is coming down. Over the past 25 years, the general level of retail prices in the UK rose by just over 415 per cent, but the increase in the money cost of air fares has been much less: in terms of constant purchasing power, the doubling of the money cost of a first-class London - New York return (from £225 in 1950 to £464.60 in 1975) represents a halving of the real cost; there are other routes where fare increases have more or less kept pace with inflation notably, intra-European routes, such as London-Paris, but the general indication is of a substantial decline in the real cost of air fares, even without taking into account the increasing availability of excursion fares. However, this decline has been from levels which, at the beginning of the post-war period, could only be afforded by the very rich, and it is still true that, in 1975, only a small fraction of people fly on international routes. But air fares have become a smaller proportion of the total money cost of overseas travel, given the rapid inflation that has taken place in the prices of commodities associated with travel, more especially of hotel accommodation and restaurant meals. But it is not only the absolute levels of fares that have come in for criticism.

Complex value-of-service tariffs have been described as discriminatory and unjust. Passengers paying normal economy fares are becoming increasingly resentful of being charged twice as much as passengers on excursions; and it is argued that this represents unfair cross-subsidization. A suggestion has been made that the airlines should reply to this criticism by offering normal economy passengers a higher quality of service than excursion passengers with, say, introduction of a third class. In the author's view, there is more to be said for replacing many of the promotional fares that discriminate by market segment with differentials more closely related to variations in operating cost. Such differentials could be between peak and off-peak, between routes of varying traffic densities and between through and "broken" journeys. With regard to the latter, there is a strong argument for fares to exhibit a sharper taper with distance flown, with the taper being based on the length of the individual sectors for which the passenger books, rather than on the total length of the journey. To be consistent with this, the mileage allowances implicit in present methods of fare construction should be abolished; and there would be no need to complicate tariffs with a series of surcharges on stopovers. A fare structure of this kind would be simpler both to market and to administer.

There would be no need for the conditions applying to fares to be as detailed as they are at present, and the problem of sharing revenue from constructed fares would in large part disappear. It would still be possible to stimulate demand from price-elastic segments of the market, by offering discounts for travel when and where it is cheaper for the airlines to cater for it.

## TABLE 1
## THE NORTH ATLANTIC FARE STRUCTURE
### 1975-76

| Fare Categories Code | Category | Length of stay (days) Min. | Max. | Stopovers permitted |
|---|---|---|---|---|
| F | First class | 0 | 365/6 | no limit |
| Y | Economy class (normal) | 0 | 365/6 | no limit |
| YE21 | Excursion | 14 | 21 | 4 |
| YE45 | Excursion | 22 | 45 | 0 |
| YGA | Affinity group (of 30) | 0 | 365/6 | 0 |
| YGC | Incentive group (of 20) | 10 | 21 | 4 |
| YGV | Group (of 10) inclusive tour | 5 | 14 | 0 |
| YGV | YGV (1 Nov - 14 Dec; 5 Jan - 30 April) | 7 | 8 | 1 |
| YGV(W) | Youth | 0 | 365/6 | 0 |
| YZ YAP45 | Apex (60 days booking) | 22 | 45 | 0 |

Return Fares (in £ Sterling), London - New York

| | Peak Season | | Shoulder Season | | Off-Peak Season | |
|---|---|---|---|---|---|---|
| | Weekend | Midweek | Weekend | Midweek | Weekend | Midweek |
| F | 464.60 | 464.60 | 464.60 | 464.60 | 464.60 | 464.60 |
| Y | 306.80 | 306.80 | 251.60 | 251.60 | 235.60 | 235.60 |
| YE21 | 250.30 | 238.70 | 216.10 | 204.50 | 216.10 | 204.50 |
| YE45 | 209.80 | 198.20 | 169.30 | 157.70 | 157.40 | 145.80 |
| YGA | 199.60 | 188.00 | 157.40 | 145.80 | 144.10 | 132.50 |
| YGC | - | - | 157.40 | 145.80 | 145.10 | 133.50 |
| YGV | 197.00 | 185.40 | 158.60 | 147.00 | 158.60 | 147.00 |
| YGV(W) | - | - | - | - | 132.10 | 132.10 |
| YZ | 186.60 | 186.60 | 165.00 | 165.00 | 155.60 | 155.60 |
| YAP45 | 171.80 | 160.20 | 135.60 | 124.00 | 130.10 | 118.50 |

# 30 The deregulation of civil aviation in Europe

*Article by M. Asteris*
*Portsmouth Polytechnic*
*August/September 1991 issue*

## INTRODUCTION

Europe's airlines have been subject to extensive state regulation since the interwar years. Now, however, the European Commission is attempting to relax controls on carriers in line with the approach of the Single European Market, which is due for completion by the start of 1993. Interestingly, America's deregulation of its domestic passenger aviation industry suggests that customers and efficient airlines have much to gain from the reform of Europe's air transport regime. The objective of this article is, therefore, to review the likely benefits and possible risks of 'freer skies' in Europe, using US experience as a benchmark.

The first part explains why nations have exercised tight control over most aspects of the industry. Following this, the American experience of deregulation is outlined and the lessons for Europe highlighted. Thereafter, the step-by-step approach of the European Community (EC) to 'freedom of the skies' is examined and the UK attitude to air transport liberalization reviewed.

The conclusion of the article is that reform of the present European air transport framework is high desirable in the interests of increased efficiency, lower prices and better services. Moreover, more open skies within the EC could be the prelude to negotiations with the USA aimed at allowing mutual access to each others aviation markets.

## STATE REGULATION

Regulation of air transport constitutes a situation where the state tightly controls entry to the industry, services offered, fares to be charged, routes to be flown and the capactity to be provided. For example, it has been the norm for air service agreements between two countries to share out capacity on a 50-50 basis; to grant each nation the power of veto over fare levels; and to specify the number of carriers allowed to operate. Indeed, with reference to the latter point, the US-UK agreement of 1977, known as Bermuda II, went so far as to name the individual carriers allowed to fly between Britain and America.

Why have nations felt it necessary to regulate air transport so closely? To answer this question one needs to refer back to the early years of the industry. During the 1920s passenger aircraft were characterized by relatively poor performance and high costs. At the same time, intense competition resulted in financial instability, difficulties in establishing route networks and concern with safety standards. Consequently, governments curbed competition via regulatory bodies such as the Civil Aeronautics (CAB) in the USA and the Air Transport Licensing Authority in the UK. These bodies controlled market entry, fares, service frequencies and capacity on routes.

Moreover, nations, were anxious to maximize the political and militai y benefits of civil aviation. Generous subsidies were therefore given to selected carriers so that they could operate scheduled services. Ever since, governments have sought to protect the market position of their national airlines. These are often perceived as more than simply a means of conveying passengers and freight: instead they are treated as though they reflect the strength of a nation. In short, national airlines (often state owned) tend to be looked at almost as virility symbols. This view is reflected in the term 'flag carriers' to describe major operators such as British Airways, Air France and KLM. Hence, governments normally adopt a partisan attitude towards the airline industry, seeking to ensure a 'fair' market share for their champions rather than the most efficient service for consumers.

Tight control has, therefore, continued to be a dominant feature of air transport even though it can no longer be considered an infant industry requiring a high degree of protection in order to survive.

# US EXPERIENCE OF DEREGULATION

By the 1970s, regulation was being called into question by mounting evidence of the relative efficiency of airlines operating in the least controlled sectors of civil aviation. In particular, American studies revealed that intrastate operations, which were not subject to CAB regulation, could offer fares of about half those of CAB regulated carriers and still show a profit. It is not surprising, therefore, that the pressure for change was greatest in the USA.

Following a series of Congressional hearings in the early seventies, the US passed the Airline Deregulation Act in 1978. This removed the framework of economic controls and the industry became competitive for the first time in 40 years. New carriers entered the market: the number providing scheduled services tripled by 1984. However, the domination of the industry by a limited number of firms continued because the new entrants were small. Hence, while in 1976 the top 12 carriers accounted for about 96 per cent of overall passenger miles, by 1984 they still accounted for 91 per cent.

Nevertheless, faced with the challenge of new efficient companies, the main carriers were compelled to reduce costs and make themselves more competitive or risk the loss of a much larger market share. Consequently, fares were reduced, service frequency improved and traffic rose rapidly - by almost 50 per cent between 1978 and 1985. At that time deregulation appeared to be an unqualified success. Since then, however, competition has diminished because the incumbent operators have had time to develop defensive strategies. The replacement of linear (point-to-point) route systems, with 'hub-and-spoke' networks has proved particularly effective in this respect.

The latter arrangement allows an airline to concentrate its operations at a central airport to which passengers are flown from surrounding cities so as to connect conveniently with outbound flights. During the early stages of deregulation this type of scheduling involved co-ordinating deals with local 'feeder' operators which were later consolidated by means of take-overs. As a result, many of the hub-and-spoke systems are now dominated by a single airline. This is able to feed traffic along one spoke into its hub airport and then out along other spokes. Passengers are thereby encourage to fly with the same carrier for their entire journey, so reducing interline traffic. It is thus more than coincidental that the most powerful and most profitable airlines, such as United and American, are also those with the strongest hub-and-spoke networks. By contrast, airlines such as Pan Am, which lack dominant positions at major hubs, have been gravely weakened.

261

Existing carriers also had the advantage that where airports were congested new firms were often unable to obtain access. The reason for this was that take-off and landing slots were awarded by scheduling committees of incumbent carriers. The allocations were based on 'Grandfather' rights, whereby carriers owned capacity at an airport merely as a consquence of having been there at an early stage in its development. Consequently, while there was no formal restriction on an airline flying a particular route, its ability to do so could be jeopardized by an allocation of slots favouring incumbents. Shortage of airport capacity was also a powerful motive for agreed mergers and takeovers involving scarce take-off and landing options.

Control of an efficient computer reservation system is second only to a dominant position at a major hub as a source of market power because travel agents tend to favour the airline supplying the reservation system. It is therefore noteworthy that the reservation systems of two giant airlines - United and American - account for over two-thirds of the terminals used by travel agents in the US. More broadly, information technology constitutes an important management tool since it provides instant market information. Consequently, those firms which can afford sophisticated systems are able to fine tune thier pricing policy, for example, by varying the availability of discount tickets. Large US carriers were able to harness IT so as to maximize the profit of each aircraft seat in a manner denied to smaller firms. Major airlines were also able to obtain pecurniary economies of scale such as economies of bulk purchase and lower borrowing costs.

The advantages enjoyed by large carriers in the US airline market are such that their share of it is now marginally greater than it was under regulation. In 1977 the five largest airlines accounted for 63 per cent of traffic: today they account for over 70 per cent. To a considerable degree this outcome reflects a highly sympathetic attitude towards takeovers on the part of the Department of Transportation, which scrutinized airline mergers following the abolition of the Civil Aeronautics Board. The refusal to allow foreign airlines 'cabotage rights' - the ability to fly internal US routes - has also played a part, by excluding a very important potential source of competition. That said, the failure to permit freer access to the US market is understandable bearing in mind the reluctance of most governments to deregulate international flights.

While America's deregulation of its internal airline industry has been flawed in some respects, it has, nonetheless, proved highly successful. Domestic airlines now have lower real costs than in the mid-1970s, partly as a result of more efficient use of labour. Overall, after allowing for inflation, fares are, on average, some 20 per cent lower. Moreover, there are far more flights and the number of passenger-miles travelled have just about doubled. Consumers have thus gained a great deal without any of the adverse effects on air safety which some critics of liberalization had predicted.

The financially fragile carrier have, however, found the last few years extemely uncomfortable with a consequent division of the industry between the strong and the weak. The most successful airlines are those such as American and United, which have consolidated their position in the market. Those at the other extreme include Pan Am, Trans World Airlines (TWA) and Eastern which have severe financial problems. In between the strong and the weak are a number of middle-ranking carriers, including Northwest Airlines and US Air. Overall the trend is towards a comparatively small number of strong firms.

## LESSONS FOR EUROPE

The US experience thus suggests two crucial lessons for Europe. First, that there are huge potential gains from deregulation in the form of increased efficiency, lower fares, improved service frequency and a substantial increase in air travel. By 1985, at 1977 prices, US consumers and producers enjoyed total gains of around $8 billion a year as a result of an open skies approach to air travel.

The second principal lesson is that deregulation does not automatically prevent the acquisition of a high degree of monopoly power by certain airlines. Measures directed towards encouraging and sustaining competitive forces are thus highly desirable. In this context, freer access to take-off and landing slots for new entrants at major airports is particularly important. So also is a firm anti-trust and mergers policy to prevent existing operators from exploiting their market position in such a way as to blunt the challenge of new operators.

In attempting to learn from American experience, it is, of course, essential to take account of certain important differences between Europe and America. To begin with, the American civil aviation industry is more than four times larger than its European counterpart, thereby presenting more opportunities for scale economies. For example, the larger US market permits more extensive use of wide bodied jets. Secondly, unlike the situation in the USA, the various computer reservation systems in Europe are owned by a number of airlines and present information in an unbiased manner. The danger that these systems will become sources of monopoly power are thus minimized. Thirdly, holiday travel in Europe is mainly the preserve of charter airlines, which account for more than 50 per cent of the total market. The relative cheapness of air charter travel goes some way to explaining why there has been less pressure for reform of scheduled services than in the United States.

By far the most significant Inter-Continental difference, however, is the fact that the US constitutes a single economic entity, while air transport in Europe is still organized as a set of national markets. The political obstacles to change are therefore substantial because some governments are fearful of even limited competition. Nevertheless, as the next section makes clear, the various obstacles are being overcome by a step-by-step approach to liberalization.


## EC AIR TRANSPORT POLICY

In accord with the commitment of Member States to complete the Single Market, the European Commission is striving to forge a less segmented and more competitive air transport sector. Protection and monopoly has resulted in many European carriers having operating costs well above US levels largely because of poor labour and capital utilization. Indeed, in 1983 overall air service costs of the 22 members of the European Civil Aviation Conference were more than 60 per cent higher than for US carriers.

There are thus considerable benefits to be reaped from freer skies. In 1988 the Commission estimated the likely gains for the Common Market states at over $1 billion per annum. The extent to which these gains are realized will be largely determined by the Commission itself since it is a supernational body acting in the interests of the community as a whole. It is therefore encouraging that there is now an agreed Community liberalization strategy. This includes freeing carriers to compete in each others markets; permitting more competition on fares; and the ending of bilateral agreements for sharing revenue and capacity in the case of airlines flying the same routes.

The achievement of a single market in civil aviation is being approached in three stages. The first, agreed in 1987, was mainly symbolic. While providing for some relaxation of controls on fares, capacity and market access, its effect was comparatively modest because the main flag carriers remained largely undisturbed. The second stage came into force in November 1990 and promises to have much greater impact. In essence, the package of measures includes the relaxation of existing capacity rules so that one country can take up to a 75 per cent share, greater freedom in fare setting, and route access for more airlines.

The third and last stage provides for the ending of capacity sharing, multiple designation of carriers on all routes, freedom for an airline to set fare levels unless the governments of both airlines object, and uniform licensing. This final measure is particularly significant because it implies that any EC airline will be able to fly any route within the community. Hence, after 1st January 1993 the area within the 12 member states will be perceived as a single 'domestic' market. While foot-dragging on the part of some nations may delay aspects of the third stage beyond that date, full implementation can be anticipated in the not too distant future.

The liberalization measures clearly herald substantial change in European air transport. Even so, as noted earlier, US experience suggests that the attempt to generate a far more competitive environment could prove abortive unless two threats are dealt with vigorously.

The first is the method by which take-off and landing slots are awarded at airports especially at peak periods. As in the USA, allocation within the EC is decided by committees of incumbent airlines largely on the grandfather principle. In the presence of capacity constrains at most leading European airports, newcomers find it very difficult to acquire slots. A fairer allocation mechanism is required. In a market economy scarce capacity has a price. Slot auctions could therefore be used to solve the congestion problem, with airlines bidding for access to runways. Those wanting peak time slots at congested airports would have to pay a high price for them: conversely, space at less popular airports could be obtained relatively cheaply. A pricing system of this kind would be both equitable and efficient.

In recognition of this fact, the European Commission has looked at the possibility that airport slots be auctioned on a rotating basis. To date, however, there appears to have been little progress on this proposal. Meanwhile, the Commission is also considering allowing newcomers to obtain some slots following a two year wait at congested airports. While representing an improvement compared with the present situation, such an approach would still blunt the competitiveness of entrants.

The second obstacle to a free market is the increasing concentration of the European aviation industry. Even at this comparatively early stage of the deregulation process, major European airlines are following the example of their American counterparts in seeking to protect themselves from competition by means of mergers, cross-shareholding agreements and various kinds of commercial pacts. For example, Air France took over UTA and Air Inter, while KLM, British Airways and Sabena were planning, until recently, to create a new hub-and-spoke airline based on Brussels.

265

The European Commission is concerned that deals of this kind will stifle competition at birth.  It has therefore examined proposed mergers very closely.  On the other hand, in a global context, there is a danger that a highly fragmented EC aviation industry, consisting of small and medium size carriers, might not be able to compete with the mega airlines of the USA and Asia.  In addition, the possibility exists that, in an attempt to ensure a competitive environment, the EC could end up introducing a new range of tight regulatory devices.

In an ideal world, the dilemma of size versus competition could be solved by opening the European market to international competition. However, such a liberal policy is unlikely to be adopted unless the rest of the world reciprocates by abandoning a protectionist stance.  Unfortunately, at the present time there appears to be little chance of such a fundamental change in attitudes.  Even so, once the EC has forged an internal market, it would be possible to achieve much of the benefits of openness if Europe and America where to grant each others airlines reciprocal access.  Meanwhile, as will be explained in the next section, the rest of the European Community may shortly be set an example by the  negotiation of an Anglo-American agreement providing for mutual market access.

## THE UK'S APPROACH TO LIBERALIZATION

In contrast to some other European countries which have often appeared to pay little more than lip service to airline deregulation, the British government has sought to promote greater competition in civil aviation and to take a lead in the efforts of the EC to liberalize the industry by 1993.  Evidence of the UK's enthusiasm for deregulation is  provided by the March 1991 deal with America to partly deregulate transatlantic air travel.

Under the provisions of the 1977 Bermuda II agreement, only two named American airlines - Pan Am and TWA - were permitted to operate from London Heathrow.  In recent years, however, neither has excelled on the north Atlantic route mainly because they lack the large domestic networks which could feed them international passengers.  Furthermore, by the start of the 1990s both were heavily in debt. To raise money, they wished to sell their take-off and landing slots at Heathrow. These are highly prized because of the huge volume of international traffic handled at the airport.

Two stronger American competitors were eager to buy the slots because this would enable them to combine their extensive US domestic operation with a new presence on the north Atlantic.  United Airlines was willing to acquire Pan Am's 237 slots for $290 million while American Airlines was happy to pay $445 for TWA's services. Until March 1991, however, these deals were frustrated by two constraints: the need to revise Bermuda II and the arrangement under which the only airlines allowed to operate from Heathrow were those that were flying from there in 1977.

The latter constraint was removed on 5th March 1991 when UK restrictions on new entrant were lifted. Then on 11th March, Britain and America agreed new air service arrangements between the two countries. This deal cleared the way for United and American to take over the Pan Am and TWA slots (though the US decided not to allow the transfer of all TWA London routes to American). However, UK approval for a change in named carriers was granted only after the American government made several concessions of its own. These included the designation of a second British carrier to operate to the US from Heathrow, the right of British Airways to fly to the US via six points in continental Europe and an increase in the number of cities in Latin America, Canada and Asia to which a British airline may continue after a US stopover.

The two countries also agreed to further talks aimed at liberalizing their aviation relationship. These will address such issues as greater British access to the immense American domestic market, which accounts for almost 40 per cent of the world's airline passengers. If the joint aviation markets of the two countries were to be deregulated this would establish an important precedent for the liberalization of services between the US and the rest of the European community.

## CONCLUSION

American experience suggests that the deregulation of civil aviation may prove to be an extremely uncomfortable experience for Europe's airlines while presenting new opportunities for the more efficient, such as BA. It is also clear from the course of events in the USA that passengers will benefit very greatly from a freer air-travel market: they will enjoy lower fares and far more choice. The potential overall gains from a single internal market probably exceed $1 billion.

That said, in order to extract the maximum benefit Europe must be careful not to reproduce two major flaws in the US deregulation process. The first was the failure to ensure that an airline wishing to start operating on a popular route had a high probability of gaining access to a busy airport. Britain's recent opening up of Heathrow, the home base of BA, to greater competition has set an example to the rest of Europe in this respect. More specifically, the move has demonstrated a willingness to discomfort the national carrier in the interests of an ideology.

With hindsight, the second flaw in the US deregulation process was too relaxed an approach to anti-trust and merger controls. The European Commission is determined not to repeat this error and has made it clear that activities which could pose a threat to fair competition will not be tolerated. It is therefore on the lookout for 'predatory practices' such as artificially low fares. It has also scrutinized proposed airline mergers very closely.

Unfortunately, not to sanction mergers runs the risk of leaving the EC airline industry too fragmented to compete with the world's mega carriers. However, the scale versus competition dilemma could be neatly solved if an open skies policy in the Common Market proves to be the prelude to a North Atlantic free market in air travel embracing both Europe and America.

# 31 Airline competition and capacity constraints at hub airports

*Article by J.P. Hanlon*
*University of Birmingham*
*June 1987 issue*

Increasing liberalization of civil air transport from controls over competition is leading to some profound changes in airline routes and services. This paper looks at the growing importance of hubs and identifies runway/terminal capacity shortages as major problems for carriers seeking to enhance the complexing of flight schedules through busy airports.

One of the clearest trends to emerge from air transport deregulation in the USA is the greatly increased emphasis on hub-and-spokes networks. A similar trend is evident elsewhere, especially where controls over airline competition are being relaxed. Many airlines are realigning schedules at hub airports so as to 'bank' services into 'complexes', i.e. timing flights on the spokes so that they arrive/depart the hub at approximately the same time, with aircraft spending sufficient time together on the ground to permit the transfer of passengers and their baggage. In America the classic example is in Atlanta where Delta Airlines' operations are banked into complexes scheduled as 'waves' once every two hours, each wave involving about 40 flights. On the other side of the globe, in Singapore, activity is very much concentrated in the evenings, where SIA's European arrivals and departures link up with flights to and from the Antipodes. And at KLM's hub in Amsterdam long-haul flights arrive in the early morning in time to connect with departures on short-haul routes, the short-haul aircraft returning in the afternoon to connect with outbound long-hauls. KLM's timetable is certainly very well planned in this respect: one of its 747 flights can be linked with as many as 50 different connecting flights.

## EXPERIENCE OF THE UNITED STATES

A key feature of US deregulation since 1987 has been the substitution of intraline connections. Connecting passengers as a percentage of total passengers on US domestic routes has remained fairly constant, but intraline passengers are now about four times as numerous as interline, compared to the situation nine or ten years ago, when they were both roughly the same. Airline networks in the USA have undergone some substantial changes. American Airlines, whose main hub is in Dallas, can now claim to offer through intraline service in some 10,000 city-pairs, compared to just 1,000 in pre-deregulation days. It is noticeable that the carriers which have been consistently the most profitable in the deregulated environment are those with hubs in which they have dominant presence and through which they carry much intraline traffic. It has been largely through their dominant positions at important hubs that 'mega-carriers' like Delta, American, United, Northwest, the Texas Air conglomerate and US Air have become so powerful in US domestic air transport. Pan American per contra has no such dominant position and its performance has been comparatively poor. To reap the advantages of strategically located hubs is an underlying motive behind many of the structural changes that have occurred in the US domestic industry - mergers, take-overs, links between major and commuter airlines, code-sharing arrangements, and the increasingly important role of computer reservations systems.

## COMPETITION IN EUROPE

The situation in Europe is not in many ways directly comparable to that in the USA; but there are many indications that the same forces are coming into play. European airlines have for a long time operated networks of the hub-and-spokes shape, although this was originally more an outcome of bilateral competing for connecting traffic. But such competition is getting fiercer in Europe. KLM and Swissair have in fact been competing vigorously in this direction for years, because for them connecting traffic has always been particularly important given their relatively small home-grown demand. Under recent bilateral agreements airlines are being granted greater freedom in pricing and route access, and it is already apparent that many are seeking to use this freedom to encourage traffic to their hubs. There are also signs that major carriers are seeking to guarantee feed from the smaller regional airlines, by taking financial stakes in them. Further, there is talk of mergers between the major carriers themselves. The influence of powerful computer reservations systems is spreading to Europe, another indication that airlines expect increasing liberalization to present good opportunities to gain traffic by complexing through hubs.

## FLIGHT COMPLEXING

Complexing through hubs confers on the airline some important operational and competitive advantages. The inherent operational advantage is that it multiplies by permutation the number of city-pairs an airline can serve. From a hub with n spokes an airline can provide through connecting services for up to a theoretical maximum of $n(n-1)/2$ city-pairs. In practice of course, some possible city-pairs may require too great a deviation to attract traffic, and some may not be served because they are already well supplied with direct services. But a well-developed complexing system can endow an airline with substantial competitive strengths. The additional traffic generated by connections can support higher frequencies and through this enable the airline to achieve high market shares. Across a network covering both large and small cities, the degree of competition may vary quite a lot, giving the airline the opportunity to charge relatively high fares in less competitive markets and relatively low fares in the more competitive city-pairs. This places the hubbing airline in quite a powerful position. Frequent connecting services between two points can inhibit the development of direct services. Unless the direct service has a high frequency, passengers who wish to be at their destination at a particular time may often prefer the connecting service, despite having to change planes en route.

The essence of complexing is that the number of (useful) connections at the hub airport are maximized. The two largest British airlines have their hubs in London, BA at Heathrow and BCAL at Gatwick. But neither is currently well placed to enhance their intralining capabilities, because of shortages in runway and terminal capacities. The present system of capacity allocation based on 'grandfather rights' constrains the possibilities for reorganizing service schedules. Whatever the long-term solution to airport capacity in the London area might eventually be, there are also some important and more immediate questions concerning the operation of present facilities. Service schedules are likely to become increasingly crucial in determining the volume and value of traffic that an airline can hope to win in a more competitive environment.

## COMPETITION BETWEEN HUBS

In the competition for connecting traffic the main factors are the following: the range of services offered; the frequencies at which these services are operated; the levels and types of fares available; the reputation of the dominant hub airline; facilities in airport terminals; and the quality of transfers.

Clearly, the more destinations that are served the greater the chance of an intending passenger finding a suitable connection. And the odds shorten with every additional flight. In both respects London ranks ahead of its continental competitors, with Paris coming second, followed by Frankfurt, Amsterdam and Zurich in that order. But the lead that London and Paris enjoy in terms of range and frequency is diminished by the split of traffic between their two main airports. Heathrow is still the airport with the greatest number of destinations and frequencies, but Gatwick ranks alongside Brussels and Rome as a relatively weak hub in the international context. There is less of an imbalance in Paris, where a policy of route sectorization between Orly and Charles de Gaulle means that as individual airports both slip below Frankfurt in scale of departures and destinations.

London and Amsterdam tend to score highly in the availability of cheap excursion and discount fares, an important factor in attracting leisure travellers in particular. Punctuality and in-flight service are often of great importance to business travellers, and the consistently high reputation in these regards earned by an airline like Swissair plays a part in persuading businessmen to prefer connections in places like Zurich and Geneva. Most European airports have ample facilities for duty-free shopping but perhaps Amsterdam has the competitive edge in prices and shop sites. To connecting passengers however, facilities at the transfer point are of much less importance than the quality of the transfer itself, and in this regard there can sometimes be a conflict of interests between the hubbing airline and a profit-motivated airport authority - to whom franchises on airport shops are an important source of non-aeronautical revenues. Good connections mean less opportunity to use airport shops. (In Atlanta many connecting passengers have only some 40 to 45 minutes to change planes and spend on average not much more than a dollar while in transit there.)

Rank orders by size are reversed when it comes to transfer quality, a factor embracing not just the interval of time required to change from one aircraft to another but also the simplicity and convenience of the connection process. Here single-airport, single-terminal operating some way below full capacity are at a distinct advantage. London is a multi-airport, multi-terminal system now heavily congested. A further disadvantage is that flight schedules at Heathrow and Gatwick are mostly not well complexed.

## CAPACITY CONSTRAINTS AT HEATHROW AND GATWICK

In the overall context of government policy towards civil aviation, the issues raised by capacity shortages at Heathrow and Gatwick are none too easy to solve. This much has been amply demonstrated in various documents produced by the Civil Aviation Authority. There are some major conflicts in policy objectives. Increasing competition within UK civil aviation, to the extent that this means reducing concentration in the industry and fragmenting services between airports, is not wholly consistent with maximizing the ability of UK air transport to compete against airlines dominating hubs in other countries. Foreign airlines see the opportunities that capacity problems in London could present them.

The CAA has clearly had quite some difficulty in attempting to devise an appropriate set of 'traffic distribution rules' to deal with the peak-load pressure on runway slots. The debate so far had tended to centre on what might be done - by frequency capping, displacement of certain operations to 'reliever' airports peak-load pricing, slot trading, etc. - merely in order to accommodate the projected secular growth in traffic. The slot allocation problems are more formidable still, if the objective is also to increase the scope for hub airlines to complex flights into waves, and through this to increase both the total volume of London's connecting traffic and UK airlines share of it. Present slots used by BA and BCAL are too widely spread and too unrelated, hindering the co-ordination of flight schedules and, as indicated here, placing both airlines at serious competitive disadvantages in the increasingly important - and increasingly contestable - international - to - international transfer market. Grandfather rights and international obligations presently preclude many possibilities for slot redistribution, but perhaps the time has come to consider more fully the trading of other aeropolitical concessions in return for greater flexibility in London. Some really quite marginal changes in slot allocation could result in some potentially large benefits, especially if

273

other restrictions were to be lifted at the same time, so as to encourage innovations like through running between domestic and international routes, stabling aircraft overnight at spoke airports, closer links with feeder airlines and so on.

# 32    Third London airport

*Article by D. Spurling*
*London College of Advanced Transport Studies*
*July 1986 issue*

The demand for air transport is rising and thus we need either a new airport in the South East or an improvement in the capacity of the existing ones.

The first solution was the suggestion in the 1970s where as a Southend councillor, I was bombarded with literature about the pressing need for an airport at Maplin (Foulness) whilst the latter solution has been supported by the Eyre Report in the 1980s.

We need, however, to consider carefully what is meant by demand, how we measure it and to be satisfied that the advantages of meeting the demand are not outweighed by the disadvantages. Demand can be measured in a variety of ways, for example the number of passengers, passenger kilometres, tonnes handled, number of aircraft movements. Each of these in turn can be measured in a number of different ways, for example in terms of annual flows or peak flows on a daily or seasonal basis. Which measure is relevant will depend partly upon the purpose, for example the number of passengers in the peak will be relevant when looking at terminal facilities whereas the number of aircraft movements at the peak is important when considering runway capacity.

The capacity of runways is, however, not constant, it will depend upon the size of aircraft, the take off and landing speeds, loading or unloading time as well as improvements in air navigation. The capacity of terminals will depend purely upon the documentation procedures. There have been suggestions from time to time that some of these procedures need not take place at the airport and therefore the global village  concept may no longer be necessary. By analogy in the freight sector vehicles are often checked at inland clearance depots. Could passports, suitcases etc be checked away from the airport which might mean cheaper land could be used and perhaps more importantly there would be less problems with surges for passengers.

The capacity of terminals to handle passenger flows may well be influenced by the so called chip revolution e.g. security checks could be speeded up by the use of computers and visual demonstration units.

Unless all the relevant airports are reaching their capacity it will be worthwhile the airports considering either administrative measures or pricing methods or a combination of these to transfer traffic from one airport which is congested to another one which is operating below capacity. An alternative policy might be to try to persuade passengers or freight to move in the off peak.

If we consider the possibility of using the price mechanism to persuade people to use one airport rather than another then we have to transfer the influences on choice of airport.

The demand for an individual airport will depend partly upon cost, ease of access to the terminal (frequency of flights) variations in air fares, if any, as well as the perceived quality of the airport itself. Within the three London airports (i.e., Heathrow, Gatwick and Stanstead) the differential in the peak is probably not such as to force passengers to switch. However, if the differential were sufficiently high it could have three possible effects.

a)    that people would transfer to regional airports;
b)    that people would transfer to continental airports, e.g. Amsterdam;
c)    that people would not travel by air, eg usually because  they would divert to other modes.

The possibility (a) might well be desirable on economic grounds if the regional airports are under utilized. The environmental effects will also be beneficial if the airport is local but could be  harmful if more car travel is involved. Where the origin or destination in the UK was fixed as with most UK residents travel, the differential in airport changes would have to be much greater than the present ones for people to travel from the South East to the regional airports. However, for people living, say, in the North of England, the Midland, Manchester or Birmingham would be natural choices since it would reduce both accessibility time or cost. The main deterrent is likely to be the infrequency or inconvenience of timing of flights.

For overseas visitors, the attraction of the South East is that there is a greater frequency of flights. London Airport is much better known than most other airports. Statistics showing the large number of overseas visitors who go onto destinations within the South East should be treated with some caution as some passengers may be going on to other destinations after the first evening and the statistics do not usually show this. Others would probably use regional airports if hotel accommodation was adequate and there were greater publicity.

The regional airports have generally had higher percentage growth rates than the London ones. Success breeds success, the greater the number of passengers the more likely is access to be improved and ancillary facilities provided which in turn will lead to more flights and passengers.

Fears have been expressed that if there is insufficient expansion in the South East or airport charges are raised too much then traffic will be lost to the UK. This would seem to be implausible for most business traffic unless, for example, businessmen were doing a European tour. More plausible is the idea that businessmen might travel to the Netherlands or France for the main haul and then catch a connecting flight. For tourism, however, where, say, American travellers might wish to visit Europe without being too specific about the destination, the idea is more plausible.

Tourist demand is generally more price elastic (i.e. responds more readily to price changes). The effects on the British economy would be much greater than just the effects on the aviation industry since tourism is a major invisible export and has remained comparatively buoyant even in the recession.

In a rational economy therefore an airport would take this into account when considering its pricing policy. However, it is unlikely that the present Government or a 'privatized' British Airports Authority will do so.

# Index

traffic trends in, 4, 16
vehicle utilization problems in, 22
Busways, 30
Butlers, 36

C-5A aircraft, 236
cabotage, 50, 262
Cambrian Airways, 225, 227
canals, 4, 58, 158, 208
Canterbury, banning of lorries in, 60
Cardiff: as sea port, 158
cars, private, 4
    design of, 71
    long-lived, 72
    parking restrictions on, 21, 23
    pollution caused by, 63-4
    costs of control of, 64-73
Caspian-Volga-Balt Line, 207
catalytic convertors, 66, 71
Central Line, 146
Ceylon Shipping Corporation, 208
Chamber of Shipping, 161
Channel Tunnel, 5, 52 128, 139-43
    impact on shipping of, 211,212, 216-18
    rail transport and, 115, 125-6, 142
    road haulage and, 141
Charles, King, of Romania, 133
charter flying, 226, 227, 250, 263-4
check-in times, 229
children's fares, 20, 22
Christian Salvesen, 36
Civil Aviation Authority, 273
CL 44 aircraft, 234
coastal shipping, 154, 159

colliers, 154
Compagnie Internationale des Wagons-Lits et des Grands Express Europeens, 134
complexing, 271-2
computers, 40, 113
    reservation systems, 262, 263
    route-planning by, 81-91
Concorde, 241, 245-8, 251
cones, traffic, 79
congestion problems, 7, 68
    for bus transport, 20-21
    on motorways, 78-9
    on railways, 129
Consortium Line, 207
Container Marine Lines, 174
containerization, 6
    operation of, 179-87
    progress of, 169-77
    railways and, 113, 172, 174, 176
    road haulage and, 176
    sea ports and, 173, 176-7, 200-201, 214-15, 216
    shipping and, 169, 171-7, 181-7
    standard container sizes in, 173-4, 180
    trans-shipment and, 212, 213-15
contract hire see under road haulage
contraflow system, 79
crew of ships, 159-61, 192-3, 196
crop spraying, 230
cross-subsidization, 2, 8, 118, 256
Cunard, 172, 207
currency fluctuations, 252-3
Customs and Excise, 52, 141, 164-5, 225, 235